Postwar Europe and the Eurovision Song Contest

Postwar Europe and the Eurovision Song Contest

Dean Vuletic

BLOOMSBURY ACADEMIC
LONDON • NEW YORK • OXFORD • NEW DELHI • SYDNEY

BLOOMSBURY ACADEMIC
Bloomsbury Publishing Plc
50 Bedford Square, London, WC1B 3DP, UK
1385 Broadway, New York, NY 10018, USA

BLOOMSBURY, BLOOMSBURY ACADEMIC and the Diana logo
are trademarks of Bloomsbury Publishing Plc

First published 2018
Paperback edition published 2019

Cover design: Bruketa & Žinić OM

A catalogue record for this book is available from the British Library.

A catalog record for this book is available from the Library of Congress.

ISBN: HB: 978-1-4742-7626-9
PB: 978-1-3501-0739-7
ePDF: 978-1-4742-7627-6
ePub: 978-1-4742-7628-3

Typeset by Deanta Global Publishing Services, Chennai, India

Contents

List of Figures

Acknowledgements

This book is the result of the Marie Skłodowska-Curie Intra-European Fellowship project 'Eurovision: A History of Europe Through Popular Music', which I conducted in the Department of East European History at the University of Vienna from 2013 to 2015. I am grateful to Philipp Ther for his mentorship during this project and to Anita Biricz for her support in managing it. Through this project I also organized public events in which I brought together academics, artists, diplomats and journalists to discuss the Eurovision Song Contest (ESC) and its significance for international relations. For their participation in these and the insights that they gave me into the ESC, I thank William Lee Adams, Eldad Beck, Marie-Luise Bohrer, Claudette Buttigieg, Ismeta Dervoz, Karen Fricker, Dave Goodman, Paul Jordan, Cathrin Kahlweit, Åse Kleveland, René Kmet, David Lewis, Ivan Raykoff, Thomas Row, Maya Sar, Marco Schreuder, Vanessa Spanbauer, Sami Ukelli, Klaus Unterberger, Georg Vogt and Florian Wagner. I also thank the Diplomatic Academy of Vienna, the embassies of Australia and Slovenia and the representations of the European Commission and the European Parliament in Vienna for their contributions to these events. I am grateful to Konrad Mitschka from the Public Value centre of the Austrian Broadcasting Corporation (ORF) and to Herbert Hayduck, the head of ORF's archives, for facilitating my collaboration with ORF. This book has also benefitted from the International Federation of Television Archives' Television Study Grant, with which I was able to conduct research on the Intervision Song Contest from 2015 to 2016.

My research for this book took me all over Europe – including to Austria, Azerbaijan, Belgium, Bosnia and Herzegovina, Croatia, Cyprus, the Czech Republic, Denmark, France, Germany, Hungary, Israel, Italy, Liechtenstein, Malta, the Netherlands, Poland, San Marino, Slovakia, Slovenia, Sweden, Switzerland, Ukraine and the United Kingdom – to discuss the ESC with its artists, fans, journalists and organizers, present my research at academic conferences and visit archives and libraries. I thank all of those who shared their experiences of the ESC with me, especially Rambo Amadeus,

Sietse Bakker, Radek Banga, Nadine Beiler, Edgar Böhm, Timna Brauer, Alessandro Capicchioni, Kim Cooper, Deen, Tini Kainrath, András Kállay-Saunders, Klitos Klitou, Mario Lackner, Jakov Leon, Ira Losco, Valentina Monetta, Beatrix Neundlinger, Kobi Oshrat, Robert Pfannhauser, Tereza Radváková, Motti Regev and Jon Ola Sand. I am grateful to the staff of the European Broadcasting Union, German Broadcasting Archive, Historical Archives of the European Union, International Telecommunication Union and of Czech Television and Polish Television for assisting me in accessing archival documents, as well as to the staff of the Austrian National Library, British Library, National Library of the Czech Republic, National Library of Liechtenstein and of the libraries of the European University Institute, University of Amsterdam and University of Vienna. I was fortunate enough to be undertaking my project in Vienna when Austria won the ESC in 2014 and went on to host it in 2015, and I thank all of the journalists who interviewed me and promoted the results of my project during this time – and for giving me the nickname 'Professor Song Contest'.

My academic interest in the ESC began while I was an undergraduate student of European studies at the Australian National University, where I wrote my first ever essay on the contest. I thank my lecturer at the time, Karis Muller, for her enthusiastic response which motivated me to pursue this research interest further. She also encouraged me to spend part of my honours year at the Hebrew University of Jerusalem. It was in Israel that I was able to see my first live ESC, in 1999, and since then I have attended more of the contests live and closely watched recordings of every edition of the ESC from 1956 to 2016. I also thank my colleague at the Australian National University, Tamsin Sanderson, for organizing with me the first ESC parties at the university and for her feedback on this book. I was further able to develop my research on the ESC in the Department of History at Columbia University through my doctoral dissertation *Yugoslav Communism and the Power of Popular Music*. I thank Mark Mazower for the advice that he gave while mentoring me for this. I began developing the idea for this book as a Max Weber Post-Doctoral Fellow at the European University Institute, and I am grateful to Stephen Smith for his mentorship during my time there and for giving me the opportunity to test some of the ideas that I had for this book in the seminars that we taught together. I also thank my other colleagues at the European University Institute for sharing with me their different perspectives on the ESC, and especially for giving me insights into various national experiences of the contest. During my time in Florence I designed the world's first ever university course on the ESC, which I began teaching at New York University's campus in Florence and later continued at the University of Vienna. I thank Bruce Edelstein for encouraging me to first teach the course at New York University. In both Florence and Vienna I have had wonderful groups of students in my courses, and I am grateful to them for their enthusiasm, opinions and questions. *Grazie* also to the members of the Italian ESC fan club, OGAE Italy, and especially its president, Cristina Giuntini, for welcoming me into their group and giving me an experience of ESC fandom. I have especially enjoyed cooperating with the team from Wiwibloggs, who have given me a valuable insight into media reporting on the ESC.

My thanks also go to Helena Rosandić, Joško Jureškin, Tanja Škorić and Ivona Haban from the Vienna team of the Bruketa&Žinić OM and Startaparat advertising agencies for the design of the book's cover and map and of my website www.deanvuletic.com; I am honoured to have on my book the mark of a creative team whose work I have long admired. It has also been a pleasure to work with the staff of Bloomsbury Publishing, and I thank all of the reviewers whose feedback helped to shape this book. Colleagues and friends who were helpful in sharing their expertise and promoting the results of my project include Molly Antopol, Konstantina Bania, Mario Dunkel, Ruža Fotiadis, Magdalena Fürnkranz, Ursula Hemetek, Ana Hofman, Marios Iacovides, Teja Komel Klepec, Aleksandar Hut Kono, Suzanne Lommers, Dirk Moses, Dirk Rupnow, Claudia Schrag Sternberg, Natasha Wheatley and Heather Wokusch. I am grateful to Thea Favaloro, Angelika Gamulin, Dorothy Georgeff, Ana Kerševan, Magdalena Moś, Nicolas Seutin, Kristina Špirk, Jessica Steiger-Thorpe, Kristrún Viðarsdóttir, Ana Vukov and Ian Willoughby for their friendship and support. Finally, I thank Mirjana Perković and Kerol Režić for introducing me to the ESC in the first place.

Dean Vuletic

Abbreviations

ABC — Australian Broadcasting Commission
ABU — Asia-Pacific Broadcasting Union
ACT — Archives of Czech Television
APT — Archives of Polish Television
ARD — Arbeitsgemeinschaft der öffentlich-rechtlichen Rundfunkanstalten der Bundesrepublik Deutschland (Consortium of the Public Service Broadcasting Corporations of the Federal Republic of Germany)
ARMTV — Public Television Company of Armenia
AzTV — Azərbaycan Televiziyası (Azerbaijan Television)
BBC — British Broadcasting Corporation
BHRT — Radio-televizija Bosne i Hercegovine (Radio and Television of Bosnia-Herzegovina)
BTRC — Belaruskaja Tele-Radio Campanija (Belarusian Television and Radio Company)
CBU — Caribbean Broadcasting Union
CET — Central European Time
CoE — Council of Europe
CoEA — Council of Europe Archives
COMECON — Council for Mutual Economic Assistance
ČST — Československá televize/Československá televízia (Czechoslovak Television)
ČT — Česká televize (Czech Television)
CyBC — Cyprus Broadcasting Corporation
DDR-FS — Fernsehen der Deutschen Demokratischen Republik (Television of the German Democratic Republic)
DR — Danmarks Radio (Danish Broadcasting Corporation)
EBA — European Broadcasting Area
EBU — European Broadcasting Union

EBUA	European Broadcasting Union Archives
EC	European Community
ECSC	European Coal and Steel Community
EEA	European Economic Area
EEC	European Economic Community
EFTA	European Free Trade Association
EIRT	Ethniko Idrima Radiofonias Tileoraseos (National Radio Television Foundation)
EP	European Parliament
ERT	Ellinikí Radiofonía Tileórasi (Hellenic Broadcasting Corporation)
ERTU	Egyptian Radio and Television Union
ESC	Eurovision Song Contest
EU	European Union
FYROM	Former Yugoslav Republic of Macedonia
GPB	Georgian Public Broadcasting
HTV	Hrvatska televizija (Croatian Television)
IBA	Israel Broadcasting Authority
IBU	International Broadcasting Union
ICTY	International Criminal Tribunal for the Former Yugoslavia
ISC	Intervision Song Contest
ITU	International Telecommunication Union
ITUA	International Telecommunication Union Archives
İTV	İctimai Televiziya (Public Television)
JRT	Jugoslavenska radiotelevizija/Jugoslovanska radiotelevizija/Jugoslovenska radio-televizija/Jugoslovenska radiotelevizija (Yugoslav Radio and Television)
MEP	Member of the European Parliament
MKRTV, MRT	Makedonska radio televizija (Macedonian Radio and Television)
NATO	North Atlantic Treaty Organization
NRK	Norsk rikskringkasting (Norwegian Broadcasting Corporation)
NTS	Nederlandse Televisie Stichting (Dutch Television Foundation)

OGAE	Organisation générale des amateurs de l'Eurovision (General Organization of Eurovision Fans)
OIR	Organisation internationale de radiodiffusion (International Broadcasting Organization)
OIRT	Organisation internationale de radiodiffusion et de télévision (International Radio and Television Organization)
ORF	Österreichischer Rundfunk (Austrian Broadcasting Corporation)
OTI	Organización de Televisión Iberoamericana/Organização da Televisão Ibero-Americana (Organization of Ibero-American Television)
RAI	Radiotelevisione italiana (Italian Radio and Television)
RTCG	Radio i televizija Crne Gore (Radio and Television of Montenegro)
RTÉ	Raidió Teilifís Éireann (Radio and Television of Ireland)
RTF	Radiodiffusion-télévision française (French Radio and Television)
RTK	Radio Televizioni i Kosovës/Radio televizija Kosova (Radio and Television of Kosovo)
RTP	Radiotelevisão Portuguesa (Portuguese Radio and Television)/Rádio e Televisão de Portugal (Radio and Television of Portugal)
RTS	Radio-televizija Srbije (Radio and Television of Serbia)
SBS	Special Broadcasting Service
SR	Sveriges Radio (Radio Sweden)
SRG SSR	Schweizerische Radio- und Fernsehgesellschaft/Société suisse de radiodiffusion et télévision/Società svizzera di radiotelevisione (Swiss Broadcasting Corporation)
STV	Slovenská televízia (Slovak Television)
SVT	Sveriges Television (Sweden's Television)
TL	Télé Liban (Lebanon Television)
TRNC	Turkish Republic of Northern Cyprus
TRT	Türkiye Radyo Televizyon Kurumu (Turkish Radio and Television Corporation)
TSC	Turkvision Song Contest

TVE	Televisión Española (Spanish Television)
TVR	Televiziunea Română (Romanian Television)
UEFA	Union of European Football Associations
UK	United Kingdom
UN	United Nations
UNESCO	United Nations Educational, Scientific and Cultural Organization
USSR	Union of Soviet Socialist Republics
YLE	Yleisradio Oy/Rundradion Ab (Finnish Broadcasting Company)

Figure 1 The logo of the Eurovision Network, 1954–1993

Introduction: Europe's Greatest Television Show

It is Europe's biggest election, a platform from which the aspirations of dictators and drag queens have been projected, and upon which battles between capitalists and communists, Europeanists and Eurosceptics, and reactionaries and revolutionaries have been played out. Since its inception in 1956, the annual Eurovision Song Contest (ESC) has always reflected political changes in postwar Europe alongside cultural, economic, social and technological developments, with almost all European states having been represented in the contest at some point in its first sixty years. While it is globally one of the longest-running and most popular television shows, having traditionally reached hundreds of millions of viewers through television and even more now through the internet, the ESC has always been quintessentially European and has forged common cultural references among Europeans. The contest has involved national broadcasting organizations sending artists with original songs to represent their states, with the winning state traditionally hosting the contest the next year under the auspices of its national broadcasting organization. Apart from earning the right for a state to host the contest, no material award – except for the bouquets, medals and trophies that have been presented to the composers, lyricists and singers of the victorious entries – has ever been attached to winning the contest. There has always been the hope that the winner could achieve commercial success, and of the 1,438 songs that were performed in the ESC from 1956 to 2016, some went on to become international hits that are still heard all over Europe. That the ESC has had a huge impact on European popular culture is also heard in the contest's characteristic phrases that have infiltrated everyday speech across Europe, such as 'good evening, Europe', 'twelve points go to …' or 'zero points' (as well as their variations in French, the other official language of the contest), with the latter two respectively expressing acclamation or disapproval.

The ESC has itself been commonly derided for promoting déclassé popular music, having excessive costs and pandering to national stereotypes. The scoffing criticisms that have been made about the cultural kitschiness of the ESC are generally unfair considering that it has launched some popular music superstars, showcased a variety of popular music genres and had songs that have been politically and socially critical. Such judgements have also belittled the ESC's success as a technological feat achieved through international cooperation. The contest was conceived by the European Broadcasting Union (EBU) in the mid-1950s as a venture in developing Western Europe's emerging television services through the programme exchange and technical cooperation that was being fostered by the organization's Eurovision Network, from which the ESC got its name. The ESC is one of the leading examples of a television show that has connected Europeans via a simultaneous, transnational broadcast, especially as the EBU and other European organizations have made other, often fleeting, attempts to achieve the same. Yet, that impact has itself often been exaggerated by the contest's advocates, who have liked to emphasize how the contest brings together Europeans, yet who have also often underestimated how much this unification is based on an international competition that has arguably done more to underline national divisions than forge a European whole. Like the European Union (EU), as much as the ESC might – or, as this book also considers, might not – have aspired to contribute to the creation of a European identity, its national basis has continued to demonstrate that postwar European integration is not a teleological process. The history of the ESC and its organizer, the EBU, is also about national broadcasting organizations hoping to enter, opting into or out of or threatening to leave them, much like states have behaved towards the EU.

The EBU, however, had a temporal head start in facilitating postwar European cooperation. Set up in 1950, it emerged just after the Council of Europe (CoE) had been created in 1949, but it preceded the founding of the European Coal and Steel Community (ECSC) in 1951 and the European Economic Community (EEC) and the European Atomic Energy Community, or Euratom, in 1957, all three of which merged to form the European Community (EC) in 1967. The EBU also predated the alternative organization for economic integration in Western Europe, the European Free Trade Association (EFTA), which was established in 1960. The EBU was independent of all of these organizations and, together with the CoE, it was at the forefront of the promotion of European cultural cooperation well before the EC began to develop its own cultural policy. The EBU did, however, cooperate with EC institutions from the 1970s on the media coverage of their activities, as well as clash with them as the EC sought to regulate television broadcasting from the 1980s. The Eurovision Network's early success in forging a common market for radio and television programmes was arguably due to the EBU distancing itself from the politics of other Western European organizations, especially those with supranationalist aims. The relationship between the EBU and the EU has historically been fraught with tensions that are usually obscured by Europeanist portrayals of the ESC as an enduring symbol of a teleological history of postwar European integration.

The ESC has often been viewed by journalists and politicians as a harbinger of developments in international relations, a waiting room for aspiring candidates for other, grander European political organizations, especially the EU. Due to the geographical spread of the EBU's members and the organization's apolitical membership criteria, the ESC has offered the broadest number of people in the most states in Europe the opportunity to vote in a common event since its introduction in the late 1990s. The results of Europe's biggest election allow us to analyse interactions and sympathies in an international context of diasporic, post-colonial, regional, religious and sexual identities. Still, the ESC has always been presented as an 'apolitical' event by the EBU, which has insisted that all of the national broadcasting organizations participating in the contest must broadcast all of the competing entries, including those from states with which the state of the national broadcasting organization might not have diplomatic relations or be involved in a military conflict. Political statements in entries have, however, only been implicitly or explicitly banned in the contest's rules since 2000, a stipulation which the EBU has nonetheless inconsistently applied. The EBU has otherwise had no political standards for its members that are national, public service radio and television broadcasters. The criteria for EBU membership stipulate that a national broadcasting organization need only come from a state that is a member of the International Telecommunication Union (ITU), a United Nations (UN) agency, and located within the European Broadcasting Area (EBA), a technical region defined by the ITU that includes states from Europe and the Mediterranean rim. However, exactly because of the ESC's wearing of the emperor's apolitical new clothes, the political aims, attitudes and opinions of activists, governments and parties have been more liberally expressed in the contest than they could have been in other international organizations that are more constrained by diplomatic norms. As the journalist Jean Coucrand put it in the Belgian newspaper *Le Soir* (The Evening) in 1979: 'If the Eurovision Song Contest does not deal with politics, politics deals with it.'[1]

That there is no other international song contest in the world matching the longevity or popularity of the ESC demonstrates, however, that there is something peculiarly European about the ESC that transcends national identifications. The intrinsic Europeanness of the ESC is also underlined by the common etymology of 'Europe' and 'Eurovision', which can be read as the Greek and Latin versions of the same concept. One explanation of the etymology of 'Europe' is that it is derived from the Greek *eurys*, meaning 'broad', and *óps*, meaning 'eye'.[2] 'Vision' is also derived from the Latin word for 'seeing'. Both 'Europe' and 'Eurovision' are therefore about viewing things broadly, even diversely. The myth of 'Europa', who in Greek mythology was seduced by Zeus and taken to the island of Crete, also embodies staple themes of ESC entries: love, the sea and travel. However, postwar European integration projects, especially that of the EU, have hijacked the terms 'Europe' and 'Euro' to the extent that it is a symptom of contemporary conditioning to conflate anything bearing these appellations with European political organizations and their aims. These days, 'euro' is also most commonly associated with the EU's currency, giving this term an economic dimension that was not attached to it previously. The EU has come to overshadow the diversity of Europeanism, which has been promoted in the postwar era by various international organizations with different goals. Even though they are both 'unions', the EBU's internationalist aims should thus not be conflated with the EU's supranationalist ones.

Indeed, as the members of the EBU themselves typify, television in Europe still remains a very national affair, as does popular music. Even though the ESC has unified Europeans by creating shared cultural references, it has arguably been more successful in forging national icons and refashioning national identities rather than transnational ones. The patriotism expressed in the barracking for national entries at the ESC reflects the resilience of national identities despite – or because of – processes of European integration.

Yet, the ESC also demonstrates that those national identities have not been pure or unique phenomena, but have rather been refashioned through cultural transfers. One of the striking features of ESC entries is, in fact, that they have always expressed social diversity through the biographies of their artists, which usually have an element of international migration based on whatever combination of economic, educational, intimate, political or professional reasons. The national label that these artists have appeared under at the ESC has often been deceiving, especially as, in some cases, the artists themselves have not even been citizens of the states that they have represented. However, even a win by a non-national has been greeted with patriotic fervour, as the example of Canada's Celine Dion, who won the 1988 ESC for Switzerland, demonstrated. So, while the extent to which the ESC has shaped a European identity is arguable, it is more obvious that it has refashioned national identities and made them appear more attractive and modern through new media, technologies and, of course, fashions. I often prefer the term 'nation fashioning' over 'nation building' or 'nation branding' as 'fashion' invokes the interdependent recognition of the aesthetic and the temporal as well as the appropriation of successful models, considerations which are also crucial for the production of ESC entries.

As it has never adopted political criteria for its membership, the EBU's remit has always been greater than that of other postwar European organizations. During the Cold War, the perception that the ESC developed harmoniously parallel to Western European integration was magnified by the contest's exclusion of Eastern European national broadcasting organizations. These had their own equivalent of the EBU, the International Radio and Television Organization (OIRT), whose Intervision Network organized the fleeting Intervision Song Contest (ISC). However, the participation of national broadcasting organizations in the ESC also did not strictly mirror their states' involvement in other Western European organizations. The EBU has included as active members – which have voting rights in the organization and can participate fully in the Eurovision Network – national broadcasting organizations from authoritarian and liberal democratic states, as well as from states that are members of the North Atlantic Treaty Organization (NATO) or neutral. Neutrality made Switzerland, for example, willing to host international organizations yet suspicious of entering them: although it joined the CoE in 1963 and the UN in 2002, Switzerland has never entered the EU. Yet, Switzerland was a founding member of the EBU and is the site of its headquarters, and the state hosted the first ESC in 1956, which it also won with Lys Assia singing 'Refrain'. The EBU has also admitted as associate members, which are not part of the Eurovision Network, national broadcasting organizations from states outside of the EBA with various political systems, including Australia, China and Iran.[3]

The ESC has from its very beginning been appropriated in the cultural diplomacies of states with varying foreign policies and political systems as cultural propaganda, nation branding or soft power. For the active members of the EBU, as well as an Australian one, which have participated in the ESC, the potential innocuousness of the popular music typically performed there has made the ESC appropriable for the cultural diplomacies of governments of various political shades. As the writer Milan Kundera puts it, '[k]itsch is the aesthetic ideal of all politicians and all political parties and movements.'[4] Sometimes just participating in the contest has been a reflection of a state's aspirations for European integration, from the case of Spain in the 1960s and 1970s when it was ruled by the rightist dictatorship of Francisco Franco, to the examples of Central and East European states that joined the ESC after the Cold War. For authoritarian states that have been represented in the ESC, such as Greece, Portugal and Spain in the 1960s and 1970s and Azerbaijan, Belarus and Russia after the Cold War, participation in the contest has been used by their governments to whitewash their suppression of media freedom and political opposition and make their international images more palatable to a European audience. In authoritarian states in which governments have exercised direct control over the national broadcasting organizations, the connection between foreign policies and the appropriation of the ESC in cultural diplomacies has been clearer than in liberal democracies in which the national broadcasting organizations are ideally meant to be free of government interference. However, the ESC has even in liberal democracies had a political symbolism in the context of domestic conflicts between political parties, and the accountability and transparency of their national broadcasting organizations has been questioned when their officials have decided not to choose entries through a national selection based on a public vote. In liberal democracies, artists, music industry representatives and officials from national broadcasting organizations have also used the contest as a vehicle not only to achieve commercial aims but also to make political statements – and despite not always having a democratic mandate to do so. Domestic political battles have been waged through the ESC as national broadcasting organizations have entered artists who have been politically symbolic because of their ethnicity, gender, nationality, race, religion or sexuality.

The ESC has thus been a highly flexible tool of cultural diplomacy that has had different meanings for different states at different times, which can also be read from the affiliations and rankings of the politicians who have attended the contest when it has been held in their state. The contest has varyingly been used to express Europeanism or Euroscepticism, or neither. In the United Kingdom (UK), for example, which has had postwar Europe's biggest popular music industry, the ESC was during the Cold War approached principally as a commercial endeavour, much as the policies of British governments favoured Western European integration more for its economic benefits than as a cultural or political project. And some of the most Eurosceptic states have in fact had some of the most fervent national audiences for the ESC: an Iceland that has withdrawn its application for EU membership; a Norway that won the contest just after it rejected EU membership; and a Sweden that has one of the biggest national audiences for – and whose popular music industry has profitted immensely from – the ESC, but which nonetheless has not adopted the euro. Voting in the ESC has infamously reflected regional blocs – Balkan, Nordic, former Soviet and Western – yet the contest's organization has been dominated by the commercial ambitions and technological superiority of Europe's north. In states that have variously been on a geocultural, geoeconomic or geopolitical periphery at a certain historical point, journalists and politicians have interpreted poor scores in the contest to explain their states' cultural, economic and political marginalization in European affairs. In all states, public reactions to national results in the contest have generally viewed failure at the ESC in terms of a cultural and political distancing from 'Europe', while success has been perceived as acceptance by it. Still, while the enthusiasm of national audiences for the contest has ebbed and risen in accordance with the success of their national entries, the ESC remains Europe's greatest television show. That this was neither the expectation nor the intention of its founders reflects how national sentiments and public desires have often been misjudged or undervalued by the technocratic establishments that have been at the vanguard of postwar European integration.

This book examines the relationship between postwar European politics and the ESC, from the soft-power use of the ESC in cultural diplomacies to refashion the images of states, to how the contest has been a subject in political battles within states. Although the ESC has been such a massive cultural phenomenon lasting some six decades so far, there has not yet been a systematic scholarly attempt to research the history of the ESC. The articles, books and websites on the history of the ESC that have been produced by the EBU, fans and journalists have tended to focus on the content of the contest itself – such as the entries, hosting and voting – rather than address the ESC in the broader context of cultural, economic and political international relations. They have sometimes also perpetuated clichés, exaggerations or unsubstantiated facts about the history of the ESC – or expressed fantasies about a unified Europe imagined through the contest.[5] As a result, a hagiographic, popular history of the ESC has emerged which overemphasizes the contest's positive function for European integration without considering the EBU's complex relations with international organizations and national governments that are explained through archival sources, especially those from the CoE, EBU, ITU and OIRT that this book pioneeringly draws on. The popular historiography of the ESC has also underplayed the role that the contest has had in the less positive aspects of postwar European history, such as in the cultural diplomacies of authoritarian states or how it has been used as a symbolic battlefield for actual wars that have taken place in Europe or elsewhere in the world. Regarding academic literature, there has been a growing scholarly interest in the ESC in the past decade, but the research has focused overwhelmingly on the post-1989 period. The Cold War era has consequently received little attention: there is hardly any literature, for example, on the ISC, the Eastern European attempt to create a global and communist alterative to the ESC. Based on the aforementioned archival sources together with an analysis of the recordings of all of the editions of the ESC from 1956 to 2016 and every artist and entry in them, this book builds on the extant scholarship and connects the Cold War era with the ESC's history from 1990 to 2016. It argues that the cultural, economic, political and social issues that were highlighted at the ESC from 1990 to 2016, such as cultural diplomacy, economic disparity, European integration, military conflict and social diversity, have historically been constant features of the contest.

The financial cost of the contest has always been criticized, the voting system has always been debated and reformed, and national societies have always argued about the merits of the songs that have represented their states.

With an emphasis on the diplomatic history of the ESC, the first part of this book, 'The Cold War, 1945–1989', focuses on the role that the ESC played in relations between states in both Eastern and Western Europe during that period. The first chapter, 'The Western European Arrangement', begins with the section 'Organizations', which discusses the international organizations whose policies and regulations have defined the remit of the ESC. Following the Congress of Vienna in 1815, the first international telecommunications organizations were established in the nineteenth century. The International Broadcasting Union (IBU), the direct predecessor of the EBU, was formed in 1925. The EBU was thus not an entirely new phenomenon in terms of promoting cooperation among national broadcasting organizations, and the ESC also had its roots in earlier transnational radio programmes. During the interwar era and in the first postwar decade, new political arrangements and telecommunications technologies required new forms of international cooperation, and this mantra also defined the development of separate international broadcasting organizations for Eastern and Western Europe. The second section, 'Integration', looks at the relationship between the ESC and Western European organizations, namely the CoE and the EC. While the CoE was important for facilitating the cultural cooperation that the ESC epitomized, the EC only began to develop a cultural policy from the 1970s and it briefly appropriated the ESC in this in the late 1980s. Considering that the ESC had by then already established itself as Europe's most popular television show, the EBU was during the Cold War earlier at the forefront of the production of shared cultural references among Western Europeans than the EC was. The third section, 'Anglo-Americanization', argues that the ESC needs to be considered in a global context as well, and not just as a European phenomenon as its name suggests. From its very beginning, the ESC reflected American cultural influences which arguably united Western Europeans more than any other cultural trends. Although the contest was not regularly broadcast in the United States, it did help to launch the careers of artists who would become successful in North America. Yet, the ESC's global influence from 1956 to 1989 was not limited by Anglo-Americanization: for example,

Portuguese and Spanish artists had, for linguistic reasons, markets in Latin America. The ESC was even broadcast to South American states that together with Australia – which was also connected to Europe through immigrant and imperial ties – were the main non-European areas to experience the ESC during the Cold War.

The second chapter, 'The Show of Nations', looks at the role that the ESC had in national politics during the Cold War. The first section, 'Fashioning', examines how the ESC refashioned national identities through the media of popular music and television. As ESC entries were usually more successful nationally than internationally, this section argues that the contest has been more effective in fashioning national identities rather than shaping a European one. The next section, 'Mapping', considers how national audiences viewed other European states through the ESC. This section demonstrates that cultural affiliations have defined the phenomenon of bloc voting throughout the contest's history, although not in all geographical or linguistic regions; it also shows that political ties have not played such a decisive role in the voting, with the major exceptions being those between Greece, Cyprus and Turkey. The section 'Revolutions' examines how national political conflicts were played out in the ESC. In many states there was an identification of the contest as something that belonged more to the left or right wings of national politics. Leftist protests in Sweden, for example, opposed the Anglicization and commercialization of the ESC in the late 1970s. The rightist dictatorships of Portugal and Spain, meanwhile, appropriated the contest in their cultural diplomacies in the 1960s and 1970s to whitewash their international images, although there were also attempts by political dissidents in these states to use the ESC as a platform to criticize these authoritarian governments. The rise of new social movements in Western Europe from the mid-1960s also saw more varied political and social issues being articulated at the ESC, although gender and sexuality issues were apparent in the contest in the late 1950s even before the greater sexual liberalization in Western European societies in the 1960s.

The third chapter, 'A Contest for Communism', discusses the experiences of Eastern European states with the ESC. It begins with the section 'Appropriation', which examines how communist governments in Eastern Europe went from a policy of censoring Western popular music to appropriating it in their cultural policies, including through the staging of international song contests.

Already in the late 1950s, as the section 'Intervision' highlights, the OIRT was interested in its members participating in the ESC as the organization began cooperating with the EBU in the context of an easing of East-West tensions. The EBU rebuffed the OIRT's proposal for a joint international song contest but allowed Eastern European national broadcasting organizations to broadcast the ESC from 1965. The OIRT twice set up an equivalent contest, the ISC, from 1965 to 1968 in Czechoslovakia and from 1977 to 1980 in Poland, and this also sought to include Western European national broadcasting organizations and record companies. However, both of these series of the ISC were suppressed because of political upheavals in Czechoslovakia and Poland. Due to the political oppression by communist governments, some Eastern European artists emigrated to Western Europe and went on to perform in the ESC, and their cases are examined in the section 'Dissent'. Although Yugoslavia represented an exceptional case in the ESC as the only communist state to participate in the contest during the Cold War, reflecting its nonalignment and openness to Western cultural influences, censorship was also a phenomenon there until 1989, the same year that Yugoslavia won the ESC as the only communist state ever to do so. This was a harbinger for the entry of Central and East European states into the ESC after the end of communism in 1989, although when the ESC was staged in May of that year, the extent of the geopolitical changes that would befall Europe before the 1990 ESC could not have been anticipated.

The second part of the book, 'European Unification, 1990–2016', focuses on the relationship between the ESC and European politics since the end of the Cold War. The fourth chapter, 'A Concert of Europe', describes how the 1990 ESC in Zagreb reflected hopes for European unification in the wake of the Cold War, but these were soon quickly tested by the wars in the former Yugoslavia. As the section 'Wars' explains, military conflicts, from those in the former Yugoslavia to the ones between Armenia and Azerbaijan, Israel and its Arab neighbours, Russia and Georgia, and Russia and Ukraine, were a constant backdrop to the ESC after 1989. The impact of these wars on the ESC demonstrated how the contest has not just been a forum for cultural cooperation but also one through which military conflicts have been symbolically waged. Some Central and East European states, as the section 'Europeanism' shows, considered joining the ESC to be important for their cultural diplomacies as an expression of their aims for integration into other European organizations, especially the CoE and the EU. Yet, while the contest can be viewed as a stage for the articulation of Europeanist aspirations, it has also reflected criticism of European integration in states across Europe, as is discussed in the section 'Euroscepticism'. In West European states, for example, media, political and public reactions to the successes of Central and East European states in the contest were tied to anxieties over the enlargement of the EU. However, for one Central and East European state, the Czech Republic, not participating in the contest also reflected Eurosceptic sentiments in its national politics. In Iceland and Norway, though, their rejection of EU membership did not correlate with a public disinterest in the ESC, with Iceland proportionately having the largest national televiewing audience for it.

The final chapter, 'The Values of Eurovision', considers how the ESC has shaped values that have been perceived as integral to a European identity. The first is that of 'Diversity', and this section examines how the contest reflected ethnic, racial, religious and sexual diversity in Europe from 1990 to 2016. Ethnic, racial and religious minorities have a history of being represented in the contest since its early years. Sexual minorities, however, were only visibly represented in the ESC from the late 1990s, and their appearance in the contest became a point of contention between conservatives and liberals across Europe. Changes to the voting system in the contest also continued to be controversial and even prompted the withdrawal of Turkey from the ESC. One such change allowed the 'Big Five' – France, Germany, Italy, Spain and the UK – direct entry into the final without having to participate in the semi-finals that were introduced in 2004 to accommodate more participants. The Big Five were privileged because of their financial contributions to the contest and their population sizes, which also demonstrates the power of commercial considerations in the ESC, an issue that is addressed in the section 'Commercialism'. In light of the economic crisis that the EU experienced from 2009, the financial cost of just participating in the ESC became daunting for some national broadcasting organizations, while others, particularly non-EU member states like Azerbaijan and Russia, invested record amounts into hosting the contest. Although the ESC has always been controversial for its cost, it has also highlighted the economic disparities that exist in Europe roughly following a north–south divide. The establishment of the Eurovision Network and the EU's original institutions were initially motivated by economic reasoning, but some sixty years after their formation economic divergences undermined the unity among their member states. Both the ESC and the EU also continued to grapple with issues of democratic legitimacy, which is the subject of the section 'Democracy'. Although the ESC adopted public televoting in 1997, the fact that it in 2009 reintroduced an element of expert jury voting alongside the public televote reflected a distrust of direct democracy that was also evident in the technocratic approaches of the EU.

The conclusion, 'Bridges, Diamonds and Fires', reflects on the issues addressed in the previous chapters through the diamond, sixtieth edition of the contest that was held in Vienna in 2015 and the 2016 ESC in Stockholm that marked sixty years since the staging of the first ESC. The 2015 ESC was staged in the year that major historical anniversaries of the Congress of Vienna, the First World War and the Second World War were being marked. Social diversity was again highlighted as a constant theme in the ESC after the victory of Austria's bearded drag queen Conchita Wurst in the previous year's contest had provoked both joyous and hostile reactions across Europe because of her queer identity. That many Central and East European states which have had close ties with Austria through culture, economics and immigration did not participate in the 2015 ESC for financial reasons demonstrated how economic disparities continued to impact on the ESC. The 2016 ESC was held in the wake of the migrant crisis of 2015, during which over a million migrants and refugees entered Europe, many of them fleeing from wars taking place in the southeastern extremity of the EBA. Yet, the 2016 ESC was most marked by another crisis – the conflict between Russia and Ukraine over the annexation of Crimea and the war in Donbass. As issues of diversity, economics, immigration and war were once again being controversially addressed in the ESC, the contest still had a meaning in Europe's international relations. Yet, has the ESC only been a metaphor or also a catalyst for change?

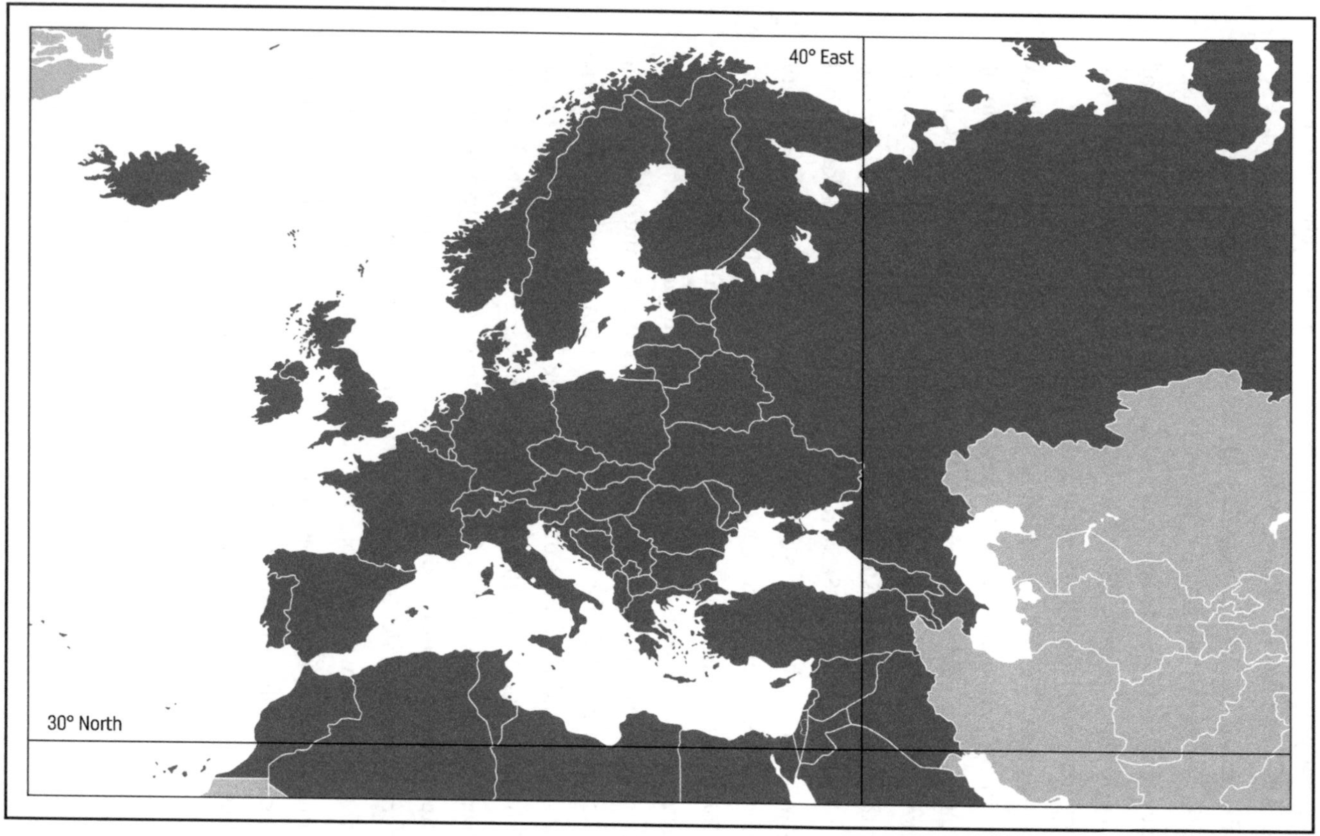

40° East

30° North

States in the EBA, 2016

Figure 2 The EBA

Part One

The Cold War, 1945–1989

Figure 3 Freddy Quinn, 1956

1

The Western European Arrangement

Freddy Quinn and Walter Andreas Schwarz were the faces of German innocence. In the first ESC that was staged in Lugano on 24 May 1956, each of the seven participating national broadcasting organizations – which all happened to come from the six founding member states of the ECSC, Belgium, France, Italy, Luxembourg, the Netherlands and West Germany, plus Switzerland – entered two artists who each performed a song. Twenty-four-year-old Quinn and 42-year-old Schwarz were internally selected within that state's national broadcasting organization, the Consortium of the Public Service Broadcasting Corporations of the Federal Republic of Germany (ARD), to represent West Germany in the ESC. Quinn and Schwarz represented West Germany not only with their songs but also through their biographies that embodied experiences which were definitive for a West German national identity. Schwarz had been born in the town of Aschersleben which, in the postwar European arrangement, would find itself in East Germany. He had studied musicology in Vienna before being interned, because of his Jewish background, in a concentration camp in Germany in 1938. After the Second World War, Schwarz resumed his career as a singer and writer; an Anglophile, he was known for his English-German translations and worked as an announcer for the British national broadcasting organization, the British Broadcasting Corporation (BBC).[1] Schwarz's ballad in the 1956 ESC, 'Das Lied vom großen Glück' (The Song of Great Happiness), advised that people should live for the present rather than get stuck in the past and risk the joys of life passing them by.

Appearing after Schwarz in the ESC, Quinn represented a different generation and sang about both the burdens and freedoms of the present. In the style of the rock and roll that was hitting Western Europe from the United States, his song 'So geht das jede Nacht' (That's How It Is Every Night) was about a girlfriend who was going out with other men who, like Freddy himself, had English-language nicknames such as Ben, Billy, Jack, Jimmy, Johnny and Tommy. Quinn hailed from Austria, and in the history of Austrian–German relations in the ESC his performance for West Germany would prove to be an unusual example of the cultural ties between the two states – especially considering that their national juries hardly exchanged points in the 1950s and 1960s, which could be interpreted as an effort to avoid any suggestion of their states' mutual association in the Nazi era. Quinn himself had been a child during the Second World War and liked to emphasize his cosmopolitan background in media interviews: his mother was Austrian and his father was American, and he had spent time living with his father in the United States before returning to Austria in 1938, the year in which it was annexed by Nazi Germany.[2]

Quinn and Schwarz were the cosmopolitan representatives of a West Germany that was distancing itself from its Nazi past and embracing an Americanized present. They challenged the stereotype of Germans as humourless, militaristic and unemotional types who speak an accordingly uneuphonious language, a cliché that lingered in the minds of other Europeans – and fuelled jokes for British sitcoms – long well after the Second World War. Quinn and Schwarz portrayed a pacified West Germany that had learned its lessons from the Second World War and was firmly in the pro-American, Western alliance as the state found itself at the centre of the Cold War. It was, after all, around a divided Germany that postwar Europe was arranged. West Germany's economic wealth, geographical location, military history, population size and technological prowess made it central to peace and prosperity in postwar Western Europe, and the state's participation was essential in the organizations that were established in the late 1940s and early 1950s for the new Western European arrangement, from the EBU to the CoE, EC and NATO.

While Western European economic, military and political organizations developed concurrently with the EBU, they – and their member states individually – often had different visions for the breadth, intensity and style of integration among their members, as well as for the role that culture should play in this. The EBU produced common cultural references for Western Europeans decades before the EC even began to develop a cultural policy, and not just through ESC artists like Quinn who would become international stars. The ESC also pioneered the use of the circle of twelve stars – a version of which the EC would in 1985 adopt as its flag – as a European symbol by utilizing it from 1954 as the logo for the Eurovision Network. As a distinctively Western European event, the ESC gave cultural expression to the economic and political integration among Western European states, but the EC only started to become directly involved with the contest in the late 1980s after Brussels realized that it needed to develop a cultural policy that would promote a European identity.

The ESC was not, however, just a cultural symbol for Western European integration in the face of Cold War division. It also expressed how Western Europeans collectively related to other parts of the world in the postwar international arrangement, especially through migration and post-imperialism. Middle Eastern and northern African states, for example, had been drawn into the EBA in the interwar era; however, they mostly did not enter the ESC in protest against the only Middle Eastern state, Israel, that regularly did from 1973, and whose participation symbolically reminded Western Europeans of the Holocaust that Schwarz had suffered in. Then there was the American superpower that led the Western Bloc and had a hegemonic influence on Western European popular culture during the Cold War, as was reflected by the Anglo-American style of Quinn's song. Some ESC songs expressed Western Europe's ambivalent response to Americanization as they criticized the exacerbation of Cold War tensions, espoused the virtues of chansons over rock and roll or glorified a European way of life. However, there were other politically charged songs that echoed the American folk music that was the soundtrack of protest movements in the United States. As the sounds of Americanization and Europeanization harmonized and clashed in the ESC during the Cold War, they reflected not only integration in Western Europe but also tensions within the transatlantic alliance.

Organizations

The ESC was a product not just of international relations in postwar Europe but also of a history of international cooperation in telecommunications that had begun in the nineteenth century. The origins of the international organizations that shaped the ESC can be traced back to 1815 in Vienna, the city that Quinn grew up in. At the Congress of Vienna that took place from September 1814 to June 1815, European statesmen redrew the map of their continent in the wake of the Napoleonic Wars and set up a system of international relations known as the 'Concert of Europe' for the maintenance of the new order. The ESC is indelibly connected to 1815 as the final defeat of France's Emperor Napoleon I at the Battle of Waterloo in that year inspired ABBA's 'Waterloo', which was declared the most popular ESC entry ever by a public televote in the *Congratulations: 50 Years of the Eurovision Song Contest* show that was staged in Copenhagen in 2005 for the ESC's fiftieth anniversary. 'Waterloo' won the 1974 ESC with its conductor Sven-Olof Walldoff dressed up as the emperor. Just as the ESC would be appropriated in the cultural and public diplomacies of international organizations and states in postwar Europe as a metaphorical 'Concert of Europe', dancing and music accompanied the negotiations at the Congress of Vienna. So much so that Prince Charles-Joseph de Ligne described it as 'the Congress dances, but does not advance'.[3] Emissaries, plenipotentiaries and royals were entertained in the Hofburg Palace, where the 1967 ESC would be staged, and composers such as Ludwig van Beethoven were commissioned to produce musical pieces especially for the Congress of Vienna.

Yet, beyond these connections, the Congress of Vienna was most significant for the ESC because it established the first intergovernmental organization, the Central Commission for the Navigation of the Rhine. This paved the way for the creation of other international organizations in the nineteenth century. Some of the earliest of these were formed for international cooperation in postal and telegraphic communications, with the International Telegraph Union being set up in 1865 as the first public international union. While the founding members of the International Telegraph Union were all European states – the first bilateral agreement on telegraphy had already been agreed between the Austrian Empire and Prussia in 1849 – the development of intercontinental telecommunications and new technologies motivated the establishment in the early twentieth century of other international organizations whose regulations would ultimately define the remit of the ESC. In 1903, the German government organized the Preliminary Conference on Wireless Telegraphy in Berlin for European states and the United States. Prince Heinrich of Prussia – an admiral, a brother of Germany's last emperor, Wilhelm II, and a grandson of Queen Victoria of the

UK – had triggered the conference after he had been prevented from sending telegrams to American and German destinations, including to American president Theodore Roosevelt, as Prince Heinrich sailed back to Europe aboard the *Deutschland* following an official visit to the United States.[4] The conference of 1903 was followed in 1906 by the International Radiotelegraph Conference, which produced the first international radio regulations and set up the International Radiotelegraph Union to administer them.

At the International Radiotelegraph Conference in Madrid in 1932, the International Radiotelegraph Union merged with the International Telegraph Union to form the ITU, which has since then been the international organization responsible for managing its namesake. The *Statutes of the European Broadcasting Union* have always stipulated that a state must belong to the ITU for its national broadcasting organization to be able to join the EBU as an active member. Another criterion for active membership of the EBU has been that the national broadcasting organization must come from a state located within the EBA, one of the world regions defined by the ITU for the purpose of allocating broadcasting frequencies. In 1932, the ITU adopted the definition of the 'European region', as it then called the EBA, as being bounded to

> the North and West by the natural limits of Europe, on the East by the meridian 40° East of Greenwich and on the South by the parallel of 30° North so as to include the Western part of the U.S.S.R. and the territories bordering the Mediterranean, with the exception of the parts of Arabia and Hedjaz included in this sector.[5]

Although the *Statutes of the European Broadcasting Union* took the EBA as being based on the definition adopted by the ITU, the EBA was originally delineated in the interwar era by the world's first international broadcasting organization, the IBU. It was established in 1925 to manage the rapid expansion of the newest technology, radio, in Europe, especially considering the increase in the number of states following the dissolution of Austria–Hungary after the First World War. By 1939, the IBU's active membership included national radio broadcasting organizations from almost all European states; the Union of Soviet Socialist Republics (USSR), the world's first and, alongside Mongolia, only communist-ruled state in the interwar era, never joined because of its political exceptionalism. As the direct predecessor of the EBU, the IBU pioneered cooperation among national broadcasting organizations on legal and technical issues, particularly the allocation of broadcasting frequencies in order to reduce interference problems. The ITU also produced the first experiments in the international exchange, joint production and simultaneous broadcasting of musical programmes. Series such as *European Concerts*, *International Concerts*, *National Concerts*, *National Nights* and *World Concerts* showcased music from states represented in the ITU, and some of these programmes were even broadcast intercontinentally.[6] As with the EBU, national broadcasting organizations from other continents joined the IBU as associate members, and the IBU also collaborated with other international organizations – including the ITU and the League of Nations – especially as it had unrealized ambitions to become a worldwide organization.

It was, however, the EBA that would be the IBU's definitive legacy for the ESC. From 1925 to 1929, the limits of the EBA were defined by the IBU through plans that were adopted at meetings in Brussels, Geneva and Prague, the same three cities that would host the headquarters of Europe's two postwar international broadcasting organizations. As the historian Suzanne Lommers has demonstrated, the debates over how exactly 'Europe' should be defined for the purposes of the IBU were settled by geographical and technical considerations – particularly the remit of broadcasting signals – rather than cultural or political ones.[7] The northern and western limits of the EBA were relatively easily defined by the Arctic and Atlantic oceans, although they would prove the most difficult to conquer technologically: at the EBA's northwestern extreme, Iceland would in 1986 become the last Western European state to join the ESC during the Cold War, mainly due to the need for a satellite connection between it and continental Europe. Regarding the eastern limit of the EBA, the 1925 Geneva Plan initially set it at 32°30' East, thereby extending into the USSR only as far as the western-most parts of Russia in order to reduce interference between Soviet radio stations and those from neighbouring European states. That was subsequently amended to 40°30' East in the 1929 Prague Plan in order to incorporate more of the USSR all the way to Moscow. This change occurred at a time when, in the early years of Joseph Stalin's rule, the Soviet government sought a rapprochement with other European states and realized that engagement with the IBU could also advance the development of Soviet radio broadcasting.[8]

Still, the eastern limit of the EBA did not extend as far as what is commonly accepted as Europe's natural eastern extremity, the Ural Mountains; if it had, it would have included the Caucasus, Iran and parts of Central Asia, as any expansion eastwards obviously went south-easterly too. Indeed, the eastward extension of the EBA in 1929 also brought the Levant into the EBA at a time when, following the collapse of the Ottoman Empire, Lebanon and Syria were under French mandate and Palestine and Transjordan were British controlled. A repercussion of this would be Israel's participation in the ESC: this has reflected the breadth of the EBA's borders, but it has ironically also limited the contest's geographical scope as some national broadcasting organizations from Arab states in the Levant and northern Africa have refused to participate in the contest because their Israeli counterpart has. Algeria, Egypt, Libya, Morocco and Tunisia were also included in the EBA in order to reduce interference between their radio stations and ones from southern Europe. The definition of the southern limit of the EBA was thus motivated more by Eurocentric, technical interests rather than colonialist ones, even though Algeria, Libya, Morocco and Tunisia were in 1932 under French, Italian or Spanish control.[9] Nonetheless, the definition of the EBA acknowledged the history of the Mediterranean basin as a single telecommunications space, the scope of which had been foreshadowed in the second half of the nineteenth century through the construction of telegraphic networks that connected the European metropoles to their territories on other continents.

The biggest swathe of territory within the EBA that was never represented in the IBU was, then, that of the USSR. However, after having achieved superpower status in the Second World War, the USSR sought a leading role in international broadcasting organizations. The Second World War had reduced cooperation among the IBU's members, especially after the organization's technical centre in Brussels had been taken over by the Nazi occupation in 1940. In 1946, the USSR proposed the establishment of a new organization, the International Broadcasting Organization (OIR), which would also be based in Brussels and include members from both Eastern and Western Europe, but with plans for it to develop into a worldwide organization. Yet, the working of the OIR became unfeasible amid rising Cold War tensions in the late 1940s: as communist parties took control of Eastern European governments, states from both blocs used international radio broadcasting as a weapon in their propaganda wars, such as through Radio Moscow and the Voice of America. Western European broadcasting organizations additionally opposed separate membership and voting rights for the broadcasting organizations of the various republics of the USSR, which would have given that state an inordinate influence in the OIR, especially in combination with the votes of other communist-controlled states in Eastern Europe.[10] A fear of Eastern European domination was thus etched into the foundations of the EBU.

Just as there would be the duplication of other international organizations for Eastern and Western Europe, such as the economic blocs of the Council for Mutual Economic Assistance (COMECON) and EC, and the military organizations of the Warsaw Pact and NATO, the EBU was established as a Western European response to the OIR. The tensions between Eastern and Western European national broadcasting organizations within the OIR led to broadcasting organizations from mostly Western European states to meet in Torquay in the UK in 1950 and form the EBU. The states that were represented at this meeting were the Western European ones of Belgium, Denmark, Finland, France, Ireland, Italy, Luxembourg, Monaco, the Netherlands, Norway, Portugal, Sweden, Switzerland, the UK and Vatican City. Yugoslavia, which had in 1948 dissented from the Eastern Bloc but maintained a communist government, was represented as well. Officials from the national broadcasting organizations of Egypt, Lebanon, Syria, and Turkey were also in attendance, while the Israeli national broadcasting organization participated as an observer; the list of attendees was completed by the broadcasting organizations from the still French protectorates of Morocco and Tunisia. The IBU was also finally dissolved in 1950, with its assets being transferred to the EBU.[11] Like the IBU, the EBU set up its administrative headquarters in Geneva and its technical centre in Brussels, the diplomatic capitals of postwar Europe. With Geneva being the site of international organizations, including the ITU and a UN office – Switzerland being an attractive location for these because of its neutrality which had been fixed at the Congress of Vienna – and Brussels the future centre of EC institutions as well as NATO, the locations of the two headquarters would serve to advance both the European and global ambitions of the EBU.

The OIR moved its headquarters to Prague in 1950 and continued to operate for the national broadcasting organizations from Eastern European states; unlike the EBU, its membership would largely be determined by political criteria, namely that of a state having a communist government. Although it was intended for states that were not allied with the USSR, the membership criteria for the EBU were nonetheless formulated to avoid subjective biases that could overly politicize the organization, as had been the case with the exclusion of the USSR from the IBU.[12] The EBU's membership criteria required only that the broadcasting organization have a national remit and public service aim, and that it come from a state that was located in the EBA and was a member of the ITU. Following the establishment of the UN in 1945, the ITU became a specialized UN agency in 1947. The ITU adopted its own membership criteria of a state being a member of the UN or having its application approved by two-thirds of the ITU's member states. Recognition of statehood by other international organizations therefore became necessary for a state to be represented in the EBU, but this did not mean that the EBU's membership criteria were not political: they were just politicized by other international organizations.

The EBU's membership criteria, and the fact that the ITU was an older international organization than the UN, meant that the national broadcasting organizations of several states could join the EBU as their states were members of the ITU but not the UN. This was especially the case until 1955, when the UN admitted Austria, Finland, Ireland, Italy, Portugal and Spain, as well as with Switzerland and West Germany, which joined the UN in 2002 and 1973 respectively, and Vatican City, which has never joined the UN. Austria and West Germany were two exceptional cases because they were under Allied occupation after the Second World War. Although Austria was readmitted into the ITU in 1945, under the Allied occupation its broadcasting organizations were decentralized on a regional level. This meant that Austria could only enter the EBU in 1953 once it re-established a national broadcasting organization, the Austrian Broadcasting Entity, although still before it regained its sovereignty in 1955.[13] ARD joined the EBU in 1952 as West Germany had to wait for permission from the Allied powers for it to first enter the ITU in the same year.[14] Cyprus and Malta had the reverse experience: their membership of the ITU was contingent upon their entry into the UN as they achieved independence from the UK in 1960 and 1964 respectively. However, because of their geographical proximity to southern Europe and status as French protectorates, Morocco and Tunisia's broadcasting organizations had already been welcomed into the EBU in 1950 after also having been previously admitted into the ITU, and before they achieved independence in 1956. Algeria was initially also included in the EBU from 1950 as its Mediterranean region was administered as an integral part of France; after Algeria became independent in 1962, its national broadcasting organization, Algerian Radio and Television Broadcasting, joined the EBU in 1970.

For most national broadcasting organizations, then, joining the EBU was less a matter of political recognition and more one of how developed their radio and television services were and what economic and technical benefits these could anticipate from membership. The national broadcasting organizations that entered the EBU in the 1950s did so first through their radio services. Their television services joined according to the introduction and expansion of these in each state until 1966, when Iceland and Israel became the last states that would be represented in the ESC during the Cold War to introduce them. Television services had limitedly begun in some European states in the interwar era, including in France, Germany, Italy, the Netherlands, Poland, the UK and the USSR, but these were interrupted by the Second World War; they were introduced in most European states in the 1950s, making the pursuit of the technical advancement of television broadcasting the principal aim of the EBU in that decade. Already in the early 1950s, pioneering milestones were reached in transnational television broadcasting that echoed the history of the EBA in royalty and telegraphy. The BBC achieved the first transnational television transmission, between France and the UK in 1950, on the occasion of the centenary of the laying of the first underwater telegraph cable between the two states. The first transnational one produced by the EBU was that of the coronation in 1953 of Queen Elizabeth II of the UK – herself a relative of the aforementioned Prince Heinrich – and it was broadcast live in France, the Netherlands, the UK and West Germany to a viewership of twenty million people.[15]

These successful experiments foreshadowed the establishment of the Eurovision Network in 1954. The EBU developed the Eurovision Network for the exchange and production of common television programmes in order to cost-effectively increase the programming material for national broadcasting organizations. An equivalent facility for radio programmes had previously been unsuccessfully proposed by Marcel Bezençon, the director general of the

Swiss national broadcasting organization, the Swiss Broadcasting Corporation (SRG SSR), to the United Nations Educational, Scientific and Cultural Organization (UNESCO) in 1947 and the IBU in 1948. He readapted his proposal to focus on television programming when he presented it to the EBU in 1950; however, such international cooperation in television programming could only be realized by the EBU as more states developed television services.[16] The first Eurovision Network programmes were broadcast between Belgium, Denmark, France, Italy, the Netherlands, Switzerland, the UK and West Germany in four weeks of experimental programming held in June and July 1954. The experimental programming began with a broadcast of the Montreux Narcissus Festival, a flower festival. Foreshadowing the importance that religious programming would have for the Eurovision Network, the first evening of the experimental programming included a speech by Pope Pius XII, who called the network 'a symbol and a promise … of union between the nations, and in one respect, to a degree, it initiates that union'.[17] EBU officials considered cooperation with Vatican City important due to the transnational Catholic audience and because religious freedom distinguished Western Europe from Eastern Europe; however, Vatican City is one of the two states in Europe that has never participated in the ESC. The most-watched programmes during the experimental programming were matches from the World Cup for soccer that was then being held in Switzerland, which was the main reason why the experimental programming was scheduled for that period.[18] This foreshadowed the importance that sporting events would have as by far the biggest category of programmes exchanged by the Eurovision Network, which would be due not only to their mass, transnational popularity, but also to the fact that they did not face the linguistic obstacles of other programmes.[19]

Yet, the most popular and successful programme that the Eurovision Network would produce, and also its only regular multilateral project, was a light entertainment programme and its namesake, the ESC. When the Eurovision Network broadcast its first programmes in 1954, discussions ensued in the EBU as to how the offerings could be made more modern and spectacular. Following suggestions put forward at the meeting of its Programme Committee – which was in 1964 succeeded by the Television Programme Committee as the decision-making body for the ESC – in Monte Carlo in 1955, the EBU decided at the session of its General Assembly in Rome later in that year to establish the ESC as well as another ultimately short-lived programme for variety acts called *Top Town*.[20] The inspiration for the ESC came from Italian Radio and Television (RAI), which had been staging the Sanremo Italian Song Festival in the seaside resort town of the same name since 1951. Members of the Programme Committee attended the Sanremo Italian Song Festival in 1955, when it was also broadcast through the Eurovision Network.[21] However, the Sanremo Italian Song Festival was not the only song contest in Italy at the time: in the mid-1950s, the City of Venice and RAI also organized the International Song Festival in Venice. The first edition of this contest in 1955 included entries submitted by the radio services of broadcasting organizations from Austria, Belgium, France, Italy, Monaco and the Netherlands: they each submitted six songs that were original and no longer than 3.5 minutes, with the entries being voted on by national juries and the winner being awarded the Golden Gondola prize. The International Song Festival was therefore more similar in its structure to the ESC than the national Sanremo Italian Song Festival was, with the major difference between the ESC and its Venetian predecessor being that the latter was broadcast only via radio and not television.[22] Still, the International Song Festival was the world's first ever international song contest based on the participation of national broadcasting organizations, and some of its participants would go on to compete in the ESC. The Italian origins of the ESC would also be reflected in the staging of the first ESC in the Italian-speaking Swiss city of Lugano, when the hosting of the contest was done entirely in Italian.

The achievements of the Eurovision Network in the 1950s were pioneering not only for Europe but also for the world. However, the history of international broadcasting organizations in the postwar era was not just about the EBU and the OIR, which was renamed the OIRT in 1959. While they were among the first international broadcasting organizations to be formed, they were just two components in a global network of these. In 1946, the Inter-American Association of Broadcasters had been formed, and in the 1960s and 1970s there was the establishment of the Asia-Pacific Broadcasting Union (ABU), Arab States Broadcasting Union, Caribbean Broadcasting Union (CBU), Commonwealth Broadcasting Association, Islamic States Broadcasting Organization, North American National

Broadcasters Association, Organization of Ibero-American Television (OTI) and Union of National Radio and Television Organizations of Africa. An organization for French-speaking national broadcasting organizations, the Community of French-Language Television Programmes, and one for Nordic ones, Nordvision, were also established. As these two demonstrate, international broadcasting organizations have been variously based on cultural and geographical regions and have not been mutually exclusive: national broadcasting organizations could be active or associate members in different international broadcasting organizations. Nordvision's members have often adopted common positions within the EBU, including on matters relating to the ESC, and their states have also been perceived as a voting bloc within the contest. However, the EBU has always been the most advanced of these international broadcasting organizations in terms of the extent of cooperation among its members in programme exchange and technological development. As such, during the Cold War the EBU cooperated with other international broadcasting organizations, as well as with international organizations such as the European Space Agency, ITU and UNESCO, on matters such as the development of satellite broadcasting. The EBU also aided extra-European national broadcasting organizations, especially ones in the Third World, in the development of their own television services.

The ABU, CBU and OTI were inspired by the EBU's models to set up not only their own equivalents to the Eurovision Network but also song contests: the OTI Festival began in 1972, and the ABU Popular Song Contest and the Caribbean Song Festival were established in the 1980s. However, no other international broadcasting organization came up with a show that could match the longevity, popularity and remit of the ESC. The ESC continually expanded during the Cold War: its seven original participants were joined by Austria, Denmark, Sweden and the UK in the late 1950s and Finland, Ireland and Norway in the 1960s. The ESC expanded in the Mediterranean with the addition of Monaco in 1959, Portugal, Spain and Yugoslavia in the 1960s, Greece, Israel, Malta and Turkey in the 1970s, and Cyprus and Morocco in the 1980s. Almost all Western European states as well as Israel, Morocco, Turkey and Yugoslavia thus participated in the ESC at some point between 1956 and 1989. The only exceptions were Andorra, Liechtenstein and San Marino – which were not yet members of the EBU as they did not have their own national broadcasting organizations, although Andorra and San Marino would establish these in the 1990s and go on to debut in the ESC in 2004 and 2008 respectively – and, of course, Vatican City. The ESC also reached beyond Europe as it was even broadcast during the Cold War in some states in Africa, the Americas, Asia and Australia. In the global context of international broadcasting organizations, the ESC was a unique Western European feat, and one of the reasons for this was that the contest's development took place in the context of a regional economic and political integration that was unmatched on any other continent.

Integration

The EBU was, however, never controlled by the CoE, EC or other Western European organizations, nor could its leading officials be interpreted as having been implementers of or mouthpieces for the policies of these. Rather than being ideological Europeanists, officials from the EBU were practical internationalists. Bezençon, for example, was initially more concerned with how programme exchange could benefit the infant television services of states – such as his small, multilingual Switzerland, where there was also significant opposition to the introduction of television because of its purported 'social dangers'[23] – than the idea of an integrated Western Europe. The EBU did for national broadcasting organizations what the EC did for states: as the historian Alan S. Milward argues, the 'evolution of the European Community since 1945 has been an integral part of the reassertion of the nation-state as an organizational concept', economically and politically buttressing states after the destruction of the Second World War.[24] Like the ECSC, the Eurovision Network was also based on the principle of pooling resources, although without the supranational elements of the ECSC: national broadcasting organizations in the Eurovision Network have always been free to decide what they will contribute to and take from it.

As Bezençon had been conceptualizing programme exchange from 1947, his proposal for the 'Stock Exchange of Television Programmes' to the EBU in October 1950 was thus not prompted by the French foreign minister Robert Schuman's proposal for the ECSC in May of that year. EBU officials were initially not so enthusiastic about adopting the snappier portmanteau 'Eurovision': in the organization's official publication of the time, the *E.B.U. Bulletin*, which was renamed the *E.B.U. Review* in 1958, the appellation was even accused of being 'somewhat barbaric' with a 'somewhat "telegraphic" style'. However, EBU officials eventually did adopt it because it quickly caught on in popular use. The name 'Eurovision' was coined outside of the EBU by the British journalist George Campey in an article in the *Evening Standard* newspaper in 1951: he first used the term to refer to a broadcast by the Dutch national broadcasting organization, the Dutch Television Foundation (NTS), of a BBC programme.[25] 'Eurovision' marked the beginning of the postwar use of the prefixes 'Eur-' or 'Euro-' for the names of international organizations and projects, and it was soon followed by Euratom, which was founded in 1957 by the member states of the ECSC.

The term 'Eurovision' was also favoured by the CoE which, from its beginning in 1949, had been considering the role that radio and television broadcasting could play in promoting the 'European Idea', and the CoE accordingly welcomed the establishment of the Eurovision Network.[26] The Eurovision Network benefitted in the 1950s from the intergovernmental cooperation initiated by the CoE, which was established to promote cultural cooperation, democratic standards, human rights and the rule of law. The CoE's spatial scope was also similar to that of the EBU, and these two organizations always had more members than the EC or NATO. The CoE's membership criteria, however, were more restrictive in geographical and political terms than those of the EBU: as they limited the CoE to Western European states and liberal democracies, they excluded Middle Eastern and northern African states as well as authoritarian governments from Greece, Portugal, Spain and Yugoslavia. Even though the CoE did not directly interfere in the operations of the EBU, the former provided a cultural and legal framework for the operations of the latter. The CoE produced the first multilateral treaty on cultural cooperation in Europe, the 'European Cultural Convention' of 1954, which promoted 'the study of the languages, history and civilization' of other member states, the protection of 'the common cultural heritage of Europe' and 'concerted action in promoting cultural activities of European interest'.[27] The CoE also collaborated with the EBU in developing two multilateral agreements that facilitated the international exchange of television programmes: the 'European Agreement Concerning Programme Exchanges by Means of Television Films' of 1958 and the 'European Agreement on the Protection of Television Broadcasts' of 1960.

There was an additional connection between the CoE and the EBU in their pioneering use of versions of the circle of twelve stars as a European symbol. The EBU became the first international organization to officially adopt a form of this symbol, which was individualized with the addition of the name 'Eurovision' and rays that symbolized the international cooperation between and local remit of national broadcasting organizations. Timothy O'Brien from the BBC created the logo for the Eurovision Network in 1954, and he had been inspired by proposals that were being considered by the CoE for its own flag and which resulted in that organization adopting the circle of twelve golden stars on a blue background in 1955.[28] For many Western Europeans, particularly those whose states joined the CoE after their national broadcasting organizations had entered the EBU, such as Austria, Finland, Monaco, Portugal, Spain and Switzerland, their first association with the circle of twelve stars was thus the Eurovision Network. The Eurovision Network introduced its programmes, and most famously the ESC, with this symbol accompanied by a wordless jingle taken from the prelude to Marc-Antoine Charpentier's composition 'Te Deum' (Thee, O God). Although 'Te Deum' would not be shortlisted by the CoE as its potential anthem – it ended up adopting Beethoven's 'Ode to Joy' in 1972 – the example that the Eurovision Network had set in popularizing 'Te Deum' as a signature tune was noted in discussions within the CoE regarding its selection of an anthem.[29]

Cooperation with the CoE also suited the EBU because of the former's intergovernmental character. With the adoption in 1957 by the ECSC member states of the Treaties of Rome that established Euratom and the EEC, the EBU was careful not to associate itself too closely with these organizations because their supranationalist aims were politically divisive. These organizations included only a limited number of states represented in the EBU: Austria, Denmark, Norway, Portugal, Sweden, Switzerland and the UK set up EFTA as an alternative economic organization in 1960. The British and Spanish applications for EEC membership were rejected in the early 1960s, with Denmark, Ireland and Norway also withdrawing their applications after France vetoed the British request in 1963. In 1957, Bezençon wrote that the Eurovision Network 'demonstrated the much discussed idea of European union in action', and the *E.B.U. Bulletin* even alluded to the EEC by describing the Eurovision Network as a 'European Television Community'.[30] However, in 1959, Bezençon emphasized the apolitical and technical nature of the Eurovision Network, asserting that it 'would still be bogged down in theoretical discussions' had it required the approval of parliaments and that 'television can also be a deadly weapon of propaganda and controlled information'.[31] In the mid-1960s, he underlined the EBU's preference for internationalism rather than supranationalism by stating that the Eurovision Network was not 'a super-State in embryo pursuing some hidden, or merely veiled, objective'.[32] He believed that the Eurovision Network could be used 'to build Europe' but that '[a] united Europe is not the same thing as a unified Europe' and '[t]he European game is therefore a dangerous one to play' because 'conceptions of Europe vary'.[33]

When Bezençon wrote about the Eurovision Network, he only sparsely mentioned the ESC as he saw it as just one aspect of the network's production, albeit a desirable one for its internationalism, liveliness and modernity. The ESC was thus not conceived or discussed by the Programme Committee as a generator of Western European integration or even the EBU's flagship project, but as an experiment in cultural exchange and technical cooperation whose continuation would be determined by its audience reception and financial viability. The EBU did not even consider the contest to be a fixed event in its early decades: until the late 1970s it was never taken for granted that the contest would continue, and this was decided on a yearly basis. There was also always discussion in the Television Programme Committee about how the ESC should be improved, modernized and reformed: the representatives of the national broadcasting organizations felt pressured by the extensive attacks on the ESC in their national media to address issues such as the contest's biased voting, excessive length, high costs, mediocre music and undistinctive artists. Bezençon would appear in the 1980 ESC to award the prize to the winner and his name would from 2002 be carried by a set of awards in the contest decided by artists, commentators, composers and journalists. However, even he acknowledged to the Television Programme Committee in 1965 that the ESC was 'a most controversial programme', popular among viewers but widely criticized in the media, and that the committee needed to decide whether it should be reformed – or abandoned altogether.[34] In the 1960s and 1970s, the national broadcasting organizations made various suggestions to the Television Programme Committee, often threatening to withdraw from the ESC if it was not reformed, and sometimes even suggesting that the contest be ended. Yet, what convinced the Television Programme Committee to continue the ESC was the fact that, already in the early 1960s, its officials were noting that it was one of the most popular television programmes in Western Europe. In its first research on the viewership of the ESC which it conducted in 1971, the EBU found that ratings admittedly varied across states and years – ranging in 1969 from 7 per cent of the audience in Italy to 66 per cent in Sweden and in 1971 from 38 per cent in Switzerland to 75 per cent in Malta – but they were nonetheless typically high, representing about half of the total audience of all of the states participating in the contest.[35]

Western Europeans were being united by the ESC not only as a result of the simultaneous development of their national television services, but also because of the transnational consumption of the products of the other cultural industry that was essential to the contest – that of popular music. The Western European popular music industry did not need to promote itself through the ESC as much as the Eurovision Network relied on popular music to do this, for the popular music industry was already established in other media, including commercial, transnational radio services like the ones of Radio Luxembourg and Radio Monte Carlo. However, the original rules of the ESC never stated that an aim of the contest was the production of European cultural references, hits or stars, but 'to encourage the production of original songs in the participants' countries by bringing about rivalry between authors and composers through the international comparison of their works'. This was maintained as the aim of the contest throughout the Cold War era, albeit with some minor changes to the wording: that the songs should be of 'high quality', for example, was added to the rules for the 1966 ESC following widespread allegations – which nonetheless continued – of their mediocre quality.[36]

Although some ESC entries during the Cold War went on to become international hits in their original or cover versions, most did not. Still, whether or not they achieved commercial success as a result of the ESC, the contest's artists already usually had cosmopolitan biographies, international ambitions and transnational careers that demonstrated the existence of a common market for popular music in Western Europe. Even before their participation in the ESC, artists had already been exposed to different musical influences from across Europe and the world through film, radio and records. Indeed, it was rare to find an ESC artist whose career was formed solely within national boundaries, cultural or geographical. Many ESC entries were also produced by multinational groups of artists. Citizenship of the state that they are representing has never been required of artists in the ESC: it would be very limiting considering the transnational character of the popular music industry. Some EBU members, namely the BBC, did seek to introduce such a rule in 1965, but it was rejected in the interests of small states.[37] Luxembourg and Monaco, for example, did not have a large pool of resident artists to choose from but did have commercial stations which were popular across Western Europe and made an association with these states attractive for foreign artists.

Although it was not crucial for the development of a common popular music market in Europe, the ESC did contribute to this by internationally promoting the careers of artists and facilitating professional contacts between artists and record company officials who attended the contest. The rules that ESC entries had to conform to, especially the time limit of three minutes that was introduced in 1962 to control the length of the show, as well as the multinational audience that entries addressed, meant that the ESC also fashioned styles and tastes, and even genres, that came to be considered typical of the contest. These were often derided in national media, and sometimes even within the EBU itself. In 1973, an official from the Norwegian national broadcasting organization, the Norwegian Broadcasting Corporation (NRK), alleged that the contest had produced 'a new "illicit" breed of popular songs', 'the Eurovision song', that were neither commercially fashionable nor of high quality. In 1979, a report by light entertainment experts criticized ESC entries for trying to be too 'international' with 'repetitive words accompanied by mime and rhythm' and lacking 'local colour', thereby going against the contest's aim of promoting national diversity.[38]

Yet, it was with such songs that the ESC helped forge Europop, a musical genre that developed from the mid-1960s. Characterized by 'a bouncy beat, just one chorus hook, elementary lyrics',[39] Europop songs achieved transnational popularity because of their simple structures and universal themes focusing on consumption, fun and love. They were the 'odes to joy' of the Cold War era: as the standard genre played in discos, shopping centres and summer resorts, Europop was the mirror and product of a period of prosperity and stability. It was not a genre of activism or protest but of affluence and pleasure, although it was also challenged in the ESC in the 1960s and 1970s by several entries that were critical of an overemphasis on consumption, commerce and money in contemporary societies. The summer holiday, especially spent in the Mediterranean region, was an inspiration and medium for Europop, reflecting the growing interconnectedness that tourism nurtured among Western Europeans during the Cold War, when the industry boomed through greater prosperity, improved transport connections and expanded labour rights. The summer holiday was also something that marked Western Europe from the Eastern Bloc, where foreign travel was more restricted by the communist governments, or even from the United States, where paid holidays were shorter and less culturally and legally institutionalized than in Western Europe.

Europop also symbolized an era of relative peace, the most valuable thing that Western Europeans shared in light of the two world wars that had been waged in the first half of the twentieth century. In 'Waterloo', ABBA – the epitome of Europop – even trivialized a military battle by bringing it down to a Europop romance. In ABBA: The Museum in Stockholm, there is a recording of one of the songs' lyricists, Stig Anderson, explaining that 'Waterloo' was chosen as the title because it is something 'that everyone can relate to', just as had been done with ABBA's 'Ring, Ring', which placed third in the Swedish national selection for the 1973 ESC. West Germany's entry in the 1957 ESC, 'Telefon, Telefon' (Telephone, Telephone), had also been conceived in the same way: its singer, Margot Hielscher, confirms that her team deliberately chose an object that 'is modern and international', especially as telephone networks that had been destroyed in the war were still being reconstructed. The song furthermore incorporated multilingual lyrics in order to appeal to a pan-European audience.[40] This was the first ESC entry that demonstrated some of the gimmicks that would become typical in the contest of using international words, onomatopoeia like 'boom' and 'ding' or just 'la la la' to make entries that had to be sung in the official languages of the states that they represented more accessible to an international audience.

Indeed, as the CoE and EC wanted to unite Western Europeans through common cultural and historical references, they should have looked at the list of the ones that were included in ESC entries. Historical figures from European civilization were referred to from the very first ESC in 1956, when Adonis, Hercules and Hermes were mentioned in the Luxembourgian entry 'Ne crois pas' (Don't Believe). The 1988 Icelandic entry 'Þú og þeir (Sókrates)'

(You and They (Socrates)), performed by the group Beathoven, mentioned more historical figures than any other ESC entry, from Beethoven, Hercules and Socrates to fifteen others including the Beatles, Sigmund Freud, Pyotr Ilyich Tchaikovsky, Mark Twain and John Wayne, as well as four Icelanders, the artist Sölvi Helgason, poet Einar Benediktsson, prime minister Gunnar Thoroddsen and the 'World's Strongest Man', Jón Páll Sigmarsson.[41] And yet, one reference that was conspicuously missing in ESC entries during the Cold War, and which all of the languages in the contest etymologically shared, was to 'Europe'. 'Europe' and 'Europeans' were mentioned in only a few, mostly French-language, entries, and usually in opposition to the United States. These songs included 'Chez nous' (Where We Live), which was performed by Dominique Walter for France at the 1966 ESC and in which he explained to an American friend why it is better to live in Europe than in the United States. In the 1981 ESC, French singer Jean-Claude Pascal represented Luxembourg with 'C'est peut-être pas l'Amérique' (It May Not be America), in which he exalted traditional European music and its presence in his everyday life, insisting that it was not only the United States that produced good music (he made this point more clearly in the title of the German version of the song, 'Heut' ist vieles sehr amerikanisch' (Many Things Today Are Very American)). France sent the group Cocktail Chic to the 1986 ESC with the song 'Européennes' (European Girls), which was about how the group enjoyed American popular music but still felt European. Whether it was because neither an anti-American stance nor a European identity were gimmicks that appealed to the international audience, none of these songs were successful in the ESC: Walter and Cocktail Chic achieved France's lowest placings in the contest during the Cold War, coming sixteenth and seventeenth respectively, while Pascal finished eleventh.

The silence on 'Europe' in the ESC during the Cold War reflected the fact that there was not a major push by the EC and national governments for a cultural expression of a European identity until the 1980s. Although the European Parliament (EP), which was established in 1958 for the ECSC, EEC and Euratom, had been discussing cultural integration from the early 1960s, divisions always existed between political leaders in Western European states who prioritized national cultures and preferred integration to be mostly economic, and others who pushed for greater cultural integration and the development of a supranational European identity. The first steps towards a cultural policy for the EC were made with the adoption of the 'Declaration on European Identity' in 1973 and the subsequent development of the idea of a 'People's Europe'. These sought to bring the EC closer to its citizens through the adoption of common symbols and the promotion of civic participation; they were conceived at a time of economic crisis and institutional stagnation that were together dubbed 'Eurosclerosis'. The first direct elections to the EP were held in 1979, although they had already been allowed under the Treaties of Rome. Between 1983 and 1986, the EC and the EP adopted the anthem and flag of the CoE, which supported the adoption of its symbols by other Western European organizations.[42] In the mid-1980s, the EC also began to develop a policy towards television broadcasting and to promote the production of common European programmes, for which it sought the assistance of the EBU.[43]

In 1985, the EC also established the European Capital of Culture, which was conceived by the leftist ministers of culture of France and Greece, Jack Lang and Melina Mercouri respectively. They did not, however, jointly coordinate, after they began their ministerial terms in 1981, the withdrawal of both France and Greece from the 1982 ESC. The European Years had also begun in 1983, and 1985 was even chosen by the EC as the Year of Music, but its events focused more on classical and folk rather than popular music. Indeed, even those Western European politicians who advocated a European identity appeared too highbrow to yet consider appropriating the ESC. Their focus on high culture portrayed a European identity as being artistically and historically justified, legitimate and serious. Popular culture, however, better reflected the contemporary situation and, although the Western European politicians did not yet recognize it, it was 'European union in action', as Bezençon had described the Eurovision Network. Western Europeans had developed a shared postwar popular culture through their common experiences of reconstruction, prosperity and consumption. The Eurovision Network had demonstrated how a common market for popular culture, based on popular music and television, could function in Western Europe. Considering that the EC was based on economic integration, did it not then follow that it was popular culture that best embodied this as it was commercial in nature and popularly determined? This neglect of popular culture by Western European politicians justified the criticism that the Western European integration project was culturally and politically constructivist and elitist and not considerate of the desires and tastes of citizens.

However, by the late 1980s, the EC realized that it could gain some promotional benefit out of the ESC as the EC was seeking new ways to promote a European identity. The CoE had decided in 1964 to recognize 5 May, the date of its founding, as 'Europe Day', and in 1985 the EC took 9 May, the date of the Schuman Declaration in 1950, for the same. From 1984, the ESC found its place among these European commemorations in May as it came to be regularly held in that month rather than in March or April, as had been the case in previous years. It does not seem that this was a deliberate Europeanist move on the part of the EBU, and it was sometimes even problematic because there were clashes with national commemorations for war victims, which is why Israel did not participate in the ESC in 1980 and 1984 and the Netherlands did not in 1985. 'May' and 'spring' had in the early years of the contest been commonly referred to in ESC entries as symbols of love and youth, but the month was from the mid-1980s increasingly being associated with 'Europe', with its two Europe days as well as the commemorations of the end of the Second World War.

It was in this context that the EC's direct – and brief – appropriation of the ESC began in 1987. Although EBU officials had previously been sceptical of being associated with the EC's supranationalist politics, the ESC's costliness had come to convince EBU members that they also needed to seek sponsorship from other sources. When the 1987 ESC was held in Brussels, the EC's capital, and on the EC's Europe Day to boot, the host Viktor Lazlo congratulated 'Europe' on its thirtieth birthday, measured in EC parlance from the signing of the Treaties of Rome. The EC contributed to the 1987 ESC by sponsoring some of the postcards that introduced the entries as well as the film for the interval act, and these accordingly depicted EC symbols (and they came after an image of Waterloo was shown in the introductory film about Belgium). In the 1988 ESC, to promote the European Year of Cinema and Television the EC also sponsored the film for the interval act, which featured the Irish group Hothouse Flowers in different parts of Western Europe, including at the EC's headquarters in Brussels, singing their song 'Don't Go'. The EC did not contribute to the 1989 ESC, when the contest was held in non-EC member Switzerland, but in 1990 it used the ESC in Zagreb to promote the European Year of Tourism. That the ESC had become a part of Europeanist symbolism prompted in 1988 and 1990 the first ever questions in the EP about the contest, which focused on the EC's financial contributions to it.[44] Justifying the European Commission's support for the 1988 ESC, Carlo Ripa di Meana, the commissioner responsible for information, communication and culture, said:

> Pop music knows no frontiers and is an excellent way of reaching millions of our citizens, especially young people. I am pleased that, in this European Cinema and Television Year, television and pop music are both committed to the idea of a People's Europe. Millions of people will watch the Eurovision Song Contest and will be able to see their Europe at work and play. The European Community is more than an economic unit – it is about culture, it is about fun.[45]

The EC's direct interventions in the ESC came mostly before the fall of the Berlin Wall and the anticipated European integration of Central and East Europe, so they were not motivated by these. They instead accompanied the EC's expansion to Portugal and Spain in 1986, as well as the adoption of the Single European Act in 1986, which would lead to the Maastricht Treaty of 1992 that established the EU and institutionalized its cultural policy. The ESC had shown the EC how the latter could both 'have fun' and forge common cultural references among Western Europeans. It had additionally promoted Western European alternatives in a global popular culture that in the Cold War era was dominated by one state in particular.

Anglo-Americanization

With the technical linkage of almost all Western European national broadcasting organizations having been achieved through the Eurovision Network by the mid-1960s, the EBU became more focused on developing intercontinental connections through satellites, especially with the United States. It hoped to transform the Eurovision Network into a worldwide one which, although it was never achieved, was variously dubbed 'Globevision', 'Mondovision', 'Omnivision', 'Télémonde' or 'Worldvision'. Regarding this, Bezençon wrote in 1967 that 'Eurovision is no longer Eurovision', and in 1971, when he became president of the EBU, he declared that the EBU's goal was 'not just European, but world-wide'.[46] In 1955, the *E.B.U. Bulletin* had stated that the Americans were 'jealous of the European "Eurovision" achievements' as the American National Broadcasting Company had announced programme exchanges between Canada, Mexico and the United States.[47] Yet, the Americans were otherwise ahead of the game in developing televisual, and especially satellite, technologies. As such, the EBU always regarded American broadcasting organizations as important partners, and the International Broadcasting Division of the United States' Department of State joined the EBU as an associate member already in 1951. Any technological rivalry could not undermine the economic, military and political interdependence between the United States and Western Europe, especially in the face of global Cold War divisions.

For Bezençon, the Eurovision Network was also meant to promote 'the essential values of western civilization, which are today in greater danger than ever', such as the 'freedom of the individual'.[48] While Bezençon did not specify a difference between 'American' and 'European' values, other Western Europeans did define themselves against the United States in terms of their cultural history and living standards. The United States' economic, military and political clout in postwar Western Europe was coupled with a cultural influence that challenged both the national cultures of Western European states and the global cultural influence that the imperial powers among them had had before the Second World War. The history of anti-Americanism in Europe can be traced back to the eighteenth century, around the time when the United States – supported by France – won its War of Independence against Great Britain.[49] However, after the United States emerged from the Second World War as one of the two superpowers, cultural Americanization was viewed as a greater threat by some Western Europeans for it was combined with the United States' economic and military hegemony. In the 1950s, some Western European intellectuals and politicians lamented the emphasis in American popular culture on commercial and liberal values: rock and roll was accused of promoting promiscuity, as Quinn's ESC entry suggested, and Westerns delinquency.

The few ESC songs that exalted Europe in opposition to the United States were all by artists from France, the state that was self-consciously the proudest critic of Anglo-Americanization. At the 1966 ESC, Walter had sung his ode to the joys of the European way of life above the American just days before French president Charles de Gaulle[50] announced France's withdrawal from NATO's integrated military structure because of American and British domination in the organization. French intellectuals and politicians also felt threatened by growing linguistic Anglicization and its worldwide spread through American popular culture. The French language had been *the* language of international relations before the Second World War. In light of this tradition, French also became on official language, together with English, of Western European organizations such as the CoE and the EBU, which is why the ESC has traditionally been partly presented in French – hence the catchphrases *douze points* and *nul points*. With five French-speaking states – Belgium, France, Luxembourg, Monaco and Switzerland – participating in the ESC, it was the predominant and most successful language in the contest during the Cold War, winning fourteen times. The 1956 and 1958 contests did not even have any entries in English as Anglophone states were not represented in those years, and it was not until 1967 that an English-language song won the ESC when Sandie Shaw was victorious for the UK with 'Puppet on a String'. Due to the value accorded to French as a euphonious, romantic and world language, French was also disproportionately preferred over other, Germanic official languages in the entries of multilingual states such as Luxembourg and Switzerland, the latter achieving its only two victories in the ESC with Assia and Dion singing in French.[51] Belgium has since 1977 had separate national broadcasting organizations for Dutch-speaking Flanders and French-speaking Wallonia that reflect the state's linguistic federalism and represent Belgium in rotation at the ESC (and they have always sent separate commentators to the contest). Belgium's French-language ESC entries were more successful than its Dutch-language ones, with the only Belgian victory during the Cold War being that of Sandra Kim with 'J'aime la vie' (I Love Life) in 1986.[52] ESC entries in other languages were also often peppered with French words, such as Austria's winning entry 'Merci, chérie' (Thank You, Darling), performed by Udo Jürgens in 1966, which is one of only two German-language songs that have ever won the contest.

Despite the success of French-language songs in the ESC, the French national broadcasting organization – which was renamed and reorganized several times during the Cold War – was throughout the 1960s critical about the contest's commercial influences, high cost and mediocre quality. It did not want to organize the 1963 ESC after having already done so twice, instead handing it over to the BBC, and in 1971 it even voted in the Television Programme

Committee to end the ESC because it opposed the voting system that was then being used in the contest.[53] Although the contest remained publicly popular in France, in 1982 its national broadcasting organization withdrew from the ESC for one year based on criticisms that the contest was 'feeble' and 'mediocre' and had monotonous entries that were the 'Esperanto of song'. It was then that the critic Michel Bourdon – and not the minister of culture, Lang, as has often been stated in histories of the ESC – dubbed the contest 'an insult to French music and a monument to drivel'.[54] By then, the decline of the French language in the face of increasing Anglo-Americanization had become obvious in the ESC. The original English-language name of the ESC had even incorporated a French loanword as 'The Eurovision Song Contest Grand Prix', but 'Grand Prix' was removed in 1968 in order to avoid confusion between the contest itself and its first prize. When the language rule at the ESC was abrogated from 1973 to 1976, English was the language of choice for the participants who chose not to sing in their national languages. English names for groups and singers, as well as the use of some English words in songs even when they again had to be sung in national languages from 1977, became more apparent than the use of French or any other language for the same. As if needing to remind, the duo Baccara represented Luxembourg in the 1978 ESC with 'Parlez-vous français?' (Do You Speak French?), which was about French as the language of love and summer. However, by the 1980s, *Franglais*, a macaronic French with many English words that demonstrated how the French language itself had succumbed to Anglicization, was also used in some French-language entries in the ESC: the name 'Cocktail Chic' epitomized this, being comprised of two words that English and French have loaned from each other.

Just as the word 'cocktail' originated from the United States and 'chic' from France, the flow of cultural exports across the Atlantic was never only one way with Americans also consuming Western European popular cultural products, even though the impact of the American ones on Western Europe in the postwar era was relatively greater. Indeed, the emphasis on Americanization in political debates in Western Europe was always skewed because it marginalized the influence that Western Europeans had on American popular culture. That the ESC had the potential to have an impact on the United States was demonstrated already in the first years of the contest. Domenico Modugno's hit 'Nel blu, dipinto di blu' (In the Blue Painted Blue), popularly known as 'Volare'

(To Fly), which came third for Italy at the 1958 ESC after having won that year's Sanremo Italian Song Festival, has been one of the most successful non-English-language songs ever in the charts of *Billboard*, the trade publication of the American music industry. It was also recognized as the 'Record of the Year' and 'Song of the Year' in the first Grammy Awards that were held in 1959. 'Volare' is the only ESC entry and non-English-language song to have ever been accorded these honours, especially as the American market has historically not been receptive of songs that have not been in English, and it remains one of the most famous non-English-language popular music songs in the world.

Despite the success of 'Volare' and some other ESC entries in the United States, the EBU did not make a serious attempt to expand the ESC to the United States during the Cold War. Even when the EBU allowed Intervision members to broadcast the ESC from 1965, it did not allow North American broadcasting organizations to do so. The EBU discussed proposals for a broadcasting organization from the United States to participate in the ESC in 1967 and 1970, the second time in response to a suggestion from *Billboard*, which also regularly reported on the ESC. The Television Programme Committee rejected the proposals because it wanted to keep the ESC's European 'character' and 'flavour', although in 1968 it for the first time mentioned the possibility of staging a world song contest.[55] A technical obstacle to the participation of an American broadcasting organization in the ESC was that the United States did not have a national broadcasting organization with a nationwide public service remit. However, the EBU did permit the newly formed Public Broadcasting Service to show a delayed broadcast of the 1971 ESC, which was the first and only time that the ESC was broadcast in the United States during the Cold War.

Yet, a broadcasting organization from the United States did not need to enter the ESC for American influences to be present in the contest. Quinn demonstrates that artists of American origin have been performing in the ESC since the contest's beginning. Sue Schell from the Swiss group Peter, Sue and Marc, who modelled themselves on the American group Peter, Paul and Mary, was born in the United States to an American father and a Swiss mother; the Italian-American singer Romina Power, who sung in a duet with Al Bano, twice represented Italy at the ESC, in 1976 and 1985; and Jeane Manson, an American who had a career as an actress, model and singer in France, represented Luxembourg in the 1979 ESC. Indeed, it is rare not to find personal or professional connections with the United States in the biographies of ESC composers, conductors, lyricists and singers. Artists in the ESC were not compelled to promote musical genres that were considered typically European, and they were themselves products of cultural Americanization who consumed American popular music and incorporated its trends into their own production. For some of them, including Quinn, the opportunity to perform for American soldiers stationed in Western Europe in the wake of the Second World War helped to launch their careers. Other ESC artists reflected the history of migration between Europe and North America by studying or working in the United States in the hope of building a career there. However, there was also the phenomenon of Americans who chose to emigrate to Western Europe for professional reasons, demonstrating that Western Europe could also provide career opportunities in the popular music industry, and they often figured in the ESC as symbols of cosmopolitanism, fashionability and modernity.

After the American popular music industry, the next most powerful popular music industry in the world was in the UK, which lost its superpower status in the postwar era in the face of American and Soviet leadership of the Cold War blocs and the decline of the British Empire. However, the UK maintained its global cultural influence after the Second World War through institutions such as the BBC and the largest popular music industry in Western Europe. This was epitomized by groups such as the Beatles, which were themselves the product of a Western European common market in popular music as their career began in Liverpool and Hamburg in the early 1960s. The Beatles' pan-European popularity was also reflected by the fact that they were the subject of the Swedish entry in the 1977 ESC by the group Forbes. The UK did not, however, enter the 1956 ESC, with the BBC stating that it wanted to first establish a national contest and that it also had to resolve issues with the Musicians Union.[56] However, the UK otherwise performed strongly in the ESC during the Cold War after it debuted in 1957: it sent some of its most famous performers who usually finished high on the scoreboard, and it received the largest number of total points of any state in the ESC from 1975 to 1989.

Still, the UK's prominent position in the global popular music industry often prompted resentment of the ESC in the British media, especially when British performers did not come first. When one of the UK's most famous artists, Cliff Richard, did not win the ESC in 1968 and 1973, but came second and third respectively, this partly motivated the BBC to seek a change to the contest's voting system so that it would become more targeted towards young people who were the key market for the popular music industry. Such British reactions to the ESC demonstrated the fact that the BBC, unlike many other national broadcasting organizations, saw the ESC as more of a commercial opportunity for its popular music industry rather than a cultural expression of Western European integration, and it was not so critical of the involvement of record companies in the contest. This was also reflected in the name of the British national selection, 'A Song for Europe': whereas other states tended to have national appellations in the names of their national selections, in the UK the name suggested that the orientation was chiefly one of export. 'A Song for Europe' was adopted in 1961 when the BBC first invited record companies, in that year EMI, Decca and Philips, to submit entries to the national selection.[57]

The UK's foreign policies also preferably viewed Western European integration as an economic rather than a cultural or political project. The UK suffered an identity crisis as a declining post-imperial power and struggled to redefine itself through Western European integration, which was underlined by the Euroscepticism of many of its citizens and politicians. Although Prime Minister Winston Churchill had been one of the principal advocates of Western European integration just after the Second World War, the UK was slow to enter the EC compared to other large Western European states. De Gaulle vetoed the UK's application twice, in 1963 and 1967, as he regarded the UK as not being committed to Western European integration and was suspicious of its close ties, or 'Special Relationship', with the United States; in light of this, the UK's entry in the 1965 ESC, 'I Belong', could have been perceived as being about more than just a love between two people.[58] Despite this and French criticism of Anglicization, France and the UK did exchange points in the ESC in the 1960s and 1970s, although the UK did not award France any points in the contests just after de Gaulle's veto of the UK's EEC applications – but France then did to the UK. The UK entered the EC in 1973, and in 1975 it held a referendum on EC membership, with 67 per cent voting 'yes' to the UK remaining in the EC. This was at a time when the UK was achieving strong results in the ESC, so the contest was not as much of a target of Eurosceptic journalists and politicians as it would be around the time of the UK's 2016 referendum on EU membership.[59] Indeed, the Conservative prime minister Margaret Thatcher, who had supported the 'yes' vote in 1975 but became increasingly Eurosceptic during her prime ministership from 1979 to 1990, even admitted in 1987 that she liked watching the ESC, even though 'we haven't done terribly well recently'.[60] Actually, since her assumption of the prime ministership the UK had done relatively well in the ESC, always finishing between first and seventh place except in 1987, when it came thirteenth. It may have been the UK's worst-performing decade during the Cold War, but it was far from the poor results that it would achieve after 2000.

The UK was certainly advantaged in the ESC during the Cold War by being able to sing in English: the Anglicization of Western Europe was not only motivated by Americanization but was also a legacy of the British Empire. Ireland and Malta had been part of the British Empire and were consequently the two other Anglophone states represented in the ESC (Cyprus had also been a part of the British Empire but, after independence, it did not take English as an official language). Ireland, which had been a part of the UK until 1922 and thereafter retained English as its official language alongside Irish, developed an influence on the global popular music industry that outweighed its population size. After the UK, Ireland scored the highest number of points in the ESC from 1975 to 1989. Ireland has also won the most contests of any state: three Cold War-era wins and four in the 1990s. Despite the importance accorded to the Irish language for national identity and official efforts to promote the use of the language, Ireland has only once, in 1972, had an Irish-language entry in the ESC, but it finished in fifteenth place. Malta appeared in the ESC only three times during the Cold War; ever since its first two entries in Maltese – the first Semitic language to be heard in the ESC – came last in the contest in 1971 and 1972, it has been represented by entries that are only in English.[61] The Nordic states also benefitted from Anglicization in the ESC, especially because of the Anglophile orientation of their cultures and the high percentage of English speakers in their populations. Sweden had initially prompted the introduction of the rule on entries needing to substantially be in national languages after it became the first state without English as an official language to be represented by an entry in English in 1965, when Ingvar Wixell sang 'Absent Friend'. The Finnish national broadcasting organization, the Finnish Broadcasting Company (YLE), had sought that there be no language rule so that its entries could also be sung in world languages.[62] When the language rule was abrogated from 1973 to 1976, the Nordic states that participated in the ESC in that period – Finland, Norway and Sweden – were the only states without English as an official language that were represented by English-language entries every year.

Together with Ireland, the UK and the United States, other Anglophone states were also able to exert an influence on Western European culture through global Anglicization. Australia was a prime example, and it is one of the few non-European states in the world in which the ESC has been regularly broadcast and has had a popular following. Australia's smaller population size and its cultural connections with the UK also made it more open to popular musical influences from Western Europe, including through the ESC, than the United States was. The Australian national broadcasting organization, the Australian Broadcasting Commission (ABC), had been accepted as an associate member of the EBU already in 1950 due to its close cooperation with the BBC and other national broadcasting organizations from the Commonwealth, which reflected the British orientation that Australia maintained in its cultural and foreign policies. The last constitutional links between Australia and the UK ended only in the mid-1980s, when Australian citizens ceased to be considered British subjects, although Australia maintained the Union Jack in its flag and, as a constitutional monarchy, the UK's monarch as its head of state. In 1984, Australia adopted 'Advance Australia Fair' as its anthem in place of 'God Save the Queen', after the Labour government under Prime Minister Gough Whitlam first proposed the change in 1974.

The close relationship between Australia and the UK was also reflected in the participation in the ESC of Australian artists who had immigrated to the UK. They were motivated to do so by the opportunities offered by a bigger market, the limitations of Australia's geographical isolation, and somewhat by the 'cultural cringe' phenomenon, a post-colonial sense of cultural inferiority among Australians in relation to Europe. The first Australian to participate in the ESC was the lyricist Alan Stranks, who wrote the UK's first ever ESC entry, 'All', in 1957. Australian artists figured prominently in the UK's ESC entries in the 1970s, such as members of the New Seekers and the Shadows which represented the UK in the ESC in 1972 and 1975 respectively. Olivia Newton-John, who was born in the UK but spent most of her childhood in Australia, represented the UK in the 1974 ESC at a time when she was at the start of what would be a hugely successful career in the United States, especially with her starring role in the film *Grease* in 1978. Another personification of these postwar migration networks between Australia and the Anglo-Celtic Isles is the Australian-born Johnny Logan, who represented Ireland at the ESC in 1980 and 1987 and is the only singer ever to have won the contest twice, winning also a third time in 1992 as a lyricist. By the late 1980s, a more distinctive Australian identity was asserting itself internationally through a wave of popular cultural products, especially popular music and soap operas, that were first exported to the UK and from there springboarded into other parts of Western Europe.

The ESC was distributed to the ABC in 1956 for radio broadcasting and a first request for Australia to participate in the contest was rejected by the EBU in 1970.[63] However, the contest was only annually televised there from 1983. In that year, the Special Broadcasting Service (SBS) began broadcasting the ESC on the Sunday evening immediately after the contest was held due to the time difference between Australia and Europe. An associate member of the EBU, SBS was established as a multilingual broadcaster after Australian governments embraced multiculturalist policies that were first instituted by the Whitlam government in the mid-1970s. The Whitlam government abolished the last vestiges of the White Australia Policy that had officially favoured only European immigrants, allowing for more immigration from other continents, especially Asia. SBS's programming was originally targeted at communities from southern Europe which had immigrated to Australia in the early postwar decades after the Australian government had realized that the UK and Ireland could no longer provide Australia with enough migrants. In the 1980s, the ESC was thus particularly watched in Australia by communities from Greece, Italy, Malta, Portugal, Spain and Yugoslavia that saw it as a way of reconnecting with their homelands. This was acknowledged by the hosts of the 1991 ESC in Rome, who in their introduction explicitly greeted Italian Australians, and depicted in a film made by SBS that was shown in the first semi-final of the 2013 ESC. The existence of SBS was, however, often financially precarious because it was followed by the smallest audience of the five major Australian broadcasting organizations and was considered too 'ethnic' by opponents who did not see the need for such a broadcasting organization or even for the multiculturalist policies that had established it.[64]

The role that migrants from non-English-speaking European states played in popularizing the ESC in Australia further demonstrated that, although the contest was succumbing to Anglicization, it had an international impact through other languages, as 'Volare' had also shown. The intercontinental markets for Italian-, Portuguese- and Spanish-language popular music especially expanded the ESC's influence to Latin America, where the ESC was for the first time broadcast by satellite to Brazil, Chile and Puerto Rico and distributed by videotape to other Latin American states when the contest was held in Madrid in 1969.[65] The ESC was especially attractive in Latin America because of familiar artists from Portugal and Spain, who also epitomized the Ibero-American popular music market through their participation in the OTI Festival that was created for national broadcasting organizations from Portuguese- and Spanish-speaking states. Professional success in Latin America could, in turn, be a springboard for a career in the United States, where the growing Hispanic community – which, as a result of immigration reforms adopted in the United States in 1965, went from 2 per cent of the American population in 1950 to 9 per cent in 1990 – developed into a major market for the Spanish-language popular music industry. Julio Iglesias is the premier example of this career route: the ESC helped to launch his international career when he represented Spain in 1970, and in 1979 he moved to the United States, where he became a superstar singing in English and Spanish. There were other Spanish-language successes from the ESC in the Americas, and not just in the southern part. In 1973, the group Mocedades came second for Spain with the song 'Eres tú' (It's You), which was a hit in Europe, Latin America and also the United States, where it was one of the few non-English-language songs to reach the top ten of the *Billboard* charts. Through the Ibero-American popular music market, Latin American artists also made their way into the ESC. For example, there was the Uruguayan group Los TNT (The TNT) that represented Spain as Nelly, Tony and Tim in the 1964 ESC. Originally from Italy, the siblings Edelweiss 'Tim', Argentina 'Nelly' and Hermes 'Tony' Croatto emigrated to Uruguay in 1946, but they subsequently moved to Spain in 1962 to develop their musical careers.

And then there was the French-language popular music industry that also extended to North America, where Quebec was a major centre of it. In 1988, the French language had its final – but biggest in terms of the artist's later success – ESC victory with Dion representing Switzerland. Dion's career took off in the French-speaking world in the 1980s, but her ESC win and the premiere of her first English-language release, 'Where Does My Heart Beat Now', in the opening act of the 1989 ESC, promoted her beyond that. In the 1990s her fame grew internationally with English-language songs produced in the United States. Dion thus personified the multilingual networks that shaped the transatlantic popular music market: she was a North American import for Francophone Western Europe, who was then exported back to Anglophone North America. Also at the 1988 ESC, the Francophone Belgian Lara Fabian represented Luxembourg; in 1990 she moved to Canada, first developing a career in Quebec singing in French and then, from 1999, expanding her success in the United States with English-language songs. The careers of Dion and Fabian thus reflected both the global reach and limits of singing in the French language in the postwar era.

Several decades after Prince Henry had hoped for better telecommunication links between Europe and the United States, the world's biggest economic, military and political allies in the postwar era were better understanding each other through popular music, and sometimes even the ESC. From the success of Modugno in the United States in the late 1950s to that of Dion in Western Europe in the late 1980s, transatlantic relations were not all about America, as Pascal sung. Nor was the ESC all about Europe. The contest had been shaped by the policies of both European and worldwide organizations that had promoted telecommunications cooperation since the nineteenth century, and its global impact reflected the history of European imperialism and migration all the way to the Americas and Australia. Although the Cold War and Western European integration defined the ESC as a 'Western European' event, the EBU was careful not to overly associate itself with the supranationalist politics of other Western European organizations for fear of limiting its programmatic and technical ambitions nationally, regionally and intercontinentally. Despite reservations from both the EBU and the EC, the ESC developed into a symbol of Western European integration as the most successful international song contest in the world, representing a region that was experimenting with supranational integration unlike any other. Still, the ESC's popularity was always determined by national audiences and, as a contest based on states and without an explicit Europeanist mission, the only collective identities that the ESC consciously promoted were national ones.

Figure 4 Gigliola Cinquetti, 1964 ESC

2

The Show of Nations

Gigliola Cinquetti was the only singer during the Cold War who represented Italy in and won the ESC, even though the song contest had been invented in Italy and the state had one of the most successful national popular music industries exporting non-English-language songs. After having won the 1964 ESC with 'Non ho l'età' (I'm Not Old Enough), which was about being too young to have an intimate relationship with an older man, Cinquetti came second to ABBA in the 1974 ESC with 'Sì' (Yes). Considering that the ESC has always been about national promotion, few of the other states that were represented in the contest could match Italy in its ability to sell itself as a brand, despite its singular Cold War-era win. The successes of Cinquetti and Modugno epitomized a global fascination in the postwar era with Italian film and popular music, two media that produced a modern repertoire for Italian culture alongside classical genres such as literature, opera and painting. 'Made in Italy' also proved internationally attractive for Italy's exports in fashion, food and furniture, in cars, computers and cosmetics … And this despite the fact that Italy's regional divisions often undermined a common national identity at home, while its turnover of fifty governments from 1945 to 1989 attracted mockery from abroad (somewhat unduly, considering that there was consistency in their domination by the centrist Christian Democracy party that sought to keep the Italian Communist Party out of power). Whereas West Germany struggled in the ESC with wartime legacies and linguistic prejudices, postwar Italy could overcome the negative associations with its own fascist history through its Mediterranean identity and Romance language. Fascism could be glossed over, and nationalism reinvented, through fashion.

The Sanremo Italian Song Festival was a model for the ESC and various national song contests because it not only promoted the production of Italian popular music but also became a cultural reference that unified Italians. As Pippo Baudo, who hosted thirteen editions of the festival from 1968 to 2008, put it:

> Sanremo is a long 'Inno di Mameli' (Mameli's Hymn) [the national anthem of Italy] – whose real title, not by chance, is 'Il Canto degli Italiani' (The Song of the Italians) – that once a year, for already more than sixty years, the Italians feel obliged to sing. And it is therefore quite natural that it is closely connected to the events, situations, climate and emotions that society is experiencing, to the evolution of customs, sensibilities and tastes.[1]

Unlike 'Volare', most ESC entries have never become international hits; they have more usually just been national ones that have reflected the evolving 'customs, sensibilities and tastes' of national audiences. Although the ESC did produce common cultural references for Western Europeans during the Cold War, it was more powerful in consolidating national identities through new fashions and technologies. While Western European organizations did not always have a strong idea of how they should use culture to forge a supranational identity, states had more experience in perpetuating and reinventing national ones. Despite the shared Eurovision Network programmes, the multinational squads behind ESC entries or the experience of Americanization, popular music and television still largely developed in the postwar era within national structures and their growth was connected to national economic and technological advancements. A state's participation in the ESC was an affirmation of its fashionability, modernity and prosperity, as viewed by both the national audience as well as the international one. A national audience would interpret a placing in the contest in terms of national pride or its state's reputation in Western Europe, and the reactions of national audiences to the voting results perpetuated and shaped popular attitudes towards other states represented in the ESC and even to the idea of 'Europe' itself. A victory at the ESC could embolden a Europeanist streak in national public opinion, while a defeat could provoke a Eurosceptic one. Yet, whatever the response, it was always nationally determined.

Still, while popular music could be appropriated by cultural and political elites to fashion national identities, its 'popular' namesake also empowered it to inspire political action. Despite the EBU's professed apoliticism, the widespread appeal of popular music and television made the ESC an ideal event for drawing attention to certain political issues, and not only international ones like Americanization, the Cold War and Western European integration, but specifically national ones as well. In some Mediterranean states, namely Greece, Portugal, Spain and Turkey, authoritarian governments used the ESC to whitewash their international images in the eyes of a Western Europe that was otherwise defined by capitalist prosperity and liberal democracy, and their influence on the national selections reflected their political control over their states' national broadcasting organizations. The revolutions and wars that these states experienced in the 1970s also had an impact on their participation in the ESC. Although there were hardly any songs about 'Europe' in the ESC during the Cold War, the political issues that were highlighted in ESC entries demonstrated that there was a shared set of Western European norms and values that were being aspired to and forged.

The new social movements that arose across Western Europe from the mid-1960s and advocated anti-capitalism, environmentalism and pacifism also resounded in the ESC. One set of issues that marked these social movements concerned gender and sexuality. RAI acknowledged these when it sent Cinquetti to sing at the ESC both in 1964 and 1974. 'Non ho l'età' was about a girl who was below the age of sexual consent, a statement for a Western Europe that was experiencing greater sexual liberalization. 'Sì' was censored by RAI as the song was perceived as advocating a position on the issue of divorce just as Italy was about to hold a referendum on this. Modugno himself took seriously the political influence that his musical fame could have: he became an advocate in Italy for social issues, including in the pro-divorce campaign, and was from 1987 to 1992 a member of the Italian parliament for the leftist Radical Party.[2] As such, he was one of several ESC artists who embarked on a national political career and personified how the ESC could not only be a stage for international relations but also a battleground for national politics.

Fashioning

Music has historically been used to differentiate national identities: in the eighteenth century, early nationalist thinkers such as the German philosopher Johann Gottfried Herder looked to similarities in the instruments, languages and styles of folk music to identify members of a national group.[3] In the postwar era, the unifying power of music was enhanced through its coupling up with new technologies, especially radio and television. The nation-building power of popular music and television was seen in Italy, where the two acted as a consolidating force in a state characterized by regional divisions, especially dialectal ones. Yet, this power was nowhere more pioneering than in Israel, which was established as a state in 1948 and thus developed a national identity and cultural infrastructure beginning from the early years of the postwar era. Inspired by the Sanremo Italian Song Festival, the annual Israel Song Festival was set up in 1960 to produce a musical repertoire for the emerging national culture; it was initially broadcast by the radio services of the Israel Broadcasting Authority (IBA) and then on television from 1969. Together with Iceland, Israel was the last state represented in the ESC during the Cold War that introduced television services, doing so in 1966. Israel's political leaders had generally regarded television as an unnecessary luxury for a state that had to secure itself economically and militarily; radio, they thought, was sufficient enough of a medium for nation building. Even after 1966, there was political resistance to the introduction of colour television in Israel, which the IBA was ultimately compelled to do partly because it had to broadcast the ESC in colour when the contest was held in Jerusalem in 1979.[4] However, Israel did set one technological precedent in the ESC: because of Israel's geographical distance from Europe and the political barriers to developing a terrestrial network with its neighbours, when it debuted in the ESC in 1973 it became the first state to be connected to the contest via a satellite, Intelsat, and the 1979 ESC was also the first ESC that was broadcast to all participating states via satellite.[5]

Together with typifying the role that radio and television could play in nation building, the Israel Song Festival also promoted the production of songs that would become staples of Israeli culture. Many of the composers, conductors, lyricists and singers who produced Israel's ESC entries were also famous for creating other hits that emerged from the Israel Song Festival and became a part of Israeli folklore. The transformation of the Israel Song Festival into the national selection for the ESC reflected, as the sociologist Motti Regev and the musicologist Edward Seroussi put it, 'the gradual transformation of Hebrewism into global Israeliness'.[6] The ESC provided the IBA with an opportunity to promote Israel's national identity abroad as well as to accordingly make political statements, through both its entries and the edition that it hosted in 1979. One of the Israeli ESC songs that became iconic in Israeli culture was 'Hi' (Alive), sung by Ofra Haza, which came second at the 1983 ESC in Munich. The lyrics of 'Hi' stated that the song had been passed down through the generations and affirmed that the Israeli nation still exists. The political symbolism of 'Hi' was particularly powerful as it was performed in Munich, the city in which the Nazi Party was founded in 1920 and just outside of which, in Dachau, the Nazis set up their first concentration camp in 1933. It was also in Munich that the Palestinian Black September Organization murdered eleven Israeli athletes and officials during the 1972 Summer Olympic Games, an event that led to increased security measures at the ESC from 1973 when Israel first entered the contest.[7] Security measures were further increased for the 1979 ESC in the wake of attacks in Israel by the Palestine Liberation Organization and riots by Israeli Arabs who opposed Israel's peace treaty with Egypt, with the venue of the contest being protected by police armed with M16 rifles.[8]

Although 'Hi' was itself replete with historical symbolism, the song had of course not been passed down through the generations because that would have made it ineligible for entry into the ESC. Entries in the ESC have always needed to be new and original, with a cut-off release date of some months before each contest always being specified in the rules. However, how 'new' they could actually be was undermined by the fact that they were nationally representative. 'Hi' demonstrated how music has historically played a role in the construction of national identities while it also encapsulated the contradictions of nationalism: the song highlighted the core elements of national identities, including ancestry, history and myth, yet it also underlined how national identities could be consolidated and fashioned through modern genres and technologies. Several other Israeli entries in the ESC in the 1980s also reflected this with their Biblical references that underlined the ancient history of the Jews, such as 'Ben adam' (Human Being), 'Hora' and 'Derekh ha-melekh' (The King's Road). As with 'Hi', folk influences sometimes appeared in the ESC entries of other states or folk music was showcased in interval acts and postcards in order to give them a national touch amid the seemingly internationally homogenous genres of Europop, jazz or rock and roll. Genres such as *Austropop*, Greek *laïkó* and Norwegian *visesang* also appeared in the ESC and reflected the international development of hybrid genres of folk and popular music.

The hybridization of folk and popular musical styles in the postwar era was not a new historical phenomenon, however, and to make an opposition between classical, folk and popular music is deceiving as their historical development has been intertwined. The ESC epitomized this through its inclusion of conductors and orchestras until 1999, even as new genres of popular music developed that did not find such typically classical accompaniments fitting. With the development of political nationalism in the nineteenth century, European composers incorporated folk elements and historical themes into their symphonies in order to promote national movements. Opera, the major musical fashion of the nineteenth century, was also used for nation building: national cultures that wanted to be seen as fashionable and modern had to have operas composed in their native languages, while the construction of ornate opera houses all over Europe further reflected the grandeur and prestige attached to the genre. As the historian Philipp Ther states, '[t]he question of whether there were sufficient means or a public to maintain an opera house was secondary to the goal of being one of the cultured cities and refined peoples of Europe, of being a part of "European civilization".'[9] Something similar could also be said for states of various economic standing eagerly investing into their hosting of or participation in the ESC.

National operas did not isolate themselves within national traditions but were marks of a cosmopolitanism and modernity led by the French, German and Italian traditions, in the same way that the Anglo-American dominance of popular music in the second half of the twentieth century inspired but did not thwart the development of national popular music cultures. Just as opera had forged a pan-European audience a century beforehand, the ESC did so in the postwar era. Both the ESC and opera in the nineteenth century were housed by the latest architectural fashions of their times: the settings for the ESC were mostly not grand old constructions but modernist congress centres and television studios that were built in the postwar era, with one exception being the Royal Theatre in Madrid which was opened in 1850 as an opera house. Classical musical traditions were promoted in the ESC entries of some states, which was also a way of fashioning national identities through musical genres associated with historical eras that preceded the political instability and wars in the first half of the twentieth century. The best example of this was Austria, which has traditionally been promoted internationally through its classical music heritage: the New Year's Concert of the Vienna Philharmonic, for example, has been one of the Eurovision Network's other popular relays.[10] During the Cold War, Austria's ESC entries included 'Nur in der Wiener Luft' (Only in the Viennese Air), sung by the opera singer Eleonore Schwarz in 1962, and 'Du bist Musik' (You're Music), performed by the group Blue Danube in 1980 and which mentioned twenty-six classical music composers. The 1967 ESC in Vienna also began with the orchestra playing Johann Strauss II's waltz 'Wiener Blut' (Viennese Spirit) and the interval act was performed by the Vienna Boys' Choir.[11] Turkey was represented by the entry 'Opera' in the 1983 ESC, which was also a symbolic affirmation of Turkey's belonging to the European cultural sphere. The development of opera in Turkey had been advanced in the interwar era under the cultural policies of President Mustafa Kemal Atatürk who, after the fall of the Ottoman Empire, sought to Europeanize Turkey through democratization, industrialization and secularization.

In the second half of the twentieth century, new styles of popular music became genres that were used to fashion national cultures as folk music and classical music had been previously. Popular music songs developed into fixtures of national musical repertoires as Western European states sought to improve the standard of living of their citizens through economic growth and the welfare state. The boom in popular music industries and television services in the 1950s and 1960s reflected the growing prosperity of the 'economic miracles' in Western Europe states that followed postwar reconstruction. With citizens having more money for consumer goods and entertainment, there was a rapid increase in the ownership rates of radios, record players and televisions. Still, while television services developed across Western Europe during the 1950s, the ownership of televisions was not so widespread even into the 1960s, and radio remained the most important medium until then. Citizens had already been exposed to national programmes on the radio in the interwar period, when popular music programmes had usually been among the most popular broadcasts. For many Western Europeans, their first experience of the ESC in the late 1950s and early 1960s was thus usually through radio services – which the EBU allowed to broadcast the ESC while insisting that the contest was conceived primarily as a televisual event – or by watching it in groups where a television could be found. With the increase in television ownership, ever more citizens watching the same television programmes in ever more places, especially as there were not so many different television channels available at the time, meant that public opinion was significantly shaped by the national television service. Accordingly, events such as the national selections and the ESC were usually more collectivist national experiences in the 1960s and 1970s than from the 1980s onwards, when the Western European television market became more open to commercial services.

The ESC refashioned national identities and even invented new national traditions not only through the collective act of watching the final of the ESC itself, but also through the organization of the national selections. The methods of these – as well as the financing of the wining song's participation in the final – have always been left up to the national broadcasting organizations, reflecting the international rather than supranational style of cooperation within the EBU. The ESC provided a forum in which the public could directly participate in Western European cultural cooperation unlike any other event staged by a Western European organization, especially when there was public voting in the national selections. In the contest's early years, when telephone ownership was not so widespread, public voting was also often done by the sending in of postal mail. From the very first ESC, the staging of national competitions was promoted by the EBU in its rules for the contest but not spelled out as compulsory, meaning that different selection procedures were varyingly adopted by the national broadcasting organizations. In choosing singers who would represent their state at the ESC, the national selections played a role in determining national representatives who were or had the potential to become national celebrities if not icons. Yet, the process of selecting these figures was often controversial. A tension that has always been inherent in the ESC is that between the platitudinous acknowledgment of the demos and public suspicions that commercial and political interests are more crucial in choosing the entries. In the Cold War era as well, national broadcasting organizations sometimes did not even hold national selections but their officials internally selected an entry themselves. However, the national representatives who were chosen by a public vote had more democratic legitimacy than the ones appointed internally by the national broadcasting organizations, whose officials were also not directly elected by the public.

One of the reasons why commercial and political interests were seen as interfering in the national selections was because national broadcasting organizations and record companies thought that they could recognize a more competitive ESC entry than the national audience could, as the public was often suspected of being limited by parochial and patriotic tastes that would choose an entry lacking international appeal. And this despite the fact that the EBU consciously appealed to patriotic emotions by having entries appear under the names of states rather than those of the national broadcasting organizations, as it thought that 'the public hardly knows the name of an organization and would therefore lose interest in the whole competition'.[12] Apart from 'Hi', there were some other ESC songs that had a patriotic theme. The 1956 ESC itself began with such a song, the Dutch entry 'De vogels van Holland' (The Birds of Holland), which had a patriotic message that praised the natural beauty of the Netherlands and the faithfulness of its girls. However, like songs that were too folkish, explicitly patriotic entries never did well in the ESC during the Cold War because they were too parochial to appeal to a broader international audience, and often even to those national audiences with which they shared close connections in their folk or popular musics or languages.

Indeed, the ESC presented an interesting dilemma for national identities: as the ethnomusicologist Philip Bohlman asks, '[h]ow can a popular song evoke the spirit of the nation and yet suppress all traces of nationalism?'[13] On the one hand, entries had to appeal to an international audience in order to be successful, with the national jury not even being allowed – after the Swiss jury had in 1956, when it voted in lieu of the Luxembourgish one that could not participate in the contest – to vote for its own state's entry in the final. Nationalism is usually motivated to appeal to members of a national corpus, which in the ESC process really only needs to be done in the first stage if there is public voting in the national selections. Nationalisms are usually studied for being constructed against 'others', be it other national groups, sexual minorities or races. At the ESC, however, entries need to be constructed to appeal to those outside of the national group in order to be successful and become a matter of national pride. This is why entries that are too national in style or theme have usually not done well in the contest or, in other words, why patriotic songs in the ESC do not result in patriotic victories.

In order to make entries more appealing to an international audience by being more cosmopolitan, ethnic, national, racial and religious 'others' have often been appropriated in ESC entries. Public opinion could sometimes be critical of its own state's ESC entries if they were produced by artists who were not considered nationally authentic or sung in a foreign language. Yet, the possibility of choosing international artists benefitted the nation fashioning of states that sought to overcome negative reputations associated with fascism and the Second World War. Two of the states that used this strategy, and which had to make the most efforts to refashion their postwar national identities due to their experiences of Nazism, were Austria and West Germany. Their national broadcasting organizations tried from the very beginning of the ESC to represent their states in a cosmopolitan manner, as was demonstrated by Quinn and Schwarz in 1956. In the early 1960s, Austria and Switzerland were even represented in the ESC by Israeli citizens, which, especially in the case of Austria, was a strong political statement after the Holocaust. The first Israeli singers appeared in the ESC ten years before Israel entered the contest, when in 1963 Carmela Corren represented Austria and Esther Ofarim performed for Switzerland.[14] During the 'Waldheim affair' in the mid-1980s, when the Austrian president and former secretary-general of the UN, Kurt Waldheim, was embroiled in a debate about his role in the German army during the Second World War, an Austrian-Israeli singer, Timna Brauer, represented Austria at the 1986 ESC. In 1961, Austria was also represented by the first ever Greek singer to appear in the ESC, Jimmy Makulis, who at that time was developing a career in the German-speaking world and was a symbol of the emerging economic emigration of guest workers from southern to northern Europe. That emigration also found a voice at the 1962 ESC in the West German entry 'Zwei kleine Italiener' (Two Little Italians).[15] Although Italians were used as a symbol of cosmopolitanism in the ESC entries of other states – Denmark sent Dario Campeotto, the son of Italian immigrants, in 1961, and Switzerland's Assia had sung about her Italian lover 'Giorgio' in 1958 – Italy was one of the states with the least nationally diverse artists representing it during the Cold War, with almost all of its entries being performed by Italian-born nationals.

A prominent exception in Italy's entries was the black American singer Wess, who sang the duet 'Era' (It Was) with Dori Ghezzi in the 1975 ESC. This was socially provocative at the time as it presented the duo as being in a multiracial relationship, and it suggested changing social attitudes in Italy that had also been reflected in the approval of divorce in the referendum of 1974. Italy also had a black British conductor, Del Newman, in the 1980 ESC. There had been black artists in the ESC since the 1960s whose participation expressed different political and social messages. For West Germany, black singers, such as members of the Les Humphries Singers and Silver Convention who represented it in the ESC in the 1970s, were a sign of the size and wealth of the West German popular music industry which could offer international artists career prospects, as well as, again, a distancing from Nazi racism. Like Wess, Rhonda Heath and Ramona Wulf from Silver Convention also attested to the important role that black Americans have played in popular music cultures in both Europe and the United States. In the case of the Netherlands, which was represented by the first black singer in the ESC, Milly Scott, in 1966, and whose Dutch Rhythm Steel and Showband and Lee Jackson Dancers, which had black Surinamese members performing Caribbean music, performed as the interval act in the 1980 ESC in The Hague, black artists reflected emigration from the Netherlands' former colonies and official policies of multiculturalism.[16] However, when Portugal, whose rightist dictatorship resisted decolonization, was represented by a black singer form Angola, Eduardo Nascimento, in the 1967 ESC, this underlined that, unlike other Western European states, Portugal was still bent on maintaining an empire (however, as the Angolan War of Independence was then happening, Nascimento's song 'O vento mudou' (The Wind Changed) could have been an allusion to British prime minister Harold Macmillan's 'Wind of Change' speech from 1960 in which he supported British decolonization in Africa). Simone de Oliveira, who sang for Portugal in the 1965 and 1969 contests, was the first artist with black African origins in the contest due to her father's ancestry from the then Portuguese colony of São Tomé and Príncipe. The performances of these Portuguese artists also reminded viewers that colonial Europe's cultural and political borders extended much further than the geography of Western Europe or the technical boundaries of the EBA.

Another demographic development that the ESC reflected in its early decades was the growing cultural, economic and political power of youth. In the 1950s, teenagers became an important consumer category as economic growth also meant that they too had more money to spend, and they were one of the key groups motivating the growth of the popular music industry (the English word 'teenager' was itself first mentioned in the ESC in 1959 in the West German entry 'Heute Abend wollen wir tanzen geh'n' (Tonight We Want to Go Dancing)). Yet, the ESC shared the same dilemma as nationalism: it relied on classical elements to give it a historical justification but also needed to legitimize itself in modern ways. This was seen in the concerns expressed in national media commentaries as well as by some officials from the national broadcasting organizations over the outdated musical styles in the contest and the mediocre quality of the entries in the late 1960s and early 1970s. Although most ESC performers in the 1950s and 1960s were relatively young, the styles of popular music that they largely performed, like chanson and schlager, sounded out of fashion amid the rock and roll that was the real hit among young people. These singers themselves often sang more modish styles in other contexts, but at the ESC they opted for more traditional styles in order to appeal to the transgenerational audience and juries. However, in light of falling viewership ratings in some states, especially among youth, from the early 1970s the EBU sought to modernize the contest through the inclusion of more young people in the national juries and by allowing instrumental backing tracks that reflected the growing popularity of electronic music. Indeed, whereas the ESC had always reflected technological advancements in television, it was relatively slower to make way for those in popular music.

The national broadcasting organization that most ardently pushed for these changes was the BBC, which is unsurprising considering that the UK has had the largest export popular music industry in Europe. Another state which during the Cold War began developing a highly successful popular music industry in terms of exports is Sweden. The victory of ABBA in the 1974 ESC set the foundations for the consequent emergence of Sweden as a global force in popular music, which has also become inherently connected to Sweden's national identity and soft power. The Melody Festival, staged since 1959 as the national selection for the ESC, remains one of the most popular events on the Swedish national calendar. Sweden was one of the rare exceptions, especially among the smaller states participating in the ESC, whose national popular music industry managed to become an international force. One of the reasons for this has been the high level of English-language proficiency in Sweden, considering that its popular musical exports have been overwhelmingly in the English language.[17] Another reason lies in the social democracy that has been the dominant political ideology in Sweden in the postwar era, and Swedish governments have generously supported music activities and education through grants and subsidies. Social democracy also shaped a mindset of making well-designed goods for broad consumption, as the expansion of H&M and Ikea stores outside of Scandinavia from the 1970s demonstrated even before the boom in the Swedish popular music industry.

However, although Sweden now has one of the most fervent national audiences for the ESC, this was not always the case. In the 1960s and 1970s, there were major criticisms made by the Danish, Norwegian and Swedish national broadcasting organizations that record companies were unfairly influencing the ESC. These criticisms, together with ones from the Danish Broadcasting Corporation (DR) about the voting system and those of a group of Danish leftist artists and intellectuals about the unedifying quality of the songs, even prompted DR to withdraw from the ESC from 1967 to 1977.[18] Norway was also represented in the ESC by a few entries in the 1970s which protested against the culture of consumption and money, namely 'Lykken er' (Happiness Is) and 'Småting' (Little Things). There were also protests within Sweden itself by leftist groups in the 'Progg' (a contraction of *proggresiv musik*, or musical progressivism) movement that opposed the commercialism of popular music and were critical of groups such as ABBA that allegedly undermined national culture by singing in English. The Progg movement also opposed Sweden's participation in the ESC because of the financial costs of participating in and hosting the contest, especially after it was held in Stockholm in 1975, and this pressure compelled the Swedish national broadcasting organization, Radio Sweden (SR), to withdraw from the contest for one year in 1976.[19] However, a survey conducted by SR in 1975 found that 71 per cent of those Swedes polled wanted SR to continue participating in the ESC.[20]

As the criticisms by the leftist movements in Denmark and Sweden showed, popular music did not unproblematically unite the populations within states, either through fashion, language or sound. And the ESC has also never seamlessly united Europeans. Not only has it never attracted the same proportion of viewers in all states, but it has also always had different national commentaries.[21] The EBU was conscious of the challenges that linguistic diversity posed for the Eurovision Network from its very beginning and, realizing that it could not broadcast only images across Western Europe, the EBU opted for different national commentaries in the ESC and its other programmes. Commentators have always been sent by the national broadcasting organizations to personally view the ESC, which has meant that the biggest difference in how national audiences have consumed the contest has been in the commentaries that they have heard. Different styles of national commentary, as well as different personal styles, have shaped how national audiences variously relate to the contest. The most famous example was that of the BBC's Terry Wogan, whose ESC commentaries beginning in the 1970s mocked the contest and also fed British Euroscepticism: in his commentary for the 1983 ESC, he said that the contest was referred to by some as the 'Eurobore' or 'Euroyawn'. Which parts of the hosting or songs are translated, or what information about the artists is shared, have also been left up to the discretion of the commentators, making them especially powerful in the period when such information could not be accessed via the internet. Unlike in the entries themselves, nationalism could also be effectively used in the commentaries as these have been targeted at a national audience. The ESC has thus always been an international event with national limitations: European viewers have collectively watched but not listened to the same show, and what they have heard has always had an impact on how they have viewed each other.

Mapping

Together with the national commentaries, the voting has been the other major medium through which mutual perceptions between states at the ESC have been interpreted and shaped, being ritually read in the media as an indicator of how national audiences mentally map Europe. Since the late 1990s, political interpretations of the voting results have carried more weight considering the adoption of public voting; during the Cold War era, the voting was only done by national juries. Still, that there were six different voting systems used in the ESC from 1956 to 1974, with national juries varyingly being composed of two, ten or twenty members and different points scales being adopted, demonstrated that the EBU felt pressured to respond to the political and technical controversies generated by the voting – including allegations of rigging – from the contest's very beginning.[22] There were constant discussions within the Programme and Television Programme committees over how the voting system could be made fairer while adding to the excitement and suspense of the show.

Who exactly should be allowed to sit in the juries was also always a matter of debate within the EBU. Although a jury always took the appellation of the state that it represented, and its votes were presented under such, the national representativeness of the juries was questionable as they were made up of individuals with their own interests and predilections. While the ESC's rules left the selection of the jurors up to the national broadcasting organizations, as they did with the method of selecting the entries, various changes were progressively incorporated into the rules in order to make the juries more representative and transparent. From 1966, for example, the rules banned officials from record companies in the juries, as several national broadcasting organizations felt already in the 1960s that the contest was being excessively commercialized. This ban was also extended in 1972 to employees of the national broadcasting organizations themselves. From 1974, the rules also called for each national jury to be representative of the public and to have a gender balance. How the jurors were selected was, however, still left up to the national broadcasting organizations; therefore, in the early 1970s, the jury selection was being done randomly by some organizations, but by one of them it was being done with the help of a sociologist.[23] This meant that there was no democratic, scientific or standardized method for the selection of the jurors across all states, which always needs to be recalled when we consider who was voting as the representative of a state and how much the voting could therefore be construed as reflecting a national sentiment.

That the national broadcasting organizations themselves had the liberty to select jurors also meant that accusations were made about 'diplomatic' or 'political' voting between the juries from the early years of the contest, especially in national media.[24] In 1970, the EBU's scrutineer for the ESC, Clifford Brown, responded to these by stating that there were indeed voting biases between juries, but that these were based on cultural and linguistic affinities and not political motivations.[25] Yet, the voting results have always been influenced by a mixture of culture, language and politics. When it came to language, there was not a strong tendency for national juries to consistently give high scores to other entries with which they shared linguistic ties until the 1980s – although the 1980s had the most diverse winners with only one being repeated, Ireland. So the five Francophone participants did not ensure each other victory every year, nor was there a strong connection between Belgium and the Netherlands when the former sang in Dutch; indeed, it is striking how often the Belgian and Dutch juries gave each other's entries no points in the 1950s and 1960s. Regarding the Anglophone states, the British and Irish juries also did not consistently trade high scores, but what was most telling was that they did award each other points despite the violent riots in and the deployment of British troops to Northern Ireland in 1969 in the early years of the conflict there between British unionists and Irish republicans. Ireland won its first ESC in 1970, and despite a protest by the pro-republican political party Sinn Féin, the contest was held in Dublin in 1971 (the party then even issued a statement in which it called for a boycott of the contest, claiming that it was expensive and 'sterile' and criticizing the cooperation between the BBC and the Irish national broadcasting organization, Radio and Television of Ireland, (RTÉ); security was also heightened at the 1971 ESC because of terrorist threats from the Irish Republican Army).[26] The voting relationship between Ireland and the UK in the ESC reflected how Irish artists were part of the Anglo-American popular music market.[27] In its three participations in the 1970s, Malta, the only other state in Western Europe that had English as an official language, always gave points to Ireland and the UK, but they ironically gave Malta points only when it entered its first two songs in Maltese.

When it came to the five states having German as an official language and that participated in the ESC during the Cold War – Austria, Belgium, Luxembourg, Switzerland and West Germany – there was also no strong connection between them in their voting. Austrian juries awarded West German entries few, and West German juries gave Austrian entries no, points until the early 1970s.[28] Scandinavian states also did not consistently award each other high scores in the first two decades of the contest, despite the impression given by the 1963 ESC, when the victory of the Danish entry 'Dansevise' (Dance Song) was decided by the Norwegian jury. Due to a technical problem, the Norwegian jury had to be called back at the end of the voting, by which time it had decisively changed its points for the Danish entry from two to four.[29] There was a more consistent voting relationship between Portugal and Spain, but only from 1966 after their first two joint appearances in the contest, to 1974. Cultural, linguistic or neighbourly voting was thus not such a strong phenomenon in the ESC in the early decades of the Cold War. Still, in states which then experienced a string of low scores in the ESC, such as Finland, Malta, Norway, Turkey and Yugoslavia, there were complaints – and even symptoms of 'national trauma'[30] – that these states were marginalized because of their geographical, linguistic and political, and, in the case of Turkey, religious, peripherality in relation to Western Europe. In West Germany, meanwhile, which had more bordering neighbours in the ESC than any other participating state, failure in the ESC was often linked to lingering prejudices in other participating states stemming from its Nazi past.

Nonetheless, there were unexpected results at the ESC in terms of political voting, and not between states which had close cultural, economic and political ties, but rather between ones that did not. Where the voting would be expected to be most predictable, that is in authoritarian states whose governments exercised control over the media, it was perhaps freer than any other election in these states. Points were given by Portugal and Spain to Yugoslavia and vice versa, despite the official anti-communism of the governments of the former two. This was especially mutual in the early 1970s, when Yugoslavia did not have diplomatic relations with Portugal and Spain, which only came in the late 1970s after the fall of their right-wing dictatorships. However, from the 1960s, Spain was also seeking to develop diplomatic relations with Eastern European states – one expression of which was Spain's entry into the 1968 ISC – so the points given to Yugoslavia reflected a political rapprochement in the context of Madrid's desire for improved relations with Eastern Europe. Spain and Yugoslavia's cultural affinities from their belonging to the Mediterranean sphere could also have trumped the political.

As the last jury to present its voting results in the 1968 ESC, the Yugoslav one also determined the Spanish victory by voting for neither Spain nor the UK – to the disappointment of Richard, who came second by one point.[31] The voting results between Spain and the UK also coincided with political tensions, especially regarding their dispute over Gibraltar, which London has controlled since 1713. In 1967, a referendum was held in Gibraltar in which its citizens voted to remain under British sovereignty, and Spain subsequently closed their common border. In the late 1960s, there were no points awarded between Spain and the UK in the ESC, even as they both had winning or highly ranked entries. After the end of the Franco dictatorship in 1975, the politicization of the voting between Spain and the UK was conjecturable: when the 1982 ESC was staged in the British town of Harrogate at the time of the Falklands War between Argentina and the UK, when Spain took the side of Argentina, the Spanish jury awarded the British entry one point, but the British jury awarded no points to the Spanish entry Él' (He), which was based on the tango, an Argentinian dance. 'Él' was furthermore symbolic in the context of the abolition of laws against adultery and divorce in Spain in 1978 and 1981 respectively, as it spoke of a woman choosing between two men and their respective offers of a casual relationship or a serious one.

The year 1975, being the time around the fall of the rightist dictatorships in Greece, Portugal and Spain, was a turning point in Mediterranean Europe. The mid-1970s also marked the ESC's expansion to Greece, Israel and Turkey, meaning that almost all of the states that participated in the contest at some point during the Cold War had by then appeared in it. Regarding Nordic Europe, its participation in the ESC was strengthened with the return of Denmark in 1978 and the debut of Iceland in 1986. The year 1975 was furthermore a turning point for the ESC because it was then that a voting system was introduced that would be used for the rest of the Cold War and into the 1990s. That system had eleven – and from 1988 sixteen – jury members who would select their top ten songs and rank them according to the 1-8, 10, 12 points scale (the 12 and 10 points were adopted to differentiate the top songs and help to avoid a tie, especially after the 1969 ESC had controversially resulted in four winners). Under this system, more points were given out to more entries by more jurors, which meant that the juries had more opportunities to award points based on different motivations. They may have chosen to give their highest scores to entries based on their musical qualities, but to also award some points to the entries of states with which they shared cultural and political affinities.

It is for these reasons that the first ever scientific studies of voting in the ESC begin with the post-1974 period, and they were produced by the sociologists Gad Yair and Daniel Maman in the late 1990s. Based on the voting results in the ESC from 1975 to 1992, Yair and Maman concluded that there were three voting blocs that were apparent in the contest: the Western, Northern and Mediterranean. For all of these blocs, they noted cultural, historical and political ties as being the reasons for the greater connections between some states and not others. However, they also observed that there were stronger ties within the Northern and Western blocs than the Mediterranean one, with the Northern bloc being based principally on cultural affinities, the Western bloc on political grounds and the Mediterranean one on common maritime and historical experiences. So there was no strong voting connection between Yugoslavia and Finland, another non-aligned country, but there was between Yugoslavia and non-aligned but Mediterranean Cyprus. Finland and Portugal were noted by Yair and Maman as isolates, together with Austria, which even after 1974 did not have a strong voting connection with its Germanophone neighbours, let alone its other ESC neighbour, Yugoslavia.[32]

Yair and Maman identified the Western bloc – comprised of France, Ireland, Israel, Luxembourg, Malta, the Netherlands, Switzerland and the UK – as the most prominent. Indeed, when the ESC winners during the Cold War are geographically mapped, there is a clear concentration in the northwest and a wane southwards. Ireland, France, Luxembourg, the Netherlands and the UK took almost two-thirds of the ESC victories during the Cold War. For Ireland, France, Luxembourg and the UK, their success in the ESC can be partly explained by the fact that their entries were performed in world languages with related large popular music industries. Still, although there was a higher concentration of wins in northwestern Europe, the victors in the post-1974 period were more diverse than in the previous decades, as there were more representatives from all of Western Europe's geographical regions in the ESC and the voting system allowed juries to differentiate more between entries. From 1975 to 1989, the ESC winners stretched from Ireland and Norway in the north to Yugoslavia and Israel in the south, with Israel, Norway and Yugoslavia all winning for the first time and Ireland winning twice.

Yair and Maman argued that Israel was, for historical and political reasons, more a member of the Western bloc than the Mediterranean one. As Israel has always been the most politically controversial participant in the ESC because of Europe's history of anti-Semitism and the wars between Israel and its neighbouring states, we can also measure how political the contest was considering the votes that were given to it. For the Western European audience, Israel, the only ESC participant during the Cold War that geographically lay outside of Europe, was variously mapped as Western, Mediterranean and Middle Eastern. Israel and West Germany often awarded each other points in the 1970s and 1980s, including some high scores for the political songs of Haza and Nicole, who won the 1982 ESC for West Germany with 'Ein bißchen Frieden' (A Little Peace). There were points exchanged between Israel and

Spain in the 1970s and 1980s even though they did not establish diplomatic ties until 1986 because of the pro-Arab policies of the Franco government and subsequent Spanish ones (the Spanish jury's vote in 1979 even decided the victory for Israel over close runners-up France and Spain). Yugoslavia, which did not have diplomatic relations with Israel from 1967 until the early 1990s because of the former's support for Arab states through the Non-aligned Movement, gave Israeli entries some high scores, as did Israel to Yugoslavia, especially in the 1980s. These voting results were quite a political statement for the national audience when they were broadcast on Yugoslav television, especially as the Yugoslav media was otherwise highly critical of Israel. However, one of the reasons for Yugoslavia not participating in the 1979 ESC was the contest's staging in Israel, and in the late 1970s officials from the Yugoslav national broadcasting organization, Yugoslav Radio and Television (JRT), also criticized the ESC voting as being biased in favour of Israel.[33]

The Arab world, then, also had an influence on the ESC during the Cold War, even though just one Arab state, Morocco, has ever participated in the contest. This occurred only once, in 1980, when Morocco was represented by the entry 'Bitaqat hob' (Love Card), a song about world peace that was also symbolic in light of the conflict in which the Moroccan army was then involved in Western Sahara, as Morocco sought to annex that territory after Spain had ended its control over it in 1975. Arab states have mostly boycotted the ESC because of Israel's participation in it: Tunisia had considered entering the ESC in 1977 but withdrew because of Israel, while Morocco appeared in 1980 when Israel declined to host the contest for financial reasons and did not participate because the date clashed with Israel's Memorial Day for fallen soldiers.[34] When the ESC was broadcast in some Arab states in 1978, their national broadcasting organizations did not show the winning Israeli entry 'A-ba-ni-bi' but had a commercial break or, in the case of Jordan, showed an image of flowers, instead.[35] In Egypt, which in 1979 became the first Arab state to establish diplomatic relations with Israel, the ESC was broadcast from 1981. After it became an active member of the EBU in 1985, the Egyptian national broadcasting organization, the Egyptian Radio and Television Union (ERTU), also enquired about joining the ESC in 1989, but only if it could be excluded in advance from a first-place result as it did not want to have to host the contest.[36]

This left Turkey as the only predominantly Muslim state that, after its debut in 1975, regularly participated in the ESC. Unlike Arab states, Turkey was willing to compete alongside Israel in the contest as it had recognized the State of Israel in 1949 and had diplomatic relations with it from 1950. However, in 1979, when the ESC was held in Jerusalem, the Turkish national broadcasting organization, the Turkish Radio and Television Corporation (TRT), withdrew from the contest after coming under political pressure from Arab states.[37] The 1979 ESC was held just five days after the signing of the peace treaty between Egypt and Israel, which other Arab states opposed. Turkey had become more dependent on Arab states for petroleum supplies during the oil crisis that was provoked by the Iranian Revolution earlier in 1979, and the Turkish entry in the 1980 ESC, 'Petr'Oil', itself alluded to the oil crisis. Turkish juries had awarded Israeli entries six points in 1975 and twelve points in 1978. However, in the 1980s they gave no points at all to Israel: during this decade, the relations between the two states deteriorated because of Israel's annexation of East Jerusalem in 1980 (in the introductory film for the 1979 ESC, images of East and West Jerusalem were shown, including one of an Israeli soldier in the Old City). Still, Israeli juries awarded points to Turkish entries twice in the 1980s.

Political voting in the ESC during the Cold War was most apparent in the relationship between Cyprus, Greece and Turkey, due to tensions over the Turkish invasion of Cyprus, historical animosities between Greece and Turkey, and the cultural, linguistic and political ties between Greek Cypriots and Greece. As the centre of the Greek-language popular music industry is in Greece, Greek Cypriot singers like Anna Vissi have relocated there, and she has even represented both Cyprus and Greece in the ESC. The relationship between Cyprus and Greece has become the cliché example of bloc voting in the ESC, and since the early 1990s they have usually awarded each other maximum points. However, in the 1980s that was not the case: the Greek jury even gave the Cypriot entry no points in 1983 after Cyprus had awarded Greece only six points when Cyprus debuted in the ESC in 1981. For the rest of the 1980s their juries also often did not have the opportunity to vote for the other's entries, as Greece was not represented in the 1982, 1984 and 1986 contests and Cyprus was not in 1988. The complexities in the cultural, economic and political ties between Cyprus and Greece is also obscured by their clichéd 'twelve points': there have been different political views within each state regarding *enosis* (union) between them, especially considering Cypriot anxieties over being dominated by a much larger Greece. Still, both Cyprus and Greece share historical tensions with Turkey, and neither Cypriot nor Greek juries awarded Turkish entries any points during the Cold War, with Turkish juries acting likewise except for once in 1988, when the Greek entry was awarded three points.

What analyses of the voting results do not explain is the agency behind why national juries voted the way they did. Explanations based on cultural affinities and historical connections can be distorted by stereotypes. If the relationship between Cyprus and Greece versus Turkey is the only one during the Cold War with a consistently strong negativity bias, then the cultural affinities themselves were not so constantly decisive. Indeed, bloc voting could have even been a self-fulfilling prophecy: after all, voting blocs were not so apparent in the early years of the contest. As the ESC expanded and as reasons were sought to explain the poor results of entries, officials from the national broadcasting organizations began to both fear such blocs and search for a position in one of them. Indeed, if the same cultural and political factors were always at play, then this would have led to the same winner or few winners once the ESC's participation stabilized from the mid-1970s, which was not the case. It is impossible to determine the motivations for any juror's or jury's votes without documentary proof, or to determine the extent of organized vote trading among the delegations, which was another popular suspicion. In the end, this means that the voting is most interesting for how it was interpreted by the media and public: it is this, rather than the scores themselves, that tell us more about how Europeans perceived each other during the Cold War. Considering that, first, jurors did not have the democratic legitimacy to express the views, say, of the general public or political factions and that, second, the EBU always presented the ESC as apolitical, it is striking that these voting results were given more attention than they really deserved. The ESC was accorded a power that outweighed its actual significance: after all, it has never had a decision-making function in international relations but has remained in the realm of symbolic acts.

That national stereotypes and touristic images were regularly used in the ESC to depict the participating states also did not help to change mental maps. National broadcasting organizations that hosted the contest often began their broadcasts with films about their states, which were usually conceived with the purpose of promoting tourism and were sometimes even financially supported by tourism organizations. In 1959, images of famous national sites were used in the ESC for the first time as the backgrounds for each of the entries. States were also visually depicted in the promotional videos that were made for the entries, in the postcards that were produced from 1970 to introduce each entry (and which more practically allowed time for set changes as performances became more elaborate after the rules were changed to allow instrumentation and more artists onstage), and sometimes in the interval acts (which allowed time for the voting). One of the paradoxes of the ESC has been that the national stereotypes that have been traded in it have tended to draw on a state's cultural heritage, even though the aim of the contest has been to promote modern cultural production. So, in the Cold War era there were the usual touristic images of Paris to represent France, Rome for Italy, London for the UK, classical music for Austria, tulips for the Netherlands and mountains for Switzerland. That there was not much attention given to presenting states more innovatively could have also been due to the time limits: visual messages had to be peacefully harmless, politically inoffensive, quickly effective, universally understood and visually pretty. This was significant because it demonstrated that, despite Western European integration and the new technologies that were allowing Europeans to have more cultural exchange with each other, they were still relating through historicized, simplified messages and stereotypes. History was still being used to formulaically shape contemporary views of each other, including through the use of folk influences, and paradoxically even more so as a way to distinguish nations from each other considering that they were increasingly sharing the same modern cultural phenomena.

As the ESC developed into a stage for promoting tourism, there were also commercial motivations behind the depiction of states through their famous attractions, which was especially the case with Mediterranean states. As there was only one Eastern European state, Yugoslavia, in the ESC during the Cold War, Europe's east-west axis did not significantly function as a geocultural divide in the contest then. However, the north–south one was apparent in the ESC and politically definitive for Western Europe during the Cold War.[38] There was an exoticization and romanticization, even a fossilization, of the Mediterranean that both northern and southern Europeans played to. Entries from the north, for example, sometimes sang about travelling to the south to find love: in the 1960 ESC, Austria's Harry Winter wondered whether he had fallen in love in Madrid, Paris or Rome in the song 'Du hast mich so fasziniert'

(You Fascinated Me So Much), and in the 1961 ESC Norway's Nora Brockstedt sang 'Sommer i Palma' (Summer in Palma), which was about having a summer romance in the Spanish city of Palma de Mallorca. Indeed, whenever songs from northern Europe sang of the south, the references were always positive. Entries from the south also fed northern European fantasies for the sun, sea and love: the first Greek entry in 1974 was called 'Krasi, thalassa ke t' agori mou' (Wine, Sea and My Boyfriend). Yet, southern Europeans rarely sung about the north during the Cold War. Even Paris, the clichéd city of love which was the city most mentioned in ESC entries during the Cold War, was never sung about in entries from other Mediterranean states (except in some Monegasque entries, which were anyway usually produced by French artists). The only entry that sang about Stockholm and being in love there was from Sweden in the 1963 ESC: 'En gång i Stockholm' (Once Upon a Time in Stockholm) was also the only Swedish entry in the ESC that received no points at all.

The Swedish capital was, however, one of the stops mentioned by Vissi in 'Autostop' (Hitchhiking), with which she represented Greece in the 1980 ESC. Just as 'Autostop' was more an ode to travelling rather than automobiles, songs that glorified technology were more of a northern thing: only entries from northern European states sang about aeroplanes, satellites, telegrams, telephones and videos. The national broadcasting organizations from Mediterranean states technologically lagged behind northern European states from the 1950s to the 1970s, which is also why they mostly joined the ESC later. The Spanish national broadcasting organization, Spanish Television (RTE), required assistance from its West German counterpart to produce the ESC in 1969: this contest was the second to be broadcast in colour after the 1968 ESC that was staged in the UK, but it was not seen in colour in Spain as RTE only began the colour broadcasting of all programmes in 1977. Like Israel and Spain, most southern Europe states, including Italy, introduced colour television amid political controversy. They did so later than northern European states did, where colour broadcasting had begun in Belgium, France, the Netherlands, West Germany and the UK in 1967, while the 1971 ESC was a pioneering colour broadcast for RTÉ. Colour television changed the way that ESC performances were conceived by putting more emphasis on their visual aspects, especially the artists' costumes, and therefore had an impact on how national audiences and juries judged the entries. Yet, black-and-white technological differences symbolized other ways in which northern and southern Europeans differed from each other, and that was in their national politics, especially in their attitudes towards gender and sexuality issues and liberal democracy.

Revolutions

That the ESC was also a battleground for national politics was evident in the choices made to send artists with particular ethnic, national, racial or religious backgrounds or political affiliations. These decisions reflected the attitudes of officials from the national broadcasting organizations, or the public when it was allowed to vote in the national selections, towards contemporary political issues and social changes. As Western European societies were experiencing changing attitudes towards gender and sexuality issues in the 1950s and 1960s, these were also expressed in the ESC: in those decades entries were mostly about love and hardly about peace, making Europeans seem more united by sex than by Western European integration. Female singers have never been underrepresented in the ESC: they have always outnumbered, and won more times than, male ones in the contest, although they have been less numerous as conductors, composers and lyricists. Although entries in the first years of the contest appeared conservative with women wearing dresses and gowns and men in dinner jackets and suits – as they were instructed to dress by the EBU[39] – the themes of some of them were socially provocative, with few songs about traditional notions of the family and marriage. The first decade of the ESC was not simply a conservative era but rather a time in which societies faced both re-traditionalization and sexual liberalization, although the latter would be more palpable in the contest from the mid-1960s. There were ESC entries in the late 1950s that dealt with dating and unfaithfulness, including Quinn's song and the Dutch winner 'Een Beetje' (A Little Bit) in 1959. This was also the time when the ESC had its longest onstage kiss ever, between Denmark's Birthe Wilke and Gustav Winckler, a twenty-year-old divorcée and a thirty-one-year-old married man, in 1957. These entries represented, as the historian Dagmar Herzog has defined it, an era 'of great contradiction in the West: rising prosperity, but also ongoing ambivalence about pleasure as an end in itself'.[40] In the late 1950s and early 1960s, the EBU was not yet pushing the idea that the ESC should be watched by the whole family, and the contest even began as late as ten o'clock Central European Time (CET), and only from 1963 was it constantly staged on a Saturday.[41]

Even though the ESC always exhibited camp aesthetics that made the contest extremely popular in gay culture in Europe – the writer Susan Sontag in her 1964 essay 'Notes on "Camp"' describes homosexuals as being 'the vanguard – and the most articulate audience – of Camp'[42] – gay artists in the ESC during the Cold War could hardly be open about their sexuality. The ESC has been especially popular among gay men and its artists and songs have been staples in gay bars and clubs around the continent. Gay men have also played a prominent role in the national ESC fan clubs that were from 1984 connected through the international network of the General Organization of Eurovision Fans, commonly referred to by its French-language abbreviation 'OGAE'. However, in the 1950s and 1960s, homosexuality was not openly discussed in Western European societies and was still even criminalized in some states, a situation which could not be categorized simply according to a north–south axis (in 1966, for example, homosexuality was legal in Greece, Italy and Turkey, but still not in Norway, the UK and West Germany). Homosexuality became a more public issue from the 1970s, when it became decriminalized in more states and as gay rights movements developed. Yet, even in the 1980s it was still rare for a public figure in Western Europe to openly declare their homosexuality. Under the Thatcher government, a law was even adopted in the UK in 1988 that forbade the public promotion of homosexuality by local authorities and schools, which was ironic considering that Thatcher herself had come out as an ESC fan.

Still, the ESC manifested latent connections with gay culture already in the late 1950s and early 1960s. The first known gay man to perform in the ESC was Bob Benny, who represented Belgium in 1959 and 1961; he first publicly declared his homosexuality in 2001. The 1960 West German entry 'Bonne nuit, ma chérie' (Goodnight, My Darling) was written by Kurt Schwabach. In 1920, he had co-written the song 'Das lila Lied' (The Lavender Song), which became one of the first ever gay anthems during a period of sexual liberation in Germany, and especially Berlin, before the coming to power of the Nazis.[43] In 1961, Pascal won the ESC for Luxembourg with 'Nous les amoureux' (We, the Lovers). Although Pascal could not explicitly articulate it then, the entry could be read as being about homosexual love.[44] The song was gender-neutral and about maintaining love despite social hostility; it also, however, expressed a sense of helplessness against these prejudices, reflecting the fact that gay activism was not much of a phenomenon at the time. This was also the first song in the contest to mention 'God', which it did by referring to a God-given right for the lovers to be happy together. The poet Ary dos Santos, a communist opponent of Portugal's dictatorship, wrote several of the Portuguese entries in the late 1960s and 1970s; he was the most openly gay artist in the ESC during the Cold War as he did not conceal his homosexuality even as it remained criminalized in Portugal until 1983.[45] The first obviously queer entry in the ESC was in 1986 with 'Romeo', which represented Norway and featured Jonny Nymoen, a member of the drag troupe the Great Garlic Girls, in drag dancing onstage. In 1981, Norway had become the first state in the world to adopt laws against the discrimination of sexual minorities, even though it had decriminalized homosexuality relatively late in 1972. Nella Martinetti, who wrote some of the Swiss entries in the 1980s, including 'Ne partez pas sans moi', entered into a registered partnership with her female partner in 2009.

With the beginning of a new wave of feminist activism in the 1960s, heterosexual issues became even more apparent in the ESC. The costumes also accordingly changed as gowns and suits gave way to more casual and modish attire: in 1966, Norway's Åse Kleveland became the first female singer to perform in the ESC wearing pants. Southern European artists and juries were not necessarily more conservative than their northern European counterparts. Sexual issues were championed by French- and Italian-language entries in the 1960s. A year after Cinquetti won with 'Non ho l'età', the winner of the 1965 ESC was the French singer France Gall, who represented Luxembourg with 'Poupée de cire, poupée de son' (Wax Doll, Sound Doll). Like 'Non ho l'età', it referred to a girl on the verge of her sexual awakening; it also criticized the appropriation of teenage pop singers by the popular music industry, which played a major role in promoting liberal sexual attitudes in Western European societies. 'Poupée de cire, poupée de son' was composed and written by the artist Serge Gainsbourg, who was renowned for the sexual innuendo in his films and songs, such as the 1966 hit 'Les sucettes' (Lollipops), which was also sung by Gall and alluded to oral sex. He also composed and wrote Monaco's 1967 entry, 'Boum-badaboum', sung by Minouche Barelli, which spoke about being free to live and love amid the threat of nuclear war. In the 1968 ESC, France came third with the song

'La source' (The Source), sung by Isabelle Aubret, which was about rape. None of these songs was censored by the EBU, nor were they even discussed in its meetings as being controversial.

Another example of an ESC entry making a political statement about a social issue, and which highlighted a major difference that did exist between Catholic southern Europe and Protestant northern Europe regarding divorce, was Cinquetti's 'Sì'. RAI censored it and other songs by Italian artists that were perceived as advocating a position regarding the national referendum on the abrogation of a law adopted in 1970 that allowed divorce; the referendum was to be held in May five weeks after the staging of the 1974 ESC.[46] 'Sì' was about a woman being in love with a man, but because *no* and *sì* were the options on the referendum ballot, RAI considered it inappropriate for broadcast during the referendum campaign (a *sì* vote on the referendum ballot was actually in favour of abrogating the law allowing divorce). RAI had already received approval from the EBU to delay its broadcast of the ESC by one day as RAI's transmission time had been shortened to 10.45pm due to the energy crisis that Italy and other Western European states were then facing. Yet, one week before the 1974 ESC, RAI decided that, because of 'Sì', it would not broadcast the contest until after the referendum was held.[47] 'Sì', however, came second to ABBA in the 1974 ESC, and the day after the contest the Italian media duly reported on this, Italy's biggest successes at the ESC since Cinquetti had won in 1964.

Concerning women's rights, Liechtenstein even sought to enter the ESC in 1976 at a time when it was under international pressure, including from the CoE, for being the last state in Europe to not allow women's suffrage. This was also occurring at a time when Liechtenstein was seeking membership in the CoE, which it achieved in 1978 after it had been admitted as an observer in 1974. In 1976, the front page of the national newspaper *Liechtensteiner Vaterland* (Liechtenstein Fatherland) reported that, although Biggi Bachmann and her song 'My Little Cowboy' had been selected to represent Liechtenstein in the 1976 ESC by the government's Culture and Youth Committee, she would not be able to participate in the contest because Liechtenstein did not have a national broadcasting organization that could join the EBU. The article appeared alongside another about women's suffrage which compared Liechtenstein with other states in the world, such as Saudi Arabia, that did not allow women to vote (both Liechtenstein and Saudi Arabia are also among the few states in the EBA that have never been represented in the EBU).[48] Women's suffrage was finally introduced in Liechtenstein after a national referendum in 1984.

Despite the fact that social issues were being addressed in the ESC, and even by artists who had a reputation for being sexually provocative, the contest was not attractive to younger viewers in the late 1960s and early 1970s, as the surveys conducted by the EBU in the early 1970s found. The contest had been declining in popularity across Western Europe in the late 1960s, a major reason being because its songs were widely considered to be mediocre and outmoded. After the student movements in Western Europe in 1968 that called for liberalizing political and social reforms, national broadcasting organizations were also compelled to modernize the ESC and make it more culturally and politically recognitive of youth tastes, such as by ensuring in the contest's rules that the national juries be half composed of persons under the age of twenty-five. The hippy culture and new social movements which developed in Western Europe from the mid-1960s also had an impact on the aesthetics and themes of ESC entries in the 1970s. In the 1971 ESC, Peter, Sue and Marc referred directly to youth issues in their folkish 'Les illusions de nos vingt ans' (The Illusions of Our Twenties), in which they called for older generations who had fantasized about spring and waltzing to now let young people live and love. Youthful freedom was also the theme of the entry that was meant to represent France in the 1974 ESC, 'La vie à vingt-cinq ans' (Life at the Age of Twenty Five), but due to the sudden death of President Georges Pompidou, who had as prime minister negotiated an end to the student and workers' protests of 1968, France withdrew from the 1974 ESC just days before it was staged.[49] The impact of the hippy movement was, however, evident in the 1974 ESC with the Dutch entry 'I See a Star', which was performed by the duo Mouth & MacNeal and alluded to drug use. The debate on drugs policy that was occurring in the Netherlands at the time resulted in that state adopting the world's most liberal laws on soft drugs, decriminalizing the personal use of cannabis from 1976. Environmental issues also became more apparent in the ESC in the 1970s and reflected the development of the green movement, beginning with the West German entry 'Diese Welt' (This World) in 1971. In the 1980 ESC, the Norwegian entry 'Sámiid ædnan' (Sami Land) referred to the autonomy movement of the indigenous Sami people and public protests in the late 1970s against the construction of a hydroelectric power plant in their region.[50]

Together with the Dutch and Italian entries, the symbolism and themes of the ones from Greece, Portugal and Yugoslavia made the 1974 ESC the most politically charged edition in the contest's history. While the 1970s were revolutionary in northern Europe in terms of social liberalization, in southern Europe it was also a revolutionary decade as it saw the end of rightist dictatorships in Greece, Portugal and Spain. The ESC featured in these political changes as these states were represented in the EBU because of its apolitical membership criteria; the CoE and EC, for example, rebuffed their authoritarian regimes for suppressing media, personal and political freedoms. In Greece, Portugal and Spain, the ESC was a battleground for competing political factions not only because of the dictatorships' political control of the national broadcasting organizations, but also because the contest could draw international attention to opposition political causes. For these Mediterranean states, as well as Turkey and Yugoslavia, participation in the ESC was also a chance to promote their growing tourism industries that were key for their economic development, and these states were often represented by entries with maritime or touristic themes. Such entries underlined these states' belonging to and acceptance by a Western European consumer culture, while using the innocuous, fun and transnational genre of Europop to whitewash the images of their non-democratic governments that otherwise did not belong to the Western European political standard. The EBU's apoliticism meant that it never criticized or sanctioned the authoritarian governments of Greece, Portugal, Spain or any other state that was represented in its organization. There was a protest against Spain and Portugal in the 1964 ESC in Copenhagen, when an audience member from the leftist Group 61 youth organization held up a sign saying 'Boycott Franco and Salazar' – but that was deliberately not shown in the broadcast.[51]

The year 1968 would in hindsight be a turning point for the ESC in terms of its impact on the modernization and rejuvenation of the contest in the 1970s, but the win of Spain in that year also demonstrated how the contest could be appropriated by authoritarian regimes. Spain's victory was considered important by the Franco government for the state's cultural diplomacy in Western Europe and especially the promotion of Spain's growing tourism industry (Spain even had a joint ministry for information and tourism). Franco ruled Spain after his Nationalist faction defeated the leftist Republicans in the Spanish Civil War of 1936 to 1939. As Franco's Nationalists had been supported by fascist

Germany and Italy during the Civil War and his government had supported them during the Second World War, although Spain remained officially neutral in that conflict, Spain was isolated by the Western powers in the aftermath of the Second World War. However, the development of the Cold War saw a rapprochement between the West and anti-communist Franco in the 1950s. Spain joined the EBU in 1955 after it had re-entered the ITU, but it would never be accepted into any other Western European organization until after the death of Franco in 1975; Spain's first application for EC membership was in 1962, but this was rejected because of its political system.

Spain won the 1968 ESC with Massiel singing 'La, la, la'. Although she would later protest against Franco' policies by refusing to receive an award from him after her win, Massiel herself had symbolized the politics of the Franco government because she had been a last-minute choice to represent Spain in place of Joan Manuel Serrat. He had wanted to sing in the ESC in Catalan but was thwarted from doing so as Franco's policies promoted a unitarist national identity and suppressed regionalisms.[52] The 1969 ESC was held in Madrid and TVE invested so much into staging the contest that it caused a budgetary crisis for the organization; Salvador Dalí was even employed as the designer of the promotional materials and an onstage sculpture.[53] The Spanish government imposed no political restrictions on the participants in the 1969 ESC. The only national broadcasting organization that boycotted the contest out of political protest was the Austrian Broadcasting Corporation (ORF), which was continuing its political activism at the ESC after it had the previous year sent the Czechoslovak singer Karel Gott to represent Austria in the contest during the Prague Spring. SR, however, criticized ORF's move in 1969 for politicizing the EBU.[54] Spain scored another victory in the 1969 ESC when its singer Salomé tied for first place with the Dutch, French and British entries. The four winners, and not the Franco regime, turned out to be the biggest scandal of the 1969 ESC and resulted in changes to the contest's rules – as well as a boycott by more national broadcasting organizations of the 1970 ESC.

Although Spain's neighbour Portugal also had a right-wing dictatorship in the early postwar decades, it was not excluded from Western European organizations to the same extent because it had not supported Germany and Italy during the Second World War. The Portuguese dictatorship had arisen already in the interwar period and was headed by António de Oliveira Salazar from 1932 until 1968 and thereafter by Marcelo Caetano. Under Salazar, Portugal joined Western European organizations such as EFTA, NATO and the Organization for Economic Cooperation and Development as well as the EBU. The Portuguese national broadcasting organization, Portuguese Radio and Television (RTP), first participated in the ESC in 1964. In 1970, RTP boycotted the contest to protest against the voting system that had resulted in four winners in Madrid, and its counterparts from other members of EFTA – Austria, Norway and Sweden and associate member Finland – also joined the boycott. However, as with the national broadcasting organizations from other authoritarian states, the EBU never sanctioned RTP for political reasons – even when Portugal was excluded from the ITU in 1973 after Africans states rallied against it because of its colonialist policies, as they simultaneously did against South Africa because of its apartheid system.[55]

Upon coming to power in 1968, Caetano instituted some political reforms which included an easing of media censorship, and one repercussion of this was that the leftist opposition played a more prominent role in the production of Portugal's ESC entries, especially with the songs written by dos Santos for the 1969, 1971 and 1973 contests, such as the patriotic 'Desfolhada portuguesa' (Portuguese Husking) and the politically critical 'Tourada' (Bullfight). The ESC also played a symbolic role in the Carnation Revolution of 1974 that toppled the dictatorship and introduced multiparty democracy. The Portuguese entry in the 1974 ESC, 'E depois do adeus' (And After the Farewell), was sung by Paulo de Carvalho and written by José Niza, who after the revolution became a socialist member of the Portuguese parliament. The song was broadcast on national radio on April 23, just weeks after the 1974 ESC, as the first of two songs that were the signals used by an organization of military officers to launch the coup that started the revolution. One of these officers, Duarte Mendes, went on to perform 'Madrugada' (Dawn), an ode to the revolution, in the 1975 ESC; the Portuguese entries in 1976 and 1977, 'Uma flor de verde pinho' (A Green-Pine Flower) and 'Portugal no coração' (Portugal in My Heart), also had patriotic themes. Portuguese entries thereafter did not have such explicit political messages – until 1986, when the song 'Conquistador' (Conqueror) glorified the colonial empire that Portugal had once had, and which it entirely relinquished in 1987 when it ceded Macao to China. During the Cold War, Portugal had the most nationally politicized entries in the history of the contest, perhaps explaining why it never won the ESC then.[56]

While an ESC entry was used to start a military coup in Portugal, a military junta entered Greece into the ESC. Like Spain, Greece also had recent experience of a civil war, in its case between government and communist forces from 1946 to 1949. With the victory of the government army, Greece's position in the Western Bloc was ensured, and it entered the CoE in 1949, the EBU in 1950 and NATO in 1952. From 1967 to 1974, Greece was ruled by a military junta which came to power in what it defined as a 'revolution' to save Greece from a communist takeover. The military junta was criticized by Western European governments and organizations for suppressing human rights, leading Greece to withdraw from the CoE in 1970, although it remained in NATO. Leftist artists were censored and, as in the case of Mercouri, even exiled from Greece. However, the military junta did not suppress Western popular culture – the ESC was first broadcast in Greece in 1970 – and it also encouraged the development of tourism, especially for the Western European market. These two factors in particular explain the interest of the Greek national broadcasting organization, the National Radio and Television Foundation (EIRT), in entering the ESC, which EIRT first expressed in 1972.[57] EIRT's decision in 1973 to enter the 1974 ESC was made at a time when the military junta was attempting political liberalization and seeking to improve its image in Western Europe. Marinella, one of Greece's biggest stars at the time, represented Greece at the 1974 ESC with 'Krasi, thalassa ke t' agori mou' (Wine, Sea and My Boyfriend). After free elections that restored multiparty democracy were held in November 1974, Greece boycotted the 1975 ESC in protest against Turkey's debut in the contest after the Turkish invasion of Cyprus in 1974. The invasion had also been a factor that had contributed to the downfall of the Greek military junta, which had tried to overthrow the Cypriot government through a military coup that aimed for enosis. In the 1976 ESC, the Greek entry 'Panagia mou, panagia mou' (My Lady, My Lady) explicitly protested against the Turkish invasion of Cyprus, leading TRT to complain to the EBU about the song's political message. However, the EBU did not agree that the song violated the contest's rules and, indeed, there was not yet a stipulation in the rules against entries with political messages. TRT consequently withdrew from the 1976 ESC and did not return to the contest until 1978; it censored the Greek entry in its broadcast of the 1976 ESC by replacing it with a Turkish protest song.[58]

Greece's 1976 entry was the first expression of solidarity between it and Cyprus in the ESC. During the Cold War, non-aligned Cyprus joined the CoE in 1961 and its national broadcasting organization, the Cyprus Broadcasting Corporation (CyBC), entered the EBU in 1969, but it was not a member of any Western European economic organization. Cyprus' participation in the ESC has only meant the involvement of the Greek Cypriot-controlled part of the island, the Republic of Cyprus, which is internationally recognized – except by Turkey – as the legitimate government of the whole island. Despite the fact that both Greek and Turkish are official languages of the Republic of Cyprus, it was during the Cold War represented in the ESC only by entries in Greek. The Turkish Republic of Northern Cyprus (TRNC) was declared in 1983 and has only been recognized by Turkey; it has lacked the international recognition required for it to join the EBU, but its citizens have been able to watch the CyBC's or TRT's broadcasts of the ESC, while Turkish Cypriot artists have also participated in some Turkish ESC entries. Turkish Cypriot Bayrak TV made a request to join the ESC in 1987, complaining that Greek Cypriots should not be the only Cypriots to represent Cyprus and that it 'prevents the Turkish people of Cyprus from making its contribution to the cultural diversity of the Continent of Europe', but the request was obviously denied by the EBU due to the TRNC's lack of international recognition.[59]

That Turkey was, together with Israel, the only Middle Eastern state to appear in the ESC during the Cold War was a consequence of Atatürkist Europeanization as well as the state's geopolitical role in the Western Bloc. Turkey had been included in the Western Bloc in the late 1940s through the Marshall Plan, through which the United States provided economic assistance to Western European states to aid their postwar reconstruction and shore them up against the spread of communism. Considering their strategic position in the eastern Mediterranean, both Greece and Turkey were admitted into NATO in 1952. Turkey joined the CoE in 1949 and became an associate member of the EC in 1964; it applied for membership of the EC in 1987. TRT was also a founding member of the EBU, but because it only began regular television services in 1971 and was connected to the Eurovision Network from 1973 – when it first broadcast the ESC – it first participated in the ESC in 1975.[60] TRT's participation in the ESC from 1975 thus paralleled Turkey's efforts to become more economically and politically integrated with Western Europe. However, even though some of Turkey's most famous artists performed in the contest –

such as Ajda Pekkan who sang 'Petr'Oil' – the generally low placings of Turkish entries in the ESC during the Cold War were popularly attributed to cultural and religious differences with Western Europe as well as domestic political problems that harmed Turkey's international image.[61] From 1980 to 1983, Turkey was ruled by a military junta which had come to power in a coup under the pretext of ending armed conflicts between leftist and rightist political organizations in Turkey; this was the last of three military coups in Turkey during the Cold War. Turkey's relationships with some Western European governments were consequently strained but the state was not expelled from the CoE. TRT continued to participate in the ESC in the early 1980s, but some artists who had previously represented Turkey in the ESC protested against the military junta: the lyricist of 'Petr'Oil', Şanar Yurdatapan, was also a human rights activist who was exiled to Germany after the military coup and stripped of his Turkish citizenship.

As the ESC was conceptualized from its beginning as a competition between states, it always reflected both national politics within these states as well as the bilateral relations between them. Popular music and television figured prominently in the efforts of states to fashion national identities during the Cold War. Some of the national broadcasting organizations took an activist role in trying to present their states as cosmopolitan or liberal, such as through the inclusion in their ESC entries of ethnic minorities or non-nationals and the promotion of women's rights or other issues that were articulated by new social movements. In southern Europe, the national selections were themselves arenas in which critics of the rightist dictatorships expressed their opposition towards the government, as in Portugal and Spain, especially as these governments sought to appropriate the ESC to legitimize, normalize or rehabilitate their images in Western Europe. However, despite the north–south political differences that were apparent between Western European states for much of the Cold War, these states were still united by economic and military structures, as well as through the cultural and technical cooperation in the EBU, that were created in opposition to Eastern Europe. The main axis dividing Europe during the Cold War was still the east–west one, which was reflected in the separate international broadcasting organizations – and their separate international song contests – for Eastern and Western Europe.

Figure 5 Helena Vondráčková, 1977 ISC

3

A Contest for Communism

Communism is an atheistic ideology, but it also produced its own idols in Eastern Europe. One of them was Helena Vondráčková, the winner of the 1977 ISC. Together with her counterpart Karel Gott, Vondráčková was among the biggest pop stars in Czechoslovakia during the communist era. Born in 1947, the year before Czechoslovakia came under communist control, Vondráčková began her artistic career in the mid-1960s with Czech-language covers of Western hits. In the 1970s, she sang covers of ESC winners and ABBA's songs, but she was ahead of ABBA in singing about Waterloo: her 'To je tvý Waterloo' (That's Your Waterloo) was released in 1970, well before ABBA's 'Waterloo' won the 1974 ESC. Czechoslovakia had met its own Waterloo in 1968, when on 21 August a Soviet-led military invasion by Warsaw Pact forces quashed the Prague Spring, the movement that had sought to liberalize the communist system in Czechoslovakia and make it more independent from the USSR. Some months after the invasion, Vondráčková formed the English-named pop group Golden Kids with Marta Kubišová and Václav Neckář. However, Kubišová had recorded the patriotic song 'Modlitba pro Martu' (A Prayer for Marta) just days after the invasion to protest against it. During the period of 'normalization' that ensued in Czechoslovakia, the reforms of the Prague Spring were reversed and retribution was enacted on the movement's supporters. Kubišová was in 1970 consequently forbidden by the authorities from performing in public because of her stance against the invasion. Golden Kids disbanded, and all of Kubišová's contracts with record companies were scrapped.[1]

Kubišová's folk nationalism had irritated the authorities more than Vondračková's pop internationalism. Vondráčková went on to develop an international career that spanned other parts of Eastern Europe and she even had some success in Western Europe. After she came top of the bloc in the 1977 ISC, she entered the West German national selection for the 1978 ESC, finishing twelfth out of fifteen entries with 'Männer wie du' (Men Like You). Vondráčková's ability to even travel to Western Europe, let alone to seek to represent a Western European state on the international stage, was contingent upon her not publicly criticizing Czechoslovakia's communist government. In her autobiography published for the German market after the fall of communism, Vondráčková is critical of Czechoslovakia's communist government but acknowledges that it used her 'to show the whole world how liberal it was in the CSSR [Czechoslovak Socialist Republic] after 21 August. I travelled more than before, also to Western countries. Paris, Rio, Tokyo'.[2] The government appropriated Vondráčková at a time when it was being criticized by Western European intellectuals and politicians for its suppression of dissidents. These dissidents included Kubišová and the playwright Václav Havel, who were part of the Charter 77 initiative that protested against the government's human rights record. Gott and Vondráčková were in January 1977 mobilized by the government in a countermovement that attacked Charter 77. Their careers depended on it: Vondráčková would not have appeared at the 1977 ISC had she declined.

Vondráčková's biography epitomized how Eastern European popular music industries fashioned national identities and sought international success during the Cold War much like their Western counterparts. While there was more political censorship of popular music in Eastern than in Western Europe, in Eastern Europe there was also the appropriation of Western European trends, the imitation of Western European hits and even the export of domestic stars to Western Europe. As national popular music industries developed in Eastern Europe with their own celebrities, festivals and record companies, they reflected the failures and successes of the cultural and economic policies of the communist parties in satisfying citizens' desires for consumption and entertainment. In the cultural and economic contest between the Cold War blocs, popular music played a prominent role in the cultural propaganda, soft power or 'bloc branding' in states of both Eastern and Western Europe. However, Eastern European popular music would ultimately not be as internationally successful as its Western counterpart because of Eastern Europe's economic and technological backwardness relative to Western Europe as well as the cultural censorship by communist governments. The Iron Curtain was officially penetrable only for Eastern Europeans who performed popular music that did not challenge communist rule.

Vondráčková's ambitions in Eastern and Western Europe also demonstrated that the relationship between the two blocs was never simply binary and hostile. The EBU and OIRT, for example, cooperated in programme exchange from 1960. Through this, Eastern European audiences could from 1965 watch the ESC via their own national broadcasting organizations which were connected through the Intervision Network. The ISC also included artists from Western European states who sought to expand their careers in Eastern Europe. As Eastern European audiences watched the ESC and artists from Eastern and Western Europe sought careers that spanned the Iron Curtain, East–West relations were not black and white during the Cold War era: they more colourfully allowed for appropriation, cooperation and exchange. However, the ESC did send some political messages to Eastern Europe, such as when Gott represented Austria at the 1968 ESC; some Eastern European artists who had emigrated to Western Europe because of their opposition to the communist governments also appeared in the ESC. And the participation of one communist state, non-aligned Yugoslavia, was the result of its early dissent from the Eastern Bloc, which allowed JRT to become a founding member of the EBU. JRT would later also become an observer member in the OIRT and participate in the ISC. The experiences of Yugoslav entries in the ESC typified how the categories of 'East' and 'West' were used to view the contests: domestic reactions to the results of these entries in the contest considered Yugoslavia to be orientalised by Western Europeans in the ESC while it was otherwise occidentalised by Eastern Europeans. The notions of 'East' and 'West' defined hierarchies among communists as well and, as they too competed among themselves to be fashionable, some of them wanted to be more 'Western' than the others. However, to become so attractive, a dose of rebelliousness was always required.

Appropriation

For the states that were defined as 'Eastern Europe' – those states lying between, on the one side, Austria, Italy and West Germany, and, on the other, the USSR – the appellation of 'Eastern' was a Cold War-era branding. During the interwar era, their geographical location – especially with Europe's only communist government at the time on their eastern flank – and their historical inclusion in the Austrian, Italian and German empires and adherence to Western Christianity had rendered them 'Central European'. In his 1984 essay 'The Tragedy of Central Europe', Kundera argued that communism had 'kidnapped, displaced, and brainwashed' Czechoslovakia, Hungary and Poland from the West.[3] Prior to the Cold War era, Central Europe's inclusion in the Germanophone sphere had been a cultural legacy of the Austrian and German empires and an extant reality of the millions of Germans who lived in the region's newly established states after the First World War. It was also reflected in a shared affinity across the region for *Schlager*, a genre of popular music that developed in the interwar era and had its origins in operettas. Central Europe is the *Schlagerraum* (schlager sphere), and the German word for the genre often appears as a loanword in the non-German local languages. This linguistic and musical heritage would prove important in the Cold War era for cultural exchange between East and West, and despite the expulsion of millions of Germans from Eastern Europe at the end of the Second World War. With his Czech first name and German last name and his songs in Slavic languages and German, Gott epitomized the multilingualism that had before the Cold War era characterized the Central European space.

The Central European states were also exposed to cultural influences from other parts of the West during the interwar era, including American jazz. However, this and other popular music originating from the Allied powers were censored in Germany and the European states that were under Nazi occupation during the Second World War. The Nazis considered jazz to be politically inappropriate due to the war with the Americans and racially 'degenerate' because of the genre's African American origins and the Jewish ethnicity of some of its leading artists. Some schlager artists were also censored by the Nazis, such as Lale Andersen and her song 'Lili Marleen';[4] her career would be rehabilitated after the war, and she represented West Germany at the 1961 ESC. The Communist Party of the USSR displayed varying approaches towards American popular music in the interwar era, rather tolerating it until 1936, suppressing it between 1936 and 1941, and then allowing it to thrive during the Second World War as an expression of the wartime alliance with the United States.[5] Jazz was again censored in the USSR in the first decade of the Cold War era. The Soviets' treatment of jazz foreshadowed how the political attitudes of Eastern European communist governments towards popular music would be crucially shaped by what their allies and opponents consumed and produced, which would not make for ideologically consistent policies throughout the region.

After the end of the Second World War, communist parties progressively came to dominate the governments of Eastern European states until 1948, when Czechoslovakia was the last state to come under full communist control. In Albania and Yugoslavia, their communist parties had already come to power in 1944 and 1945 respectively through the victories of their antifascist, pro-communist National Liberation armies in the war, while in Bulgaria, Czechoslovakia, East Germany, Hungary, Poland and Romania the communist parties rose to power through elections, coalitions and political manoeuvring in territories that were under the control of the Red Army. As the communist parties took control and implemented Stalinist systems in Eastern European states, Western cultural influences, including jazz, were censored, and Soviet – and especially Russian – cultural products were privileged. Cultural policies were tuned to the socialist realism articulated by Andrei Zhdanov, who was effectively the cultural commissar in the USSR, and schlager were accordingly censored for being 'decadent', with folk or classical music and mass songs being promoted instead.[6] However, Western cultural institutes, such as the British Council or the United States Information Service, still tried to penetrate these states with Western popular music by making it available on the premises of their local representations. Radio stations from the two blocs also infiltrated each other's states, and the musical programmes of Western radio stations, especially the BBC, Radio Free Europe, Radio Luxembourg and the Voice of America, proved to be the most popular Western broadcasts in Eastern Europe in the late 1940s and 1950s.[7]

It was in this context that the separate international broadcasting organizations were established for Eastern Europe and Western Europe in 1950. However, although the USSR was the political centre of Eastern Europe, the OIR did not move its headquarters from Brussels to Moscow – but to Prague. Czechoslovakia was one of the most industrialized and technologically advanced parts of Eastern Europe, despite major disparities between the more industrialized Czech lands and Slovakia.

Czechoslovakia's telecommunications infrastructure had suffered relatively less wartime destruction in comparison to other Eastern European states. Geography was also a factor in making Prague the OIR's headquarters: Prague was, after Berlin, the most geographically Western city of the Eastern Bloc, giving it a technical advantage for the relaying of propaganda broadcasts to the West; Czechoslovakia had also been the target of the first broadcasts of Radio Free Europe from West Germany in 1950.[8] Yet, Czechoslovakia was also central enough in Eastern Europe to function as a regional telecommunications node, especially to connect what would always be the most technologically advanced states of the Eastern Bloc, namely Czechoslovakia, East Germany, Hungary and Poland. And the Communist Party of Czechoslovakia had honed its skills in cultural propaganda through its control of the ministries of information and the interior in coalition governments after the Second World War, which had aided its complete takeover of the Czechoslovak government in 1948.

With the death of Stalin in 1953 and the emergence of the Thaw under his successor Nikita Khrushchev, communist governments in Eastern Europe began to liberalize their cultural policies and, as they sought a political rapprochement with the West, they permitted more cultural exchange with it. The year 1956 was a major turning point for Eastern European popular music, and not only because of the beginning of the ESC. It was then that Khrushchev made his 'On the Cult of Personality and its Consequences' speech, in which he denounced Stalin for his cult of personality, forced deportations and state terror. Khrushchev's speech heralded the beginning of the de-Stalinization period in Eastern Europe that was marked by cultural, economic and political reforms as well as 'peaceful coexistence' with the West. Cultural policies were adopted that sought to emulate the West in the production of film, popular music and radio and television programmes, especially as Eastern European governments saw that Western popular culture was attractive to their own citizens and that they needed to offer ideologically suitable as well as popularly appealing alternatives. Eastern European governments also began to place more emphasis on the production of consumer goods, as it was also clear that the capitalist systems in the West were more successful in producing popularly fashionable products – and enough of them to satisfy market demands. The economic plans of the Eastern European governments had largely succeeded in attaining economic growth in the 1950s through the expansion of heavy industry. The adoption of new economic policies from the late 1950s that promoted the production of consumer goods contributed to the expansion of radio services and popular music industries in Eastern European states, with the purchase of radios, records and record players booming and popular music festivals being established in every state. Like in Western Europe, television services were also introduced in most Eastern European states during the 1950s, with Albania being the last of them to do so in 1960.

However, Khrushchev's liberalizing policies were tested in Eastern Europe both by political leaders who did not think that they went far enough, as well as by others who thought that they went too far. The first two challenges that Khrushchev faced were from Hungary and Poland, where some political leaders, emboldened by popular support, wanted to liberalize their political systems and make their states more independent from Soviet control. In the case of Hungary, a revolution was suppressed in November 1956 when Soviet forces invaded the state and ousted a government that had sought to introduce a multiparty system, withdraw Hungary from the Warsaw Pact and declare the state neutral. However, while the Hungarian communist party's subsequent leadership under János Kádár never again challenged the USSR's domination, it did prove to be more liberal in cultural and economic matters: its system of 'goulash communism' allowed for some free market principles that gave Hungary a more developed consumer society than other states in Eastern Europe and also made it more open to Western popular cultural trends. This was also seen in the production by the Hungarian national broadcasting organization, Hungarian Television, of its own national song contest with juries that included representatives of Western broadcasting organizations and record companies who, it was hoped, would foster opportunities for Hungarian artists in Western markets.[9] However, due to its linguistic unlikeness, Hungarian-language popular music would never be able to have as wide of an impact in Eastern Europe as its counterparts in German and Slavic languages.

Also in 1956, mass protests in Poland over economic conditions, religious suppression and Soviet domination compelled Khrushchev to agree in October to the reinstatement of Władysław Gomułka and his reformist government. Under Gomułka, Poland became more open to Western cultural influences than any other part of the Eastern Bloc. Soon after the ESC had been inaugurated in 1956, the first international popular music festivals in the Eastern Bloc began to be staged in Poland. The ISC may have been the most famous of the Eastern European song contests because it modelled itself on the most famous one in Western Europe, but it had its local precedents. In August, during the period of political unrest, Polish jazz artists established the Sopot Jazz Music Festival as the first of its kind in Eastern Europe (although it was not the first popular music festival in a communist state: the Zagreb Festival had begun in Yugoslavia in 1953). In 1961, the Sopot International Song Festival was formed for popular music, and it included both Polish and international artists – including ones who participated in the ESC – and had different finals for Polish-language entries and those in other languages. The Sopot International Song Festival was created by the composer and pianist Władysław Szpilman, a Holocaust survivor who is the protagonist of the film *The Pianist*, directed by Roman Polanski. The festival's first three editions were staged in a hall in the Gdańsk Shipyard, renamed the Lenin Shipyard from 1967 to 1989, a location that would be fateful for Poland's communist government and the ISC in the early 1980s. From 1964, the Sopot International Song Festival moved to the open-air Forest Opera amphitheatre in the seaside resort town of Sopot, following the model set by Sanremo in staging a song festival in a town synonymous with entertainment and tourism.

The Sopot International Song Festival was broadcast through the Intervision Network in the 1960s, as were two international song contests from Bulgaria and Romania, which also included artists from both Eastern and Western Europe, among them ones who also performed in the ESC. As with the Sopot International Song Festival, tourism was a motivation for the establishment by the Bulgarian national broadcasting organization, Bulgarian Radio and Television, of the Golden Orpheus festival, named after the legendary musician of ancient Greece. First called 'Songs About the Bulgarian Black Sea Coast', the festival was held from 1965 in Slanchev Bryag, or Sunny Beach, a Black Sea resort that was developed from 1958.[10] In 1968, Romania's leader Nicolae Ceaușescu was also convinced by these precedents elsewhere in Eastern Europe to allow the Romanian national broadcasting organization, Romanian Radio and Television, to establish the Golden Stag festival in Brașov, a city in a region renowned for its mountain resorts. This was also a sign of his government's desire to reduce Soviet influence over Romania and improve relations with the West. Although Cliff Richard was hired to perform in the 1969 Golden Stag, this second edition of the festival otherwise had a deliberate emphasis on the

French language in the host's script and the songs that were performed. This reflected the traditional Francophilia of the Romance-language Romanians as well as the new orientation in Romania's foreign policy; de Gaulle had also visited Romania in 1968. An article in *Le Monde* even praised the 1969 Golden Stag for being more impressive than the ESC. As this was the first edition of the festival that was held in the wake of the Prague Spring, the 1969 Golden Stag also took place after the first series of the ISC was stopped, and it symbolized not only Romania's continued openness towards Western cultural influences but also Ceauşescu's opposition to the quashing of the Prague Spring, with Romania having been the only Warsaw Pact state not to have participated in the invasion. However, unlike the Golden Orpheus, which was held annually throughout the Cold War from 1965, the Golden Stag was stopped after its 1971 edition for financial and political reasons, as Ceauşescu adopted more autarchic and nationalist cultural and economic policies, including a return to socialist realism and greater censorship.[11]

Due to the postwar division of Germany, East Germany's communist leaders faced different challenges to their counterparts elsewhere in Eastern Europe in formulating their cultural policies, especially with regard to their degree of openness towards the West. In the first decade of the Cold War, popular music was already established as a cultural battleground between East and West Germany, in terms of the differing political attitudes of their governments towards, as well as debates within each of their societies about, the impact of American jazz and rock and roll.[12] Berlin lay at the centre of a popular music industry that had in the interwar era had one of the largest markets in Europe, and it was in that city that some of the key cultural battles of the Cold War were fought. When the Berlin Wall was built in 1961 to prevent the immigration of East Germans to West Berlin, this also prevented East Germans from physically accessing Western cultural products there. However, West German radio and television services continued to penetrate most of East Germany throughout the Cold War era, despite efforts by the East German government to sanction the consumption of West German broadcasts, which it finally permitted from 1972. As the majority of East Germans tuned into Western programmes daily, they remained familiar with current trends in Western popular music. However, as East Germany's national broadcasting organization, Television of the German Democratic Republic (DDR-FS), had to compete with West

German broadcasting organizations for the East German audience, DDR-FS's programmes were within the OIRT often considered to be of a higher quality compared to those of other members of the Intervision Network.[13]

Although some of the earliest popular music festivals that were broadcast by the Intervision Network were staged in East Germany, that state never produced an international song contest like the ones in Czechoslovakia or Poland that would be the basis for the ISC. This was due to the fact that the East German government was more politically orthodox than other Eastern European ones because it felt especially threatened by West Germany culturally, economically and politically. East Germany accordingly became the host of Eastern Europe's most politically defined international song contest for popular music, the Dresden International Schlager Festival of Socialist Countries, which began in 1971 but was preceded by the Schlager Festival of Friendship from 1968 to 1970. The Dresden International Schlager Festival's organizers included the DDR-FS and the East German government's State Committee for Broadcasting.[14] Although it was billed as an international song festival only for 'socialist countries', including ones from outside of Eastern Europe, entries were not politically engaged – for that there was the Festival of Political Song in East Berlin – but they were not politically critical either. So Tereza Kesovija, for example, represented Yugoslavia there in 1971, the year before she did so at the ESC. While the two series of the ISC were ended by political censorship in Czechoslovakia and Poland, the Dresden International Schlager Festival continued throughout the 1970s and 1980s. In 1989, however, it was not held because of the political changes that were occurring in East Germany that led to the fall of the Berlin Wall, only then making it yet another example of an Eastern European international song contest that was stopped due to political upheaval.

The development of these different international song contests in Eastern Europe reflected cultural multipolarity and nationalism within the Eastern Bloc. They also underlined how the USSR failed to exert itself as a cultural superpower. These international song contests were often inspired by cultural, economic and foreign policies that sought to assert their states' autonomy from the USSR and their openness to the West.[15] However, these international song contests could not exclude the USSR, as the ESC did the United States. The USSR was present in all of the Eastern European international organizations: for example, a Soviet official always headed the OIRT's technical centre, while the other part of the organization, the general secretariat, was headed by a Czechoslovak. The USSR also contributed the most programmes to the Intervision Network.[16] Yet, the inclusion of the USSR was not the priority for most of the organizers of the international song contests in Eastern Europe. The USSR did have its own nationally televised song contest, the Song of the Year,[17] but the archival documents of the OIRT never mention it producing an international song contest, let alone a Soviet alternative to the ESC. The USSR also had its own large, multinational domestic market for its popular music industry, for which Western European markets were relatively less potentially lucrative than they were for the smaller popular music industries of other Eastern European states, which were also geographically closer to Western Europe. Still, the USSR never managed to match the cultural influence that American popular music had on Western Europe – or, for that matter, on Eastern Europe. In East Germany, for example, it was American popular music that was central to the cultural battles that took place in the 1960s, and not the Soviet. In Yugoslavia, which was more open to cultural influences from the West than other parts of Eastern Europe, but nonetheless still had cultural cooperation with the USSR after relations between them were normalized in 1955, Soviet popular music was hardly noticeable for the rest of the Cold War. And when Czechoslovak artists adopted foreign-language names or covered foreign songs, they preferred English-language ones over the Russian, as Golden Kids demonstrated.

That the USSR did not become a popular music superpower also begs the question of whether Eastern Europe was culturally as much of an interconnected bloc as Western Europe was. In both cases, national cultures were still the most important identifications for people, despite cultural Americanization in the Western Bloc and political Sovietization in the Eastern Bloc. Eastern Europe faced less linguistic diversity than Western Europe, being predominantly Slavic, but the cultural differences even between the Slavic speakers had been historically defined by their different geographies and histories: Yugoslavia was more influenced by Italian culture than was Czechoslovakia, where the German-language culture had a greater impact. Then there were those languages that were not part of the Slavic group, such as Albanian, Estonian, German, Hungarian, Latvian, Lithuanian and Romanian, whose cultural products, with the exception of the world language of German, were even more restricted to a national context. There were also hierarchies among the states themselves in terms of cultural and economic development, with those of Central Europe being considered more developed than those of southeastern Europe or the USSR, with such differences fuelling mutual stereotypes. There were additionally more economic and political restrictions on Eastern Europeans travelling within the Eastern Bloc than there were for Western Europeans in theirs, so that tourism was not such a unifying factor for the former: unlike in the ESC, for example, singers in the ISC did not sing much about foreign places. All of these aspects demonstrated that Eastern Europe was not the homogenous, grey bloc that it was often made out to be in Western political commentaries and popular culture – and that it was not all 'Eastern'. While Western European integration generally progressed over the course of the Cold War era, the states of Eastern Europe sought to be more nationally autonomous from the USSR. Many citizens in these states still felt more of a cultural affinity with Central or Western Europe, even as their communist governments varyingly sought to control and define their cultural openness and orientation towards the West.

That the Eastern Bloc was not so culturally, economically and politically coherent explains why it failed to produce a durable challenge to the ESC. The Intervision Network was also less successful than its Eurovision counterpart because Eastern Europe could never close the technological gap among its members – let alone that with Western Europe, which became even more apparent from the 1970s with the advent of the Digital Revolution. The differences in technological development between the states represented in the OIRT were, from an Eastern European perspective, geographically defined by a north–south axis – as was the case in the Eurovision Network – and an east–west one, both in European and global terms. For example, the first television link between two Eastern European states was between Czechoslovakia and East Germany in 1956, and the founding members of the Intervision Network in 1960 were the national broadcasting organizations of Czechoslovakia, East Germany, Hungary and Poland. The USSR joined the Intervision Network in 1961, and initially only through the broadcasting organizations from its western-most republics. The television services of Bulgaria and Romania entered the Intervision Network in 1962. Austria and Yugoslavia became observer members in the Intervision Network in 1963, and YLE a full member from 1965.[18] Albania was never represented in the Intervision Network because it dissented from the Eastern Bloc in 1961 during the Sino-Soviet split, in which Albania took the side of China as the latter sought to challenge the USSR's leadership of the international communist movement.

China also consequently withdrew from the OIRT, thereby thwarting the OIRT's ambitions to become the leading international broadcasting organization in the world by being based on the membership of communist states.[19] Still, the OIRT lived up to its 'international' appellative by including national broadcasting organizations from communist, neutral and non-aligned states worldwide. Cuba, Mongolia, North Korea, Vietnam and Afghanistan were added to the Intervision Network's membership in the 1970s and 1980s, albeit too late for the last three of them to consider participating in the by then defunct ISC. Although the Intervision Network grew more slowly and had a smaller membership than the Eurovision Network, it covered a much larger expanse by stretching from Eastern Europe to as far as the Caribbean Sea and northeastern Asia. Yet, whereas the EBU was based primarily on achieving cooperation among its active, Western European members, the OIRT's territorial overreach came with further political limitations. National broadcasting organizations from some African, Asian and Latin American states joined the OIRT under socialist governments.[20] However, the membership of non-European states in the OIRT was not constant for political and technical reasons: their participation varied according to changes in their foreign policies and technical development, and not all of them could connect to the Intervision Network. Egypt and Syria, for example, left the EBU when Israel joined it and instead became members of the OIRT, but they returned to the EBU in the 1970s. In the end, the OIRT always remained a mostly Eastern European affair. And, as the ISC showed, Central Europe was central to Eastern Europe.

Intervision

Although the EBU restricted its criteria for active membership to national broadcasting organizations from states located within the EBA, the EBU's technological achievements rendered it more 'international' than the OIRT in terms of its aid to and cooperation with extra-European national broadcasting organizations. Considering the EBU's financial and technical prowess, the OIRT also sought cooperation with it as Cold War tensions eased after the death of Stalin. Building on the bilateral cooperation between national broadcasting organizations from Eastern Europe on the one side and Western Europe on the other, the first meetings between officials from the EBU and OIRT were arranged by YLE in 1957. As Finland was non-aligned and the only state to be an active member of both the EBU and OIRT, YLE was geopolitically poised to play a bridging role between the two organizations. In 1957, the USSR seemed to challenge the West's technological prowess when it launched the world's first ever satellite, Sputnik. However, in 1961 the OIRT still had to rely on the EBU's technical links to broadcast the welcome celebrations for the cosmonaut Yuri Gagarin, after he became the first person to travel to outer space, from Moscow to Eastern Europe; as there was no existing link between the USSR and Czechoslovakia, East Germany and Poland, the televised transmission went through the Eurovision Network via Finland.[21]

From the beginning of the programme exchange between the Eurovision and Intervision networks that was institutionalized in 1960, the national broadcasting organizations from the Eurovision Network would throughout the Cold War always send more programmes to their counterparts in the Intervision Network than they would broadcast from them. Although the two sides agreed that the programme exchange should be mutual and voluntary, and that the programmes involved should not politically attack the other side or be commercially motivated, the Eurovision Network's members considered many of the Intervision Network's offerings to be too politicized and uninteresting. The national broadcasting organizations individually decided which programmes they would choose from the other network, and Intervision members also rejected programmes from the Eurovision Network that they deemed were commercial, political or religious.[22] Still, it seems counterintuitive that communist Eastern Europe was more open to cultural influences from liberal Western Europe than vice versa. However, because the Eastern European national broadcasting organizations were state controlled and therefore promoted the goals and policies of the ruling communist parties, the Western European national broadcasting organizations were careful not to legitimize the communist governments' suppression of cultural and political freedoms by taking programmes from Eastern Europe that had political content. Such programmes would also not have been popular among Western European audiences.

That the OIRT felt that it benefitted more from cooperation with the EBU than vice versa was also seen in the EBU's rejection of OIRT proposals for them to jointly organize an international song contest. This, together with the fact that Eastern European national broadcasting organizations were never allowed to participate in the ESC, was a statement of political exclusion in the face of the cultural cooperation that these national broadcasting organizations aspired to under the Thaw. Already in 1958, the OIRT expressed interest in participating in the song contests organized by other international broadcasting organizations.[23] The OIRT began organizing popular music festivals for its members in 1958, when it staged the first Festival of Light and Dance Music in Prague, moving it to Leipzig in the early 1960s. Popular music programmes were considered by the OIRT's members to be a priority in the context of government policies that promoted consumption and entertainment, so much so that they organized a conference of music professionals at the second edition of this festival to discuss issues concerning the development of popular music in communist states.[24]

OIRT representatives proposed the joint organization of an international show of popular music between the members of the Eurovision and Intervision networks at a meeting of their representatives in Helsinki in 1964. The director general of Czechoslovak Television (ČST), Jiří Pelikán, reported that the EBU had rejected the proposal – although he did not explain exactly why. EBU officials suggested instead that the OIRT arrange its own contest and that the two organizations broadcast each other's contests through the Eurovision and Intervision networks.[25] The ESC was thus first relayed by the Intervision Network in 1965 to Eastern European states, which also received it for free from the EBU (even when the EBU from 1976 started requiring a participation fee both from national broadcasting organizations that entered as well as those that just relayed the contest, it did not charge OIRT members 'to avoid creating misunderstandings between the two Unions').[26] After 1965, the hosts of the ESC often mentioned in their introductions to the shows the states of the Intervision Network in which the contest was being broadcast, so viewers were aware that there was a pan-European, East–West audience watching. The ISC was also broadcast in some Western European states via the Eurovision

Network in 1965, although there was less interest for it than for the ESC in Eastern Europe, as was generally the case with the transfer of programmes from Intervision to Eurovision members.

In the mid-1960s, the Czechoslovak government began instituting economic and political reforms after having been a relative latecomer to de-Stalinization policies. It was in this context that OIRT officials decided to stage the first ISC as part of the second edition of ČST's Golden Prague international television festival, which itself attracted participation from both Eastern and Western European national broadcasting organizations. The rules that were then adopted for the ISC were largely a copy of those for the ESC, with the ISC initially being open only to members of the Intervision Network. The ISC also had just an international jury which was comprised of musical experts representing each of the participating national broadcasting organizations, with one more from Czechoslovakia as a non-voting chair, and its voting was ostensibly secret.[27] Another major difference between the ESC and the ISC was that Czechoslovakia's government, namely its Ministry for Culture and Information, organized the ISC in cooperation with ČST, artist's organizations, concert organizers and local record companies, and it also approved the selection of Czechoslovak artists. This also reflected the fact that the OIRT's membership was largely based on state-controlled broadcasting organizations.

The ISC was first staged as the Golden Clef Intervision Contest on 12 June 1965 in the Karlín Musical Theatre in Prague, and it was broadcast to six Intervision Network states, to seven Eurovision Network ones and to Finland which was represented in both networks. National broadcasting organizations from Czechoslovakia, East Germany, Hungary, Poland, the USSR and Yugoslavia were represented in the first ISC by two of their most prominent artists who each performed one song. Gott, who had qualified for the 1965 ISC through a national selection, won the contest for Czechoslovakia with 'Tam, kam chodí vítr spát' (Where the Wind Goes to Sleep). In 1966 and 1967, the ISC was incorporated into the first two editions of the Bratislava Lyre festival, which had a separate competition for Czechoslovak songs in which the Czechoslovak entries for the ISC were selected. The contest was staged in Bratislava in order to decentralize Czechoslovakia's cultural events: these were concentrated in Prague, which had since 1964 also had an international jazz festival.[28] Bulgaria, Finland and Romania joined the ISC in Bratislava, and the contest was won by Bulgaria's Lili Ivanova in 1966 and Czechoslovakia's Eva Pilarová in 1967. Kubišová and Vondráčková came third in 1966 with the duet 'Oh, Baby, Baby'.

The ISC's connections with the ESC were always apparent: Finland and Yugoslavia sometimes sent the same artists whom they had or would send to the ESC, such as Viktor Klimenko, Lasse Mårtenson, Lado Leskovar and Vice Vukov. And, as part of the Bratislava Lyre, Western European artists were invited to perform, including Udo Jürgens and Sandie Shaw after their ESC wins. Internal reports from ČST echoed criticisms made within the EBU of ESC entries as they also often criticized ISC entries for being dull, old-fashioned and slow. The ISC rules were changed in 1966 to urge national broadcasting organizations to submit more lively dance songs rather than chansons. However, these reports considered the most successful aspects of the ISC to be its coverage by Western media outlets, which compared the ISC positively to the ESC, and the contracts that Western record companies negotiated with ISC artists, especially Czechoslovak ones.[29] Gott's winning song in the 1965 ISC, for example, was released in Sweden by the West German record company Telefunken under the directly translated title 'Där vinden går till vila'. Rather than taking pride in producing an Eastern European contest, the organizers of the ISC were instead most pleased about its Western and commercial aspects.

From 1966, the organizers of the ISC continued to express an interest in expanding the contest to include Western European entries, either by allowing them to enter the ISC or by having a contest that would pit songs from the two blocs against each other.[30] The political context for that was most opportune in 1968, after the leadership of the Communist Party of Czechoslovakia was taken over in January by the reformist Alexander Dubček from Slovakia. With the establishment of the Dubček government, the liberalizing reforms of the Prague Spring began. These included the ending of media censorship, which made ČST more open to cultural and political influences from the West. The rules for the ISC were also changed in 1968 to make it the first international song contest that was open to states from both the OIRT and EBU; *Billboard* reported that this signified 'another step towards open competition and a common market in European pop music'.[31] The 1968 ISC was held in June in the spa resort town of Karlovy Vary, near the borders with East Germany and West Germany, where it was incorporated again into the International Television Festival.

EBU national broadcasting organizations from Austria, Belgium, Finland, Spain, Switzerland, West Germany and Yugoslavia, together with OIRT ones from Bulgaria, Czechoslovakia, East Germany, Hungary, Romania, Poland and the USSR, were all represented in the 1968 ISC. The participation of Spain reflected Madrid's interest in developing diplomatic relations with Eastern Europe, while that of West Germany was a prelude to the normalization of relations with Eastern European states – with which Bonn mostly still did not have diplomatic relations in 1968 – under the *Ostpolitik* (Eastern Policy) that began in 1969. Gott won the contest again with 'Proč ptáci zpívají?' (Why do Birds Sing?); Vukov, who had already represented Yugoslavia twice at the ESC, came second; Spain's Salomé, who would be a joint winner of the 1969 ESC, came third; and Paola del Medico, who would perform for Switzerland in the ESC in 1969 and 1980, also participated. The top three positions were thus each taken by an artist from the three Cold War groupings: East, West, and non-aligned. *Billboard's* Prague correspondent, Lubomír Dorůžka, noted that the organizers of 'the East European equivalent of the Eurovision Song Contest' had even bigger plans for 1969 'to invite participation from a number of independent American TV companies'.[32]

No Eastern Bloc state was ever directly represented in the ESC during the Cold War. However, in the 1968 ESC, Gott became the only resident of such a state to do so when he sang 'Tausend Fenster' (A Thousand Windows) for Austria just months before his win in the ISC. The song lamented alienation in modern society and how people did not even know their neighbours, which also alluded to the division of Central European states by the Iron Curtain: Bratislava and Vienna are, after all, the two European capitals that are geographically closest to each other. Gott was allowed to perform in the ESC without censure from the Czechoslovak government because of the liberalizing reforms of the Prague Spring, and his selection by ORF also reflected the closer ties in co-productions, live relays and the exchange of materials that had been developing between the Austrian and Czechoslovak national broadcasting organizations since 1964. The ending of media censorship in Czechoslovakia was one of the factors that compelled the USSR and its Warsaw Pact allies to quash the Prague Spring, as they believed that the reformist movement would end the communist system in

Czechoslovakia and undermine the Eastern Bloc as a whole. ORF played a central role in relaying programmes between the Eurovision and Intervision networks, and never more urgently than when it transmitted ČST's coverage of the 1968 invasion until ČST's Prague station was taken over by Warsaw Pact troops.[33] Austria would also be the first stop for the thousands of refugees who fled Czechoslovakia after the quashing of the Prague Spring.

As a product of the Prague Spring, in particular the greater freedom accorded to ČST, the ISC had also gone too far by welcoming Western European participants. In the context of the renewal of media censorship in Czechoslovakia under normalization, the ISC would never again be held in that state: nobody would be invited in 1969, let alone the Americans. ČST never sought to revive the ISC with the international ambitions that ČST had had in the 1960s. In 1971, the Golden Clef festival was re-established as the Děčín Anchor festival and moved eastwards to its namesake on the River Elbe and the border with East Germany; however, it was no longer branded 'the ISC', was non-competitive and only included artists representing Intervision Network members.[34] Furthermore, it was the Bratislava Lyre that established itself as the major national popular music contest in Czechoslovakia, reflecting also the federalization of Czechoslovakia in 1969, which was the only significant reform that the Dubček government had aimed for that was made after the Prague Spring.

Between 1968 and the second series of the ISC in Poland, there were suggestions made within the OIRT for the organization of a new international song contest dubbed the 'Prix OIRT', but these were not realized. Other popular music festivals in Eastern Europe were still being organized in the late 1960s and early to mid-1970s, including the Bratislava Lyre, Golden Orpheus, Golden Stag and Sopot International Song Festival, and the OIRT observed that they were 'very popular among televiewers'.[35] All of these festivals continued to have an international component that attracted artists from Western Europe, including ones who performed in the ESC. However, these festivals were still not branded, flagship productions of the Intervision Network in the same way that the ESC was for the Eurovision Network. When it came to prioritizing international festivals, the OIRT would in 1980 categorize them according to their impact for the organization, with the ISC in the most important category of Intervision contests and festivals that were 'the most representative international creative events' for all Intervision Network members, followed by other international and national ones, such as the Golden Orpheus and Golden Prague, that were not directly organized by the Intervision Network.[36]

Out of all of these international popular music festivals in Eastern Europe, it was the Sopot International Song Festival that emerged as the new bearer of the Intervision brand. The decision to transform the Sopot International Song Festival into the ISC was made because it had the longest historical tradition in the Eastern Bloc; Poland was also still relatively more culturally open and technologically developed than most other Eastern Europe states. The revival of the ISC occurred in the year of the sixtieth anniversary of the October Revolution, which the OIRT sought to commemorate with specially organized events. The Radio and Television Committee, the Polish government's body that controlled and managed broadcasting, accordingly presented the ISC as an event that would promote the popular culture of communist states and models 'worthy of dissemination in the framework of socialist culture'.[37] In a letter to the minister of finance requesting financial assistance for the contest, the chair of the committee, Maciej Szczepański, stated that the ISC was also intended as an 'effective propagandistic counterweight to the Eurovision Festival'.[38]

However, as they had first imagined in 1964, officials from the OIRT wanted this new edition of the ISC to also include participants from all over the world, and not just communist states or Intervision Network members. Officials from Poland's Radio and Television Committee presented this idea to the OIRT in the context of promoting mutual understanding and peaceful cooperation in the 'the spirit of Helsinki'.[39] By this they were referring to the Helsinki Accords that were concluded among almost all European states in the Finnish capital in 1975, and which included agreements on the inviolability of borders, respect for human rights and cultural cooperation, including the co-production, exchange and joint broadcasting of television programmes. A suggestion was even made by the Radio and Television Committee in 1976 that one of the competitions in the ISC could be a contest between the winners of the ESC and ISC, but this did not eventuate.[40] This would have even been problematic when Israeli entries won the ESC in the late 1970s: considering that most Eastern European states – Romania being the only exception – did not have diplomatic relations with Israel, Israeli artists were not invited to the ISC. For the same reason, Romania was the only member of the Intervision Network that broadcast the 1979 ESC that was held in Jerusalem. The political principles that guided the ISC also meant that it did not have explicitly politically critical songs like the ESC did. Indeed, an Eastern European equivalent of 'C'est peut-être pas l'Amérique' that would have criticized the USSR was unthinkable.[41]

Still, the ISC was more international and open than the ESC, which remained closed to any entries from states that were not members of the EBU. The Polish organizers sought to limit the commercialism that characterized the ESC by having a separate international competition for entries submitted by national broadcasting organizations, mostly Intervision members, alongside one for entries sponsored by record companies from Eastern Europe and the West. The competitions were staged on different days. Voting was done in both cases by international juries comprised of the representatives of national broadcasting organizations and record companies. The winners of the competition for the national broadcasting organizations were Czechoslovakia's Vondráčková in 1977, the USSR's Alla Pugacheva – who would also represent Russia at the 1997 ESC – in 1978, Poland's Czesław Niemen in 1979 and Finland's Marion Rung in 1980. In the competition for the record companies, entries from Greece, Poland and the UK won, and Belgium's Dream Express, which had performed in the 1977 ESC, was victorious in 1978.

Surveys conducted by the Polish national broadcasting organization, Polish Radio and Television, showed that an average of around half of the people questioned watched the ISC and that they mostly considered it to be well produced.[42] However, in Finland the ISC compared poorly to the ESC in technical terms, with YLE noting that the Intervision broadcasts were of a lesser quality than the Eurovision ones. The ESC also had a greater cachet in Finland because Western popular music was generally considered by its national audience to be superior to both Eastern European popular music and the national one. YLE had joined the ESC in 1961, and throughout the Cold War the generally poor results achieved by Finnish entries in it prompted public discussions in Finland about how unmodern Finnish popular culture was and how the state was culturally, geographically and linguistically peripheralized from Western Europe. This contrasted with Finland's success at the ISC, where it was the most economically and politically Western member of the Intervision Network.[43] However, some Finnish artists regarded the ISC as a fairer competition than the ESC, which they thought was too commercialized, as the YLE had also complained about with other Nordvision members in the 1970s. Finland even won the 1980 ISC with Rung singing 'Hyvästi yö' (Where is the Night); in that same year, Finland came last in the ESC.

Apart from the commercial dimensions and technical production of the ESC and ISC, the other major difference between them was that the latter was always held in the same state, thereby avoiding the need for national broadcasting organizations to compete for the right to host the contest and all the commercial and political cachet, or expense, that that could bring. The only places that were branded were Sopot and Poland, just as it was only Czechoslovakia that had been showcased in the first series of the ISC; both the Czechoslovak and Polish organizers of the two series of the ISC recognized it as important for promoting their states. However, the problem with the fixation of the ISC in Czechoslovakia and Poland was that, from the contest's beginning to its end, it was too dependent on the political situation in those states. For the first ISC series, the Prague Spring was the coup de grâce; for the second series, it was the rise of the Solidarity movement. Political dissent and social discontent had been growing in Poland in the late 1970s amid an economic crisis; Niemen's 1979 ISC hit was, deliberately or not, titled 'Nim przyjdzie wiosna' (Before Spring Comes). A week before the 1980 ISC, a strike calling for economic, labour and political reforms began in the Lenin Shipyard in Gdańsk, where the Sopot International Song Festival had first been staged; the strikers capitalized on the already-present media attention for the ISC in nearby Sopot.[44] A week after the 1980 ISC, Solidarity, the first independent trade union in the Eastern Bloc, was formed in response to the strikers' requests. However, as Solidarity became the centre of a broader social movement and anti-government protests continued amid worsening economic conditions, the ISC was not held in its usual August slot in 1981: Poland's Radio and Television Committee stated in 1981 that 'in the current economically and socially tense situation such expenditures would not be approved by the population'.[45] The Polish government's further attempt to quell political opposition through the imposition of martial law from December 1981 to July 1983 meant that the ISC would not be held in those years either.

The Sopot International Song Festival was restarted from 1984, but never again as the ISC. However, in the late 1980s, NRK proposed the creation of an international song contest that would include Eurovision and Intervision members as well as representatives from extra-European states; the preselections would be based on regional contests organized by the various international broadcasting organizations. While this idea had original elements, it revived the proposals that the OIRT had had for a contest for both Eastern and Western European states. From 1970 to 1989, there was also a world song contest, the World Popular Song Festival, that was annually staged in Tokyo by the Yamaha Music Foundation. The OIRT responded positively to NRK's proposal, but it added that it was unsure about whether it would be restarting the ISC.[46] There was a discussion in the OIRT in 1987 about reviving the ISC at the time of the seventieth anniversary of the October Revolution, yet few national broadcasting organizations were interested in participating.[47] NRK's proposal foundered, but there would soon be no need to create another international song contest as Eastern European states would enter the ESC. Economic pressures, political upheavals and technological backwardness had made the OIRT unable to come up with an international song contest as attractive and longevous as the ESC. These issues would from 1989 contribute to the demise of Eastern Europe's communist governments, which were also made unpopular by repressive apparatuses that had turned some pop stars into political dissidents.

Dissent

The ESC began at a turning point in the relations between the Eastern and Western blocs in the Cold War with the beginning of the Thaw. However, in the late 1950s and early 1960s, several ESC entries were composed or sung by artists whose emigration from Eastern to Western Europe made them politically symbolic. There was Schwarz, who had grown up in what would become East Germany but had chosen to settle in West Germany. In the early 1950s, the Kessler Twins also emigrated from East to West Germany and went on to represent the latter at the 1959 ESC. The first Bulgarian singer in the ESC, Nora Nova, represented West Germany at the 1964 contest: she had emigrated there because of her opposition to Bulgaria's communist government and her support for the national monarchy. There were also other West German ESC artists who had origins in an Eastern Europe that had seen the expulsion of its German populations, especially from Czechoslovakia, Poland and the USSR. These artists personified the migration trends in the early postwar era that not only shaped the social composition of West Germany but also influenced its government's policies towards communist states.

However, West Germany's entries in the ESC otherwise hardly contained political messages, and there were none explicitly directed against East Germany – although the subject of being separated from a lover in the 1960 and 1961 entries 'Bonne nuit, ma chérie' and 'Einmal sehen wir uns wieder' (We'll See Each Other Once Again) could have been interpreted by Germans on both sides of the Iron Curtain as a lament over their postwar division. The only ESC entries that ever alluded to the Cold War division of Germany were Norway's 'The First Day of Love' in 1974, which mentioned 'curtain', 'wall' and 'revolution' all in one verse, Portugal's 'Um grande, grande amor' (A Big, Big Love) in 1980, which referred to the Berlin Wall, and Italy's 'Per Lucia' (For Lucia) in the 1983 ESC in Munich, which mentioned gunfire and a wall; the West German entry in the 1986 ESC, 'Über die Brücke geh'n' (Crossing the Bridge), also sang of overcoming a wall to achieve international understanding. Although the East German government in the late 1950s and 1960s considered that West German broadcasts to East Germany violated EBU–OIRT agreements on the non-political use of broadcasting between Eastern and Western Europe, watching the ESC was in itself not a subversive act in East Germany for most of the Cold War considering that programme exchange between the Eurovision and Intervision networks meant that its own national broadcasting organization could relay the contest from 1965. Watching West German television services was in any case no longer sanctioned by the East German government from 1972, in line with the Ostpolitik that normalized relations between the two states and allowed them to join the UN.[48]

The communist state that was most open to Western cultural influences during the Cold War was Yugoslavia. It dissented from the Eastern Bloc in 1948 after its political leadership under President Josip Broz Tito refused to submit to Stalin's domination, thereafter developing a non-aligned foreign policy. Yugoslavia became a founding member of the EBU at a time when other Eastern European states did not wish to cooperate with Yugoslavia nor admit it into their international organizations, including the OIR. As it courted the

West for economic and military assistance from 1950, the Communist Party of Yugoslavia also developed a cultural policy that reduced censorship and permitted Western cultural influences. An early repercussion of this was the establishment of the first popular music festival in communist Europe, the Zagreb Festival of Popular Music, in 1953, which was, of course, modelled on Sanremo's one. Like their counterparts elsewhere in Eastern Europe, Yugoslavia's political leaders realized during the 1950s that they also needed to develop a domestic popular music industry, especially as the state, which had before the Cold War been one of the poorest in Eastern Europe, was achieving some of the highest rates of economic growth in the world. That Yugoslavia did not enter the ESC before 1961 was thus not due to any political obstacles, but rather to the fact that television services were only introduced there from 1956, the year in which the ESC began. This underlined that Yugoslavia was still less technologically developed than other states that were represented in the EBU, even though the ownership of radios, records and record players was also booming in Yugoslavia in the late 1950s. In those years, Yugoslavia's political leaders called on pop singers to participate more in international concerts and festivals, as they realized that popular music could also be used in Yugoslavia's cultural diplomacy to show Western Europe that its communist system was more modern and open than that of the other Eastern European states. These political leaders also sought to promote Yugoslavia's developing Adriatic tourism industry to the key Western European market, and Yugoslav entries in the ESC often accordingly had maritime motifs and themes.[49] JRT decided in 1960 to enter the ESC, with Yugoslavia debuting the year after. Also in 1961, the first conference of the Non-aligned Movement was held in Belgrade, bringing together states from all over the world that did not want to ally themselves with either of the two Cold War blocs. At a time when Yugoslavia was playing a prominent role in international relations as one of the leading states in the Non-aligned Movement, a JRT official, Miroslav Vilček, was from 1963 to 1965 the EBU's scrutineer for the ESC.

Still, although Yugoslavia's participation in the ESC underlined it as the most culturally liberal, modern and open communist state in Europe, it remained a one-party state in which political opposition was suppressed. In terms of its governmental system, Yugoslavia never approached the multiparty democracies of Western Europe and remained securely Eastern European in this regard. Some of its ESC artists were also censored for their political views. The most famous of them was Vukov, who hailed from the Dalmatian coast and represented Yugoslavia at the ESC in 1963 and 1965 with the maritime-themed songs 'Brodovi' (Boats) and 'Čežnja' (Longing). He also came second in the 1967 ISC with another Adriatic-inspired song, 'Bokeljska noć' (Bokelj Night). In the late 1960s, Vukov emerged as the bard of the Croatian Spring, a national movement that called for more autonomy for Croatia in a reformed Yugoslav federation. The Croatian Spring was quashed in December 1971 after Tito considered its calls for autonomy to have gone too far, and the movement's key figures were arrested. Vukov managed to avoid arrest as he was touring the Croatian migrant community in Australia at the time; instead of returning to Yugoslavia, he went to live in Paris. His songs were censored in the Yugoslav media and he was not allowed to perform publicly in Yugoslavia until 1989. In an attempt to promote pan-Yugoslav values in the aftermath of the purging of liberal politicians in Croatia and other republics in the early 1970s, Yugoslavia's political leaders began urging pop and rock artists to incorporate themes such as the wartime resistance, Tito and multinational unity into their songs. This was reflected in Yugoslavia's entry in the 1974 ESC, 'Moja generacija' (My Generation), which spoke about the generation born during the Second World War under foreign occupation and how much better and freer life had become for them since. The rock group Korni grupa (Korni Group) performed the song just before ABBA, whose winning entry of course had another, more innocuous take on war.[50]

That Yugoslavia, although relatively prosperous in comparison to other Eastern European states, would never match Western European economic and technological standards was also reflected in the ESC. While its first entries did relatively well, and although JRT usually sent the state's foremost pop stars, Yugoslavia received its first *nul points* in 1964, and its entries generally finished in the bottom half of the scoreboard in the 1970s. As in Finland, this prompted discussion in the Yugoslav media over how Yugoslavia was viewed in Western Europe, with commentaries suggesting that its poor ESC results were due to its Slavic languages and communist system and exacerbated by its geographical peripherality. There were also claims that the ESC had been taken over by commercial record companies, which echoed complaints being made by Nordvision members but also smacked of Yugoslavia's ruling communist ideology.[51] After coming second last in 1976, JRT withdrew from the ESC from 1977 to 1980 and instead entered the ISC in 1977 and 1980, where Yugoslav entries were not much more successful than in the ESC. However, public opinion pressured JRT into rejoining the ESC after a poll of 107,181 people conducted by entertainment magazines in 1978 found that 98 per cent wanted Yugoslavia to re-enter the ESC.[52] This could not happen in 1979, when the ESC was held in Israel, as Yugoslavia did not have diplomatic relations with Israel because Belgrade supported Arab states through the Non-aligned Movement. JRT also did not return to the ESC in 1980 as it was first meant to be hosted again in Israel, and then due to Tito's ill health, with him passing away on May 4 (JRT did not enter the 1985 ESC either as it was staged on the anniversary of Tito's death).

Had international politics turned out differently, Eastern Europe might have had its premier international song contest in a seaside resort in Albania, which was, after Yugoslavia's expulsion from the Eastern Bloc in 1948, the only Mediterranean state that was a Soviet ally. It was also historically strongly influenced by Italy, which is only seventy-two kilometres on the other side of the Adriatic, and which occupied Albania during the Second World War from 1939 until Italy's capitulation in the war in 1943. Admittedly, as with Hungarian, songs in Albanian, an Indo-European isolate, would have been difficult to export internationally. Yet, Albania was an exceptional case in Eastern Europe for other, political reasons. Albania's leader, Enver Hoxha, opposed Khrushchev's de-Stalinization policies and the rapprochement with the West and Yugoslavia, with Hoxha fearing that the latter had pretensions towards Albania, and he accordingly dissented from the Eastern Bloc in 1961. Like Yugoslavia, Albania managed to defect from the Eastern Bloc without being invaded by Soviet forces because it was not as geopolitically strategic for the USSR. Unlike Yugoslavia, Albania would maintain a Stalinist system and pursue isolationist policies which saw it closed off to cultural influences from both Eastern and Western Europe, making it the most closed state in Europe during the Cold War; it was, for example, one of the only European states that did not participate in the Helsinki Accords. From 1961, Albania stopped participating in the OIRT, Warsaw Pact and COMECON as it took the side of China in the Sino-Soviet split. From 1961 until 1978, Albania was China's only European ally and received economic and technical assistance from it accordingly; the 1960s also saw Albania's own national cultural revolution which brutally clamped down on religion, making Albania the world's first atheist state.

This exceptional isolationism meant that Albania and Vatican City were the only European states with national broadcasting organizations that did not participate in either the ESC or ISC during the Cold War. Unlike other Eastern European states, Albania also did not develop its own international song contest. However, even as the poorest and most isolated state in Europe, Albania did develop a popular music culture of its own. This was demonstrated by the establishment of the national song contest, the Festival of Song, in 1962; held annually since then, it has from 2003 been the national selection for the ESC. The Albanian government sought better ties with Western European states in the early 1970s as its alliance with China was waning, which was also demonstrated by the fact that the ESC was broadcast in Albania for the first time in 1972. However, reflecting the typical zig-zagging of the Hoxha regime, the 1972 Festival of Song fell victim to political censure when some of its participants were censored and even imprisoned for being too 'Western' in their performances; the winning song that year was another one about spring, 'Kur vjen pranvera' (When Spring Comes), which suggested hope for a better future.[53] Despite their government's isolationism, Albanians could increasingly, yet subversively, access Greek, Italian and Yugoslav radio and television broadcasts from the early 1970s, with the ESC and Sanremo Italian Song Festival being popular programmes.[54] In predominantly Albanian-populated Kosovo, then a province of Yugoslavia, an Albanian popular music scene also emerged that was more open to Western cultural influences because of Yugoslavia's foreign policy. Albanian-language entries competed in the Yugoslav national selection for the ESC from 1973, which also reflected the increasing federalization of Yugoslavia in which each republic and province had its own broadcasting organization.

At the time of the quashing of the Croatian Spring and the persecution of artists from the 1972 Festival of Song in Albania, Czechoslovak artists and journalists who had been critical of the 1968 invasion and the subsequent normalization were also being censored. Pelikán, the director general of ČST under whom the first series of the ISC had been developed, who implemented liberalizing reforms in ČST during the Prague Spring and had also been a parliamentarian in Czechoslovakia, found political asylum in Italy. In 1979 he was elected to the EP in its first popular elections as a member for the Italian Socialist Party. Kubišová was the Czechoslovak artist whose fate most personified such censorship, as she was forbidden from performing in public from 1970. On the other hand, those artists who did not adopt such a vocal stance against the Czechoslovak government continued to develop their careers. While Kubišová was censored and not allowed to travel, Vondráčková went on to become the biggest female pop star in Czechoslovakia with a successful career in other parts of Eastern Europe and appearances at international song festivals. Like Vondráčková, Gott also managed his relationship with the Czechoslovak authorities so that he could continue to work in Western Europe, particularly in Austria and West Germany; considering his popularity at home and abroad, the government was more accommodating of him than of other artists. Gott's performance at the 1968 ESC for Austria could have been held against him had he further provoked the post-1968 communist government. He was, however, still censored: his song about councilmen, 'Hej, páni konšelé' (Hey, Messrs. Aldermen), performed at the 1969 Bratislava Lyre, was considered by the authorities to be politically critical and records of it were pulped. In 1978, Gott released a song in honour of Jan Palach, the student who had committed self-immolation in 1969 in protest against the Soviet invasion of Czechoslovakia. The song 'Kam tenkrát šel můj bratr Jan' (Where Did My Brother Jan Go Then) was a cover of Eric Carmen's 'All by Myself'; it was censored by the authorities, which subsequently put pressure on Gott to support their policies against dissident artists and intellectuals through the anti-Charter movement.[55] Gott's experience demonstrated that the relationships between individual artists and the communist governments were not always straightforward, involving elements of appropriation, compromise and negotiation on both sides.

After the Croatian and Prague springs, communist governments throughout Eastern Europe were challenged by a new genre, rock, which was not the sort of popular music featured at the ESC or ISC. In Czechoslovakia, rock music became a key medium of resistance against the communist government. This was demonstrated by the Plastic People of the Universe, a band which, like Golden Kids, was formed in 1968 just after the quashing of the Prague Spring. However, while Golden Kids played covers of innocuous Western pop songs, the Plastic People of the Universe preferred psychedelic rock and were inspired by bands like the Velvet Underground, the Fugs and Frank Zappa (the band's name was taken from the song 'Plastic People' by Zappa and the Mothers of Invention; Peter Wolf, a member of Zappa's band, composed the Austrian entry in the 1979 ESC). Niemen, the winner of the 1979 ISC, had also pioneered psychedelic rock in Poland in the 1970s; however, reflecting the differences between the cultural policies of the Czechoslovak and Polish governments in the 1970s, he was not censored like the Plastic People of the Universe was. As an underground band, the Plastic People of the Universe was surveilled by the police because of its members' non-conformist behaviour. In 1974, the police broke up a concert of the band and beat audience members – some of whom were later also tried – in what was dubbed the 'České Budějovice massacre'. In 1976, members of the band themselves and others from the underground music scene were put on trial, convicted of 'disturbing the peace' and imprisoned. This partly prompted a group of dissidents to release Charter 77, a document that called on the Czechoslovak government to respect human rights, including the freedoms of assembly and expression, in accordance with the state's constitution and international agreements, particularly the Helsinki Accords. One of the leaders of Charter 77 was Havel, the playwright whose works had been banned after the Prague Spring and who was later imprisoned for his dissident activity.[56]

While Kubišová also signed on to Charter 77, Gott and Vondráčková joined other artists who sided with the communist government in the anti-Charter movement. They signed the declaration 'For New Creative Deeds in the Name of Socialism and Peace', in which members of Czechoslovak artistic unions affirmed their support for Czechoslovakia's communist government and the USSR. The declaration supported international cultural cooperation in accordance with the Helsinki Accords, but it also criticized 'the anti-humanist forces of imperialism' that it alleged were behind those who challenged the communist system.[57] It was ironic that Gott and Vondráčková supported a document that was so critical of the West, considering that they both also had financially lucrative contracts there, but their support for the anti-Charter paradoxically secured their international careers into the 1980s when the dissenting voices of their colleagues were silenced. After signing the anti-Charter declaration in January, Vondráčková was able to secure victory for

Czechoslovakia at the 1977 ISC in August with 'Malovaný džbánku' (The Painted Jug). She also recorded some Czech-language covers of ESC songs, such as 'Save Your Kisses for Me' (the Czech version was titled 'Já půjdu tam a ty tam' (I'll Go There and You There) and was a duet with Jiří Korn) in 1977, after having done one of 'Après toi' (Jak mám spát (How Can I Sleep)) in 1972, and she of course entered the West German selection for the ESC in 1978. In 1985, Gott became the first popular music singer to be awarded the highest Czechoslovak state honour, that of National Artist.

Other artists in Eastern Europe chose to flee the repressive policies of communist governments and seek permanent settlement in the West. Waldemar Matuška, for example, who had been censored in Czechoslovakia in the mid-1960s but performed alongside Gott in the 1965 ISC, emigrated to the United States in 1986 in protest against the political situation in Czechoslovakia. The Czechoslovak government forbade the broadcasting of his songs thereafter. The emigration of artists from Eastern Europe in the 1970s and 1980s also found its expression at the ESC. While Eastern European émigrés had already performed in the ESC in the 1960s, the 1970s and 1980s saw a new wave of artists who had fled Eastern Europe because of political oppression. Their political symbolism was magnified with the ending of Détente in the early 1980s. Silviu Nansi Brandes, who conducted the Israeli entries in the 1982 and 1983 contests, had been a pop artist in Romania but emigrated to Israel in 1975 in order to escape the political repression of the Ceauşescu regime. László Mándoki had also fled Hungary in 1975 via Austria to West Germany, and he performed for West Germany with Dschingis Khan (Genghis Khan) at the 1979 ESC. He had emigrated from Hungary with another artist, László Bencker, who conducted the West German entry in the 1987 ESC. The Lithuanian-German singer Lena Valaitas, who represented West Germany in the 1981 ESC, had also arrived in that state as a refugee at the end of the Second World War.

Although the ESC continued to be broadcast in Eastern Europe in the 1980s and reported on in national media, and the 1984 ESC even had the Theatre of Animated Drawings from Prague as its interval act, some of the contest's songs were censored in Eastern Europe. Dschingis Khan appeared on a list of foreign artists who were censored in the USSR, with the group being blacklisted for 'anticommunism' and 'nationalism'; Iglesias was also mentioned for 'neofascism'.[58]

The list was published in 1985 by the youth organization of the Communist Party of the Soviet Union, the Komsomol (All-Union Leninist Young Communist League), just months before the coming to power of Mikhail Gorbachev as the party's general secretary. From 1986, Gorbachev initiated liberalizing economic and political reforms through the policies of *glasnost* (openness) and *perestroika* (restructuring), which in the late 1980s permitted Soviet artists to have more freedom of expression and contact with the West, much like the Prague Spring had done in Czechoslovakia in 1968. Gorbachev also adopted a foreign policy of non-interference in the affairs of other Eastern European states, which would facilitate the toppling of their communist governments from 1989 without the threat of Soviet military invasion. The reforms in the USSR also prompted the Singing Revolution in Estonia, Latvia and Lithuania from 1987 to 1991, during which choral, folk and pop and rock songs featured in mass singing demonstrations against Soviet rule, with national identities being asserted through patriotic songs that had been censored by the Soviet authorities.

However, the biggest political statement from Eastern Europe at the ESC in the 1980s still came from Yugoslavia, which refashioned its ESC entries in order to make them more appealing to Western European audiences, especially through a more Europop style, the use of English-language words and a thematic emphasis on romances between locals and Western European tourists holidaying on the Adriatic coast. Two of the entries – 'Džuli' (Julie) in 1983 and 'Ja sam za ples' (I Wanna Dance) in 1986 – were about locals falling in love with foreign tourists on the Yugoslav seaside, underlining the fact that Yugoslavia was still the Eastern European state that was most open to Western tourists. They were a major source of hard currency that Yugoslavia badly needed in the 1980s as it faced an economic crisis that led to a decline in the standard of living. The ESC entries from Yugoslavia in the 1980s came mostly from Croatia, the centre of the state's popular music and tourism industries, but they were never politically provocative considering the continuing censorship in that republic after the Croatian Spring. The political situation differed in Yugoslavia's republics and provinces: in Kosovo, protests in 1981 that called for greater autonomy for the Albanian-majority province turned into riots and tensions escalated between local Albanians and the Serbian minority, and it was partly because of the ongoing tensions in Kosovo that Slobodan Milošević rose to power in Serbia in the late 1980s on a nationalist platform. The Yugoslav national selection for the ESC was held for the first and only time in Kosovo in 1986, when the results of the Yugoslav jury were presented in the ESC for the first and only time by an Albanian, Enver Petrovci (who would later compete in the Albanian national selection for the 2015 ESC), and from Priština. That an Albanian-language entry never represented Yugoslavia at the ESC further highlighted the cultural marginalization of Albanians in Yugoslavia. In Slovenia, the republican leadership's liberalizing reforms made Slovenian culture and society more liberal and open than anywhere else in Eastern Europe in the 1980s, which was demonstrated by the rise of new social movements and politically critical rock bands. One such band was Laibach (the German name for 'Ljubljana'), which achieved international attention for its ironic use of Nazi-style aesthetics that were intended to highlight the totalitarian similarities between communism and fascism. In 2014, Laibach released the song 'Eurovision' which critiqued the contemporary political problems of an EU undermined by a democratic and economic crisis.

By the end of 1989, Yugoslavia was even more of a political isolate at the ESC as the only European state represented there that had not joined the CoE. However, Yugoslavia won the 1989 ESC on 6 May just months before the fall of communist governments across Eastern Europe. Yugoslavia's ESC victory with the song 'Rock Me', sung by the Croatian group Riva – an Italian loanword in Croatian meaning 'seafront promenade' – was widely unexpected, and not necessarily welcomed, by Western European media commentators. Although the British jury, as well as the Irish, Israeli and Turkish ones, awarded Riva twelve points, British commentators, including Wogan, criticized Yugoslavia's win over the second-placed UK entry. The UK had come second for the second year in a row, and it was the Yugoslav jury that had in the 1988 ESC cast the deciding vote in favour of Dion, when the UK had lost by one point.[59] These reactions portended British and West European criticisms of the success of Central and East European states in the ESC at the start of the twenty-first century. Together with Riva's win, the 1989 ESC was additionally pioneering in that Italy was represented by the contest's first singer of Albanian origin, Anna Oxa, whose real surname is Hoxha: she was born in Italy to an Albanian father.

Yet, nobody could have predicted in May the extent of political change that was about to occur in Eastern Europe, although there were some early signs. Hungary had begun dismantling its barbed-wire 'Iron Curtain' fence on the border with Austria on 2 May; Solidarity had been legalized in Poland in April and went on to overwhelmingly win the first free postwar elections held in Poland in June. In November, Kubišová reappeared in public to sing her 'Modlitba pro Martu' to thousands of anti-government protesters gathered on Prague's Wenceslas Square; their Velvet Revolution would bring down the communist government, and Havel would go on to assume the Czechoslovak presidency and make rockers, including Zappa, his advisers. Vukov was also allowed to perform publicly in Croatia again from 1989, when he released an album of traditional Italian songs called *Bella Italia* (Beautiful Italy). All of this would in hindsight add to the political symbolism of Yugoslavia's 1989 ESC win, yet it was all unanticipated in that May, the month of springtime and Europe.

Communist governments in Eastern Europe were not as hostile towards the ESC as simplistic assessments of an antagonistic, binary Cold War would assume. While the ESC and ISC reflected cultural and political cooperation between Eastern Europe and Western Europe during the Cold War, the two international song contests also showed that this cooperation was desired more by Eastern European actors than Western European ones. The ESC did not contain explicit political messages directed against the communist governments, in accordance with the principles that the programme exchanges between the EBU and OIRT were based on. ESC entries were also mostly politically unengaged, as were their Eastern European counterparts in the ISC. Innocuous pop music was suitably appropriated by the communist governments, and after the Stalinist era they mostly did not regard Western-style pop music as being a negative influence, unlike some rock music. The ESC and ISC also demonstrated how both Eastern and Western Europe shared a common popular music market in the Cold War, which was seen in the scouting that record companies from both blocs did at the two international song contests as well as in the careers of artists like Gott and Vondráčková that spanned both blocs. The broadcasting of the ESC in Eastern Europe, as well as local cover versions of ESC songs, further showed that the ESC was not an unknown in Eastern European states when they first entered it in the 1990s. It just took the fall of communism to get them in.

Part Two

European Unification, 1990–2016

Figure 6 Fazla, 1993 ESC

4

A Concert of Europe

Dino Merlin was the composer and lyricist of 'Sva bol svijeta' (All the Pain of the World), which was newly independent Bosnia and Herzegovina's debut entry at the 1993 ESC. Performed by Fazla, the subject of the song was the war that was underway in Bosnia and Herzegovina between its Bosniak, Croat and Serb populations, and it addressed a female lover who had in Sweden found refuge from the war. To get to the 1993 ESC in the Irish town of Millstreet, members of the Bosnian and Herzegovinian delegation led by Ismeta Dervoz from the national broadcasting organization, Radio and Television of Bosnia and Herzegovina, had to escape from a besieged Sarajevo. They left the city by running across its airport's tarmac – despite the threat of sniper fire – and walking to Mount Igman, a site of events for the 1984 Winter Olympic Games but which became strategically important during the war. They then took an army truck to Mostar and a bus along the Croatian littoral to Zagreb, from where they could easily reach Ljubljana for a preselection contest in April. Having passed that, they were able to get to Ireland for the final in May.[1] Dervoz and the aptly named group Ambasadori (The Ambassadors) had sung for Yugoslavia in the 1976 ESC in the Netherlands Congress Building in The Hague, just on the other side of Churchill Square where the International Criminal Tribunal for the former Yugoslavia (ICTY), which was also established in May 1993, would be located to process war crimes committed in the wars in Bosnia and Herzegovina and other parts of the former Yugoslavia.

While Dervoz was conscious of the power that the ESC could have in a state's cultural diplomacy, Merlin had experience in using music to embellish a national identity. A supporter of the Bosniak government during the war in Bosnia and Herzegovina, Merlin wrote the lyrics for the state's anthem, 'Jedna si jedina' (You Are the One and Only), which was used mostly by Bosniaks. The anthem was replaced in 1999 – the year in which Merlin first represented Bosnia and Herzegovina at the ESC as a singer – with a wordless one composed by Dušan Šestić, whose daughter Marija Šestić represented Bosnia and Herzegovina at the 2007 ESC. The new anthem was adopted in accordance with the Dayton Agreement of 1995 that ended the war in Bosnia and Herzegovina and aimed to create common state institutions and symbols for its multinational citizenry.[2] Yet, a functioning, unified state was still not a reality when Merlin returned for his second performance in the ESC in 2011: by then, Bosnia and Herzegovina was one of the few states left in Central and East Europe that was still not in the EU; indeed, it was not even a candidate for membership.

As it had done at the Congress of Vienna and in the wake of the two world wars, Europe rearranged itself in the 1990s after the end of the Cold War. With most of the states of 'Central and East Europe' – as Eastern Europe has been referred to after 1989 – that lay between West Europe and the former USSR, there was an expectation that they would be integrated into West European organizations and their applications for membership in the CoE, EU and NATO followed accordingly. Already in 1993, the OIRT was dissolved and its membership merged into that of the EBU. Just like after the Second World War, it was the international broadcasting organizations that were among the first international organizations to accommodate themselves to the new European arrangement. The new members of the EBU did not rush to participate in the ESC all at once; the successor states of the former Yugoslavia were the most eager, but they had anyway already participated in the ESC during the Cold War as one state. There was a continued increase in the number of Central and East European states entering the ESC throughout the 1990s, which was often a politically symbolic move in the context of their Europeanist aspirations. By 2007, all of the newly admitted Central and East European states of the EU had participated in the ESC.

For Central and East European states, especially if they were newly independent and relatively small, the ESC gave them a rare opportunity to affirm their international recognition and fashion their post-communist national identities in the eyes of hundreds of millions of Europeans. However, the success of some of these states in the ESC prompted annoyed reactions from some journalists and politicians in West European states. Their commentaries showed that prejudices against and stereotypes of Central and East Europeans could not be overcome as quickly as the Cold War had ended. The changing geopolitics of the ESC, especially as it was reflected in the voting results, was even referred to by some West European politicians to fuel Euroscepticism amid anxieties over the economic and social consequences of EU expansion. Such Euroscepticism was especially apparent in British commentaries on the ESC, but it also existed elsewhere. The Czech Republic, for example, was the last Central and East European state to enter the ESC, even though it could have done so from 1993, and despite having been – or because it was – among the first Central and East European states to have joined the EU and NATO.

So, while the ESC could be hastily viewed as a symbol of European unification through popular culture and technology, it also epitomized divisions in Europe that were defined by economics and wars. The call made by the Bosnian and Herzegovinian jury to declare its votes in the 1993 ESC was one of the saddest but most poignant moments of the contest's history. Just a year before the ESC introduced the on-screen presentation of the voting results by the spokespersons of the national juries via satellite link, thereby replacing the phone-in, the Bosnian and Herzegovinian jury struggled with a poor satellite connection as the war had damaged the landlines that could make international calls. And southeastern Europe was not the only part of the EBA that was not at peace. The frozen conflict between Armenia and Azerbaijan over Nagorno-Karabakh produced political scandals in the ESC, as did the war between Georgia and Russia and the military and political tensions between Russia and Ukraine. There were old and new wars in the Middle East, with Israel fine-tuning the appropriation of the ESC in its cultural diplomacy in light of the negative international media attention that its involvement in these wars often brought it. From 1990 to 2016, hot wars were an almost constant backdrop to the ESC. Hosts of the contest spoke of it as 'uniting Europe', but the era of unification did not bring inclusion, peace and solidarity to all of the continent.

Wars

Peace became a popular theme in ESC entries from the mid-1960s because of its universal appeal and the international cooperation that the contest symbolized.

Yet, such platitudes did not mean that Western Europe had somehow overcome its history of wars and that the competition between states could now be played out harmlessly in such international mega events. While there were no hot wars waged between Western European states after the Second World War, they participated in wars on other continents and there was the constant threat of the Cold War turning hot. The first ESC song that alluded to war was the French entry 'Le chant de Mallory' (Mallory's Song) in 1964, which was about a love for a soldier who had gone to fight in Ireland. Songs about war became more politically charged in the late 1960s in the context of the Vietnam War and then in the 1980s amid increasing Cold War tensions. The United States' involvement in the Vietnam War had been one of the triggers for the 1968 student movements. Lado Leskovar's song for Yugoslavia in the 1967 ESC, 'Vse rože sveta' (All the Flowers of the World), was a timely protest against war from a state that was communist and non-aligned and was at that time also experiencing its own student demonstrations against the Vietnam War. 'Ein bißchen Frieden', West Germany's winner in the 1982 ESC, was performed in the contemporary context of protests in Western Europe against NATO's plan to install missiles in West Germany as well as of the Falklands War and the Soviet–Afghan War. With its hints of American folk music, the song was symbolic of the common political causes that were shared between the 1968 student movements and subsequent social movements in Western Europe and the United States. The Finnish entry in the 1982 ESC, 'Nuku pommiin' (Oversleep), was another protest song – in this case against the threat of nuclear war – from a non-aligned state, and it was also one of the few ESC entries in the Cold War that mentioned 'Europe'.

At the first post-Cold War ESC that was held in Zagreb in 1990, joy over the end of Cold War military tensions abounded alongside Europeanist sentiment. The contest was staged on 5 May, a day after the anniversary of the death of Tito, yet on the CoE's Europe Day. The songs entered spoke of uniting Europe, of walls falling, of people's freedom: Austria' 'Keine Mauern mehr' (No Walls Anymore), Germany's 'Frei zu Leben' (Free to Live), Ireland's 'Somewhere in Europe' and Norway's 'Brandenburger Tor' (The Brandenburg Gate). The winner was Italy's Toto Cutugno with 'Insieme: 1992' (Together: 1992), which looked forward to the establishment by the EC of the European Single Market in 1992. Cutugno wore pacific white, the costume colour that has most graced winning entries in the contest. His performance also symbolically included the

Slovenian band Pepel in kri (Blood and Ashes) as backing singers: the group had represented Yugoslavia at the 1975 ESC, and its name was adopted in 1975 to honour the national liberation from fascism during the Second World War. All of this, however, was taking place in a Yugoslavia whose political future was under question. The ESC was staged in Zagreb the night before the last round of the first multiparty elections that were held in post-communist Croatia. They resulted in the victory of the nationalist Croatian Democratic Union led by Franjo Tuđman, who became Croatia's president. In 1991, his government led Croatia to independence amid a war with the forces of the state's Serb minority supported by the Yugoslav People's Army, which opposed Croatian independence and wanted to maintain a Yugoslav state. None of this was heralded by the 1990 ESC, although Tuđman had lamented that the show focused more on Yugoslavia rather than Croatia and, unlike Yugoslavia's still ruling communist leaders, he did not attend the contest.[3] For the interval act, the hosts Oliver Mlakar and Helga Vlahović compared Yugoslavia's cultural diversity to 'an orchestra' comprised of different musical instruments before introducing the touristic film *Yugoslav Changes*. Mlakar would later become a spokesperson for Tuđman's party, while Vlahović, who had also co-hosted the Sopot International Song Festival in 1968, would go on to head war reporting in the Croatian national broadcasting organization, Croatian Television (HTV).

By the time that Cinquetti and Cutugno hosted the 1991 ESC in Rome (although RAI had originally hoped to stage it in Sanremo), an independence referendum had already been overwhelmingly approved in Slovenia in December 1990; Croatia would also pass one just over a fortnight after the 1991 ESC. Yugoslavia was represented in the 1991 ESC by a singer from Serbia, Baby Doll, who sang 'Brazil' – a subject seemingly out of touch with the fashion for 'Europe' that had been evident in the contest the year before. Her win in the Yugoslav national selection that was staged in Sarajevo had been criticized by officials from the broadcasting organizations from Bosnia-Herzegovina, Croatia and Slovenia, who claimed that the broadcasting organizations from the other republics and provinces, which were under the control of governments that were allied with Milošević, had conspired to ensure a Serbian win. Reflecting Milošević's usurpation in 1989 of the Kosovan government, whose institutions were consequently boycotted by Kosovo's Albanian-majority population, there were no Albanians in the jury representing Kosovo in the 1991 Yugoslav national selection. One of the hosts also made snide remarks when the Slovenian jury presented its results as he alluded to the political tensions surrounding the Slovenian government's vanguard efforts to dissociate from Yugoslavia.[4] On the very same day that the 1991 Yugoslav national selection was staged, Milošević violently quashed an anti-government demonstration by the Serbian opposition in Belgrade. In the 1992 ESC, the Serbian singer Extra Nena represented a rump Yugoslavia comprised of Montenegro and Serbia with a song that reflected a nationalist-inspired trend for pop music infused with folk; her placing in the middle of the scoreboard was portrayed in the Serbian media as a result that 'should not be underestimated' considering the tensions in Yugoslavia's international relations.[5] With this rump Yugoslavia being considered primarily responsible for the wars in Bosnia and Herzegovina and Croatia, the UN Security Council adopted cultural and economic sanctions against the state in May 1992, three weeks after the 1992 ESC. This resulted in the first and only time that a state has ever been expelled from the ESC for political reasons which were not, of course, adjudicated by the apolitical EBU, but by the international organizations to which it outsourced such decision-making.

Following their admission into the UN in May 1992, Bosnia and Herzegovina, Croatia and Slovenia were able to join the ITU and then the EBU, fulfilling the criteria for them to enter the 1993 ESC. As there was also interest from other Central and East European states in participating in the ESC, the EBU decided to stage a preselection in Ljubljana to determine the three Central and East European entries that would participate in the ESC. The three successor states of the former Yugoslavia ended up winning the preselection, which for them was important for promoting their newly achieved independence and, in the cases of Bosnia and Herzegovina and Croatia, their war causes. Alongside 'Sva bol svijeta', the Croatian entry 'Don't Ever Cry' was about a young man called Ivan who had died in the war, with its last line referring patriotically to Croatia. These songs may have only finished in the middle of the scoreboard, but they were statements on the EC's failure, despite its diplomatic efforts, to end the wars in these states, especially as EC members were divided over how far they should develop a common foreign policy.

The 1999 ESC sent an explicit message regarding a new war in the former Yugoslavia, this time as NATO was conducting an aerial bombing campaign against Yugoslavia from March to June 1999 in response to the actions of Yugoslav forces in Kosovo during their war with the Kosovo Liberation Army that had begun in 1998. At the end of the show, all of the artists gathered on stage to sing 'Hallelujah' – the Israeli winner of 1979 which had symbolized the Egyptian-Israeli peace treaty – as a message of peace to the Balkans. After the end of the war in June 1999, Kosovo came under UN administration with a NATO-led peacekeeping force. The Milošević government was toppled in 2000, with Milošević being extradited to The Hague in 2001 to be tried by the ICTY for war crimes. The international sanctions against Yugoslavia were consequently lifted and the state, now reconstituted as Serbia and Montenegro, re-entered the ESC in 2004 with Željko Joksimović singing 'Lane moje' (My Darling). Joksimović finished in second place, and his success was interpreted in the European media as a sign of Serbia and Montenegro being reaccepted into the European mainstream. The result was even more significant as Serbia and Montenegro received top points from the states that it had been in conflict with in the 1990s – Bosnia and Herzegovina, Croatia and Slovenia. The former Serbian and Montenegrin foreign minister Goran Svilanović saw this as a positive development that would 'help improve relations between the countries in the region'.[6] The strong voting relationships between the states of the former Yugoslavia in the ESC have reflected their common market for popular music that exists on the basis of linguistic affinities and shared musical tastes and despite the legacies of the 1990s wars.

While Serbia and Montenegro still faced political tensions with their neighbours after 2000, they also had political problems between themselves as Montenegrin political leaders sought independence for Montenegro. In their loose union, Montenegro and Serbia had an equal say in state matters such as defence and foreign affairs, even though Serbia, with a population of some 7.5 million, was markedly bigger than Montenegro with its population of some 600,000. The broadcasting organizations of Montenegro and Serbia accordingly also had an equal say in their national selection for the ESC. In the national selection for the 2005 ESC, Radio and Television of Montenegro had already been criticized for tactical voting in favour of the Montenegrin boy band No Name and its song 'Zauvijek moja' (Forever Mine). In 2006, the Montenegrin government of Prime Minister Milo Đukanović scheduled a referendum on independence for 21 May, a day after the ESC was to be staged in Athens. This turned the ESC into an ideal tool for Montenegrin cultural diplomacy. In the 2006 national selection in Belgrade, No Name won again with the song 'Moja ljubavi' (My Love), whose lyrics could be read as having patriotic allusions and accordingly urging for Montenegrin independence. Sarcastic comments from the show's hosts as well as loud booing from the live audience were directed at what they considered to be biased voting by the Montenegrin jury.[7] Fortunately, the boy band's last stand epitomized Montenegro's peaceful secession in comparison to the wars elsewhere in the former Yugoslavia. However, because of their dispute over No Name, Serbia and Montenegro ultimately did not participate in the 2006 ESC.

After a successful referendum, Montenegro declared independence in June 2006 and Montenegro and Serbia debuted in the ESC as independent states in 2007. Serbia entered the song 'Molitva' (A Prayer), performed by Marija Šerifović, which was a power ballad entirely in Serbian: it was unique in being the first non-English-language entry to have won the ESC since 1998. When Šerifović won the contest, there were celebrations on the streets of Belgrade and she was received as a national hero upon her return, including with her visit to the national parliament. Her victory came at a time when the Serbian government was seeking to forge closer ties with the EU after the years of isolation in the 1990s. One of the hosts of the 2008 ESC in Belgrade, Željko Joksimović, alluded to this when he opened the first semi-final with the line '[g]ood evening, Europe, where have you been all this time?' Šerifović was even selected by the EU as an ambassador for its European Year of Intercultural Dialogue in 2008.[8] However, the Europeanist symbolism of her victory was brought into question when she supported the campaign for the opposition extreme nationalist, Eurosceptic Serbian Radical Party in the national parliamentary elections that were held some two weeks before the staging of the 2008 ESC in Belgrade, and which pro-Europeanist parties in Serbia won. The Serbian Radical Party advocated for Serbia to be more oriented towards Russia rather than the EU, and it also denounced the EU for the support it gave to the independence of Kosovo, which was declared in February 2008 and which Russia also opposed. Russia's victory in the 2008 ESC would be politically symbolic in this context. Although not all EU members recognized Kosovo's independence, most did, and some Western companies and embassies in Belgrade were attacked by protesters during public demonstrations against the independence declaration. This brought into question Serbia's ability to host the 2008 ESC, with the EBU fearing that the security of participants could be compromised. The Serbian national broadcasting organization, Radio and Television of Serbia (RTS), ensured that extra security measures would be taken for the contest and agreed that the show itself would not contain political messages. The 2008 ESC went ahead in Belgrade without any major problems and received positive coverage in the international media.[9] Still, the Serbian entry 'Oro', named after a folk dance, did manage to plug in a slight reference to Kosovo as its lyrics referred to St. Vitus' Day. This takes place on 28 June, a day which has multiple significances in Serbian history, being the date when Serbs were defeated in the Battle of Kosovo in 1389 – and when Milošević was also extradited to The Hague in 2001.

It was of course highly symbolic that the Kosovo War was marked at the 1999 ESC in Israel, a state which has itself faced many wars since its establishment in 1948. The compulsory military service that Israeli artists have served has also been formative for their musical careers through their participation in military bands and their performances for combat troops. From the beginning of its participation in the ESC in 1973, Israel's entries often touched on the theme of wars with its neighbours in order to promote a peaceable image of the state. The band Poogy sang 'Natati la haiai' (I Gave Her My Life) at the 1974 ESC: coming after the 1973 Yom Kippur War between Israel and Arab states, when Egypt and Syria sought to reclaim territories that Israel had captured from them in the 1967 Six-Day War, the song advocated their peaceful co-existence and implicitly criticized Israeli prime minister Golda Meir for not having earlier reached a peace settlement with Egypt. Meir in any case resigned from the prime ministership five days after the 1974 ESC. In 1976, the group Chocolate, Menta and Mastik (Chocolate, Mint and Gum) performed 'Emor shalom' (Say Hello), which also implicitly advocated improved relations between Israel and its neighbours. The lyrics played on the double entendre of *shalom* as both a greeting and the word 'peace', while also referring to almost thirty years of loneliness that suggested the time since the establishment of Israel. The year 1999, though, was a time of relative peace in Israel after the signing in the mid-1990s of the Oslo Accords that gave Palestine limited self-governance and the peace treaty between Israel and Jordan. However, after 1999, Israeli entries in the

ESC again reflected political divisions within Israel over how the state should develop relations with its neighbours. This occurred despite the fact that the contest's rules had come to state from 2000 that the lyrics and performances of songs should not bring the ESC into 'disrepute', which was in subsequent years qualified with clauses explicitly banning commercial and political messages. The rule would be applied upon the judgment of the Reference Group, the steering committee of the ESC that was established in 1998 comprising officials from the EBU and national broadcasting organizations. In the 2000 ESC, the song 'Sameach' (Happy), sung by the group PingPong, was criticized by the IBA and some Israeli politicians as the group insisted on waving a Syrian flag during its performance and one member sang about her boyfriend in Damascus. Five months after that the Second Palestinian Intifada began, and in the ongoing context of this Sarit Hadad sang 'Nadlik beyakhad ner (Light a Candle)', which called for hope in times of darkness and sadness, for Israel in the 2002 ESC.[10]

Over the next decade Israel would be involved in renewed wars in Gaza and Lebanon. Lebanon's national broadcasting organization, Lebanon Television (TL), which was a founding member of the EBU, had first expressed interest in entering the ESC in 1989. TL decided to enter the 2005 ESC with a song in French, but it then withdrew because it did not wish to broadcast the Israeli entry: this would have gone against a Lebanese law that forbids the broadcasting of Israeli content. TL's withdrawal was sanctioned by the EBU, which retained the participation fee that TL had already paid and banned TL from the ESC for three years, although it has since never attempted to return.[11] Then there was the nuclear threat that Israel has feared from Iran. At the 2007 ESC, the group Teapacks sang 'Push the Button', which protested against Iran's nuclear programme and came after a war in Lebanon in which the Israeli army fought the Iranian-backed Hezbollah. The song was permitted by the Reference Group despite complaints about its political content.[12] In 2009, the duo Noa and Mira Awad – the former Jewish Israeli and the latter Israeli Arab – sang 'There Must Be Another Way'. With lyrics in Arabic, English and Hebrew, the song was another call for peace in the region, and it was the second time in the history of the ESC that lyrics in Arabic were performed, after Morocco's participation in 1980. Both Noa and Awad came under criticism for the song in Israel and Palestine. Awad was especially attacked by Arab critics, who accused her of betraying her Arab background – she is of mixed Arab and Bulgarian descent, and is also Christian – by singing for Israel and allegedly whitewashing its international image just months after an Israeli military offensive in Gaza.[13] Palestine's national broadcasting organization, the Palestinian Broadcasting Corporation, made an attempt to enter the 2008 ESC, but this was rejected by the EBU because it was not an active member of the organization, which it cannot become until Palestine is accepted into the ITU.[14]

Although the expansion of the ESC in the southeastern extreme of the EBA was stifled by Arab–Israeli tensions, the ESC included more participants from the more northeasterly areas of the EBA after 2000. That expansion to states from the former USSR encompassed regions that were experiencing frozen and hot conflicts. This included the Nagorno-Karabakh War that took place between Armenia and Azerbaijan from 1988, when they were part of the USSR, until the negotiation of a ceasefire in 1994 between these by then independent states. The war was fought over the Nagorno-Karabakh region that is officially located in Azerbaijan but has an Armenian-majority population. Nagorno-Karabakh declared its independence in 1991 with the support of Armenia, although neither Armenia nor any other UN member state has officially recognized it. Armenia and Azerbaijan have since remained officially at war and clashes between their armies have marred the ceasefire. Armenia and Azerbaijan did, however, share one common goal in their foreign policies: to be admitted into the EBU despite being located outside of the EBA. They joined it in 2005 and 2007, with Armenia joining earlier as the EBU had concerns over the public service credentials of the Azerbaijani national broadcasting organization, Azerbaijan Television (AzTV); it was Public Television (İTV) that instead joined the EBU as the Azerbaijani member. The Transcaucasian states had not been admitted in 1993 with other former members of the OIRT as they were then not located within the EBA. They lobbied to have the *Statutes of the Eurovision Broadcasting Union* changed by the EBU's General Assembly in 2004 to allow any state from the CoE to also join the EBU, with Armenia and Azerbaijan having both joined the CoE in 2001. The ITU accordingly expanded its definition of the EBA to include the Transcaucasian states in 2007.[15] This was the first time that the EBU directly associated itself with a European organization in its statutes as well as changed the ITU's definition of the EBA. Although the EBU has continued to define itself as apolitical, that its membership is also determined by that of the CoE, which has political criteria for membership, now makes it implicitly otherwise.

The Armenian national broadcasting organization, the Public Television Company of Armenia (ARMTV), has used the ESC to promote Nagorno-Karabakh. The first ever Armenian entry in the ESC in 2007, 'Without Your Love', was sung by the artist André who is from Nagorno-Karabakh. The 'We Are Our Mountains' statue in Nagorno-Karabakh was shown in the first semi-final of the 2009 ESC in the postcard for the Armenian entry 'Jan Jan' (My Dear), but was edited out for the final following complaints from Azerbaijan. Nonetheless, during the presentation of Armenia's voting results in the final, images of the statue were shown in the background and on the clipboard used by the Armenian presenter, Sirusho. Armenia and Azerbaijan have also typically not awarded each other points in their voting – they have often come last place in each other's voting results – although the Armenian juries and public did give Azerbaijani entries two points and one point in 2008 and 2009 respectively. In 2009, officials from Azerbaijan's Ministry of National Security questioned citizens who had voted for the Armenian entry in the ESC even as İTV had sought to obscure the on-screen telephone number with which viewers could vote for it; the EBU subsequently fined İTV for this and introduced a rule that made the national broadcasting organizations liable for protecting the identities of people who vote in the contest. At the 2012 ESC in Baku, postcards dedicated to Nagorno-Karabakh received wild applause from the local audience. Although ARMTV had initially confirmed its participation in the 2012 ESC, due to the political tensions with Azerbaijan it eventually withdrew from the contest and, in accordance with the contest's rules, was subsequently fined by the EBU for its late withdrawal.[16]

The other Transcaucasian state that was able to enter the ESC as a result of the changes to the EBU's membership rules was Georgia. In 2003, following the Rose Revolution that deposed President Eduard Shevardnadze, a new government headed by Mikheil Saakashvili came to power in Georgia with a strongly pro-Western orientation, including aspirations to enter the EU and NATO. Relations between Georgia and Russia consequently deteriorated, having already been tense due to Russian support for the territories of Abkhazia and South Ossetia, which had declared independence from and fought wars with Georgia in the early 1990s. Georgia found itself at war with Russia for five days in August 2008, when the Russian army intervened on the side of Abkhazian and South Ossetian forces in the context of renewed fighting with the Georgian army. Russia became the first internationally recognized state to recognize the independence of Abkhazia and South Ossetia in August 2008, with Tbilisi breaking off diplomatic relations with Moscow in response. In the Georgian national selection for the 2009 ESC, Stephane & 3G's song 'We Don't Wanna Put In' won, but there were Russian protests to the EBU because 'Put In' seemed to be a reference to Vladimir Putin, who was then Russia's prime minister; the lyrics also mentioned a love for Europe. The Reference Group asked the Georgian national broadcasting organization, Georgian Public Broadcasting (GPB), to choose another entry or change the lyrics of the song because it considered them to be in breach of the contest's rules against political messages in entries. However, GPB refused and instead decided not to participate in the 2009 ESC that was, awkwardly for GPB, going to be staged in Moscow. The national broadcasting organizations of the Baltic states also considered boycotting the 2009 ESC to protest against Russia's war with Georgia, but they ultimately did not.[17]

The Georgian case was an early indication of a new phase of deteriorating relations between Russia and the West. The EU and the United States had strengthened their ties with the Saakashvili government to the concern of Moscow, which sought to maintain its geopolitical dominance in the Caucasus. There was a brief rapprochement between Russia and the West in 2009 around the time that Moscow hosted the ESC, when the American secretary of state Hillary Clinton famously wanted to 'reset' relations with Russia. When the 2009 ESC was held in Moscow, Russia was represented by a Ukrainian artist, Anastasia Prikhodko, who sang 'Mamo' (Mum) in Russian and Ukrainian, which could have been read as alluding to 'Mother Russia's' patronizing relationship towards Ukraine.[18] Subsequent Russian entries also tried to promote a peaceable and pluralistic image of Russia, such as the song 'Party for Everybody' in the 2012 ESC, which was performed by a group of grandmothers singing mostly in the Udmurt language, and 'What If' in the 2013 ESC, a peace song which was sung by Dina Garipova, a Muslim of Tartar descent. Political tensions with the West again increased over Russia's involvement in the conflict in Ukraine in 2014, which saw Moscow support Russian separatists in eastern Ukraine as well as annex the Ukrainian territory of Crimea. The 2014 ESC in Copenhagen was marked by protests against Russia's actions by the Ukrainian delegation in its media appearances, as well as booing from the live audience for the Russian artists, the teenage twins the Tolmachevy Sisters. In 2014,

Prikhodko also criticized Russia's foreign policy towards Ukraine and stopped performing in Russia.[19] It was by then clear that the tensions between Russia and an EU that had expanded to the former's borders were being played out at the ESC. However, the entries that were representing Russia in the ESC around that time were produced by an international group of composers and lyricists, including ones from EU states such as Sweden. Indeed, Russia appeared to be adopting very Swedish strategies in its appropriation of popular music in its cultural diplomacy when we consider the precedent that Sweden had set in the ESC for this. The historian Larry Wolff has traced Western anxieties and notions of 'Eastern Europe' back to the Swedish king Charles XII's wars with Russia in the early eighteenth century.[20] As the ESC was held in either northern European or former Soviet states in thirteen of the seventeen contests staged from 2000 to 2016, the notions of 'East' and 'West' were again more contested on that front than in Central Europe, even though it was in Central Europe that the expansions of the EU and NATO were most controversial.

Europeanism

Alongside the narratives of the hot wars that were a backdrop to the ESC after the Cold War, there was also that of expanding European integration, especially EU enlargement. Following a national referendum in which 52 per cent of voters supported EU membership, Sweden was in 1995 part of the first post-Cold War enlargement of the EU, together with Austria and Finland. Sweden had applied for EU membership just months after its ESC win in 1991; the 1992 ESC in Malmö was even held on the EC's Europe Day, as the hosts of the show, Lydia Cappolicchio and Harald Treutiger, reminded viewers as they acknowledged the recent geopolitical changes in Europe and stated that 'Europe has become greater' now that 'East is no longer East and West is longer West'. In the 1994 ESC, the last before their EU accession, Sweden was represented by the song 'Stjärnorna' (The Stars), which was about stars shining the way for lovers, Austria by a song about world peace, 'Für den Frieden der Welt' (For the Peace of the World), and Finland by 'Bye Bye Baby', which was about the end of a love and a new beginning. This wave of EU enlargement was thus not explicitly thematized in the ESC entries of these states: there was nothing like 'Insieme: 1992' as an ESC soundtrack to the EU enlargement of 1995.

Indeed, songs about Europe were really only fashionable at the ESC in the year after the fall of the Berlin Wall. Cutugno had won the 1990 ESC with a song that was explicitly about the formation of the European Single Market for the free movement of capital, goods, services and people, which was ultimately established on 1 January 1993 and which the host of the 1993 ESC, Fionnuala Sweeney, mentioned in her introduction to the show. The EC was transformed into the EU after the Maastricht Treaty came into effect later in 1993. 'Insieme: 1992' was performed just after the end of the Cold War at a time when there were new hopes for integrating Central, East and West Europe. The song was, however, more about West Europe, considering that none of the Central and East European states had in 1990 yet applied for membership of the EC so it was not yet known when any of them would become members of the EU. Indeed, while 'Insieme: 1992' was the first example of an ESC entry that explicitly thematized European integration, there were hardly any others until 2003, just before the EU's first enlargement to Central and East Europe on 1 May 2004, when Poland was represented by the group Ich Troje (The Three of Them) and the song 'Keine Grenzen – Żadnych granic' (No Borders) that was sung in German, Polish and Russian.[21]

While there were not that many songs in the ESC with explicitly Europeanist messages, the contest featured prominently in the cultural diplomacies of some states that were pursuing Europeanist goals. That this did not apply much to Austria, Finland and Sweden was due to the fact that they had already been members of Western European organizations such as the CoE and that, despite their neutrality having precluded them from joining NATO (and, in the case of Finland, the CoE until 1989), they did not have to prove their Western economic and political credentials as much as states that had formerly been under communist government did. For most of the states of Central and East Europe, membership in the EBU was the first example of them joining a West European organization, although Hungary, Poland and Bulgaria had already joined the CoE in 1990, 1991 and 1992 respectively, while East Germany had been incorporated into both organizations through German reunification in 1990 (the German national selections in 1991 and 1992 were even staged in cities that had previously been in East Germany).[22] Joining the EBU was a much easier process for Central and East European states than entering any other West European organization. The OIRT had already declared its intention to merge with the EBU in 1990, after which the EBU and the OIRT negotiated for all of the latter's European members and assets to be merged into the EBU on 1 January 1993 upon the OIRT's dissolution. Entering the EBU thus did not entail any economic, political or technical standards. The only significant dilemma posed was by the non-European members of the OIRT, which could not be admitted into the EBU because they were not located within the EBA.[23] Still, although the EBU was the first West European organization to take in so many members from Central and East Europe, the OIRT was actually the last Eastern European organization to be dissolved, with COMECON and the Warsaw Pact having been disbanded in 1991. The Cold War division in international broadcasting organizations thus actually ended later than in other international organizations, but only because of negotiations over the faster accession of the Central and East European members into the EBU.

Although the EBU was the first West European organization to integrate Central and East European states, the ESC was itself unprepared for the expansion. That the EBU had not planned for the entry of new members into the ESC three years after the end of the Cold War demonstrated that it was slow to integrate the Central and East European national broadcasting organizations as equal members. EBU officials were unsure of how to accommodate the organization's new members in the 1993 ESC, as they capped the number of entries at twenty-five in order to prevent the programme from becoming too long, which was one of the constant criticisms that had been made of the contest. For this reason, the preselection was held in Ljubljana to determine three out of seven states from Central and East Europe that would appear in the final: in addition to the three victorious states from the former Yugoslavia, Estonia, Hungary, Romania and Slovakia were also represented in the preselection. The national broadcasting organizations of the Czech Republic, Lithuania, Poland and Russia had also initially confirmed their participation in the preselection but later withdrew, while those of Belarus, Latvia, Moldova and Ukraine never replied to the EBU's invitation.[24]

The national broadcasting organizations of Albania and Macedonia were not invited to the preselection because they were not yet members of the EBU. The Albanian national broadcasting organization, Albanian Radio and Television, which had withdrawn from the OIRT in 1961 and therefore was not merged into the EBU together with other Central and East European states, only joined the EBU in 1999 and debuted in the ESC in 2004. Macedonia's entry into the UN was, unlike that of the other successor states of Yugoslavia, delayed until 1993 because of Greece's objections to the use of the name 'Macedonia' amid fears that this implied territorial pretensions towards Greece's own region of the same name (the toponym had, however, already had its debut in the ESC in 1990 with the Belgian entry 'Macédomienne' (My Macedonian Woman)). Macedonia subsequently joined the ITU later in that year only after both states agreed that it could internationally use the name 'the Former Yugoslav Republic of Macedonia', or 'FYROM' for short. The Macedonian national broadcasting organization, Macedonian Radio and Television (MRT), was admitted into the EBU in 1993 but, because of the name dispute with Greece, participated in the organization under the acronym 'MKRTV'. MRT had sought as early as 1993 to participate in the ESC, but it only first entered the contest in 1998 due to the EBU's changing rules on preselection and relegation. Greece's national broadcasting organization, the Hellenic Broadcasting Corporation (ERT), again voiced objections to the name that Macedonia could use in the contest. In the end, the EBU considered 'the Former Yugoslav Republic of Macedonia' to be too long to fit on the scoreboard, and 'FYROM' as being too unfamiliar to viewers, so the name that was used was 'FYR Macedonia'.[25]

After extensive discussions within the EBU, in 1994 the organization sought to accommodate its new Central and East European members in the ESC by introducing a relegation system, whereby states that finished in the bottom places of the scoreboard would not qualify to participate in the contest of the next year.[26] With this new rule in place, seven states from Central and East Europe entered the ESC in 1994 which, considering that the successor states of Yugoslavia had already participated in the contest from 1961 to 1992, was the first real post-Cold War expansion of the ESC to new participants. The Central and East European states that entered the ESC in 1994 were Hungary and Poland, which had already applied for EU membership earlier in that year, and Estonia, Lithuania, Romania and Slovakia, which would all apply for EU membership in 1995. Russia also made its debut entry in 1994, but not with the same Europeanist aspirations that these other states had. Under the presidency of Boris Yeltsin in the 1990s, the EU and Russia did sign a Partnership and Cooperation Agreement in 1994, but in light of its lost superpower status after the demise of the Eastern Bloc and the dissolution of the USSR in 1991, Moscow was also wary of European integration, especially when it came to NATO's expansion.

One could read certain political messages from the first entries that some Central and East European states submitted to the ESC, although none were as explicit as the Bosnia and Herzegovinian and Croatian entries of 1993. The first artist to perform for Estonia, Silvi Vrait, had participated in the Singing Revolution in Estonia. The songs of Tublatanka, the band that represented Slovakia in the 1994 ESC, had also been a soundtrack to the revolutionary days of 1989 in Slovakia, especially the anthemic 'Pravda víťazí' (The Truth Wins). Edita Górniak performed 'To nie ja' (That's Not Me), Poland's first ever entry, in which she sang about how she should not be viewed as a figure from the past. However, apart from such occasional symbolism, as well as the fact that the songs were performed in national languages that had not yet been heard at the ESC (some of which, like Macedonian, found themselves for the first time on such a stage, as a Macedonian-language entry had never represented Yugoslavia in the ESC or ISC), not so much distinguished the Central and East European entries from West European ones. The entries of the Central and East European states in the ESC in the 1990s usually conformed to the usual contest fare of ballads and Europop. However, one major difference was that the Central and East European entries were performed by major stars from these states, such as Pugacheva who performed for Russia in the 1997 ESC with the song 'Primadonna', whereas established artists from West Europe often shunned the contest because of the negative connotations that it had developed in their own states.

Another aspect that the Central and East European participants had in common with West European ones in the ESC in the 1990s was that they did not all consistently enter throughout that decade, because of the relegation system or withdrawals motivated by complaints about the cost or the voting. Indeed, with the exception of Poland, the other Central and East European states that were at the vanguard of EU integration did not appear in every ESC in the 1990s. That the ESC was varyingly valued in the cultural diplomacies of some Central and East European states and not others also had to do with the different challenges that they faced in their European integration. The most successful Central and East European participant in the ESC in the 1990s was not the Czech Republic, Estonia, Hungary, Latvia, Lithuania, Poland, Slovakia or Slovenia, which were the first Central and East European states to enter the EU in 2004 and NATO in 1999 and 2004. It was, rather, Croatia, which qualified for the ESC every year from 1993 to 1999 and achieved some relatively high placings on the scoreboard. As Tuđman indicated with his complaint about the 1990 ESC and as was evident at the 1993 ESC, his government considered the ESC to be important for Croatia's cultural diplomacy, especially in terms of its Europeanist aspirations.[27] Yet, because of the Tuđman government's control of HTV and other policies that were considered by European organizations to be non-democratic, Croatia's European integration efforts were stalled in the late 1990s, and it would be among the last states of Central and East Eastern Europe to enter the CoE, EU and NATO, doing so in 1996, 2013 and 2009 respectively.

On the other hand, the Slovakian national broadcasting organization, Slovak Television (STV), entered the ESC from 1994 to 1998 after having unsuccessfully competed in the 1993 preselection just months after the dissolution of Czechoslovakia. During this period, Slovakia's government under Prime Minister Vladimír Mečiar was also criticized by European organizations for its non-democratic policies, including its control of STV, which also initially stalled Slovakia's EU membership negotiations. The value that Mečiar himself accorded the ESC was demonstrated when he appeared in a video message to introduce the Slovakian entry in the 1996 ESC, with each entry that year being introduced by a politician or diplomat from its state. Croatia's prime minister Zlatko Mateša also appeared; however, unlike Croatian entries, Slovakian ones did not score highly in the ESC in the 1990s and Slovakia was consequently relegated every second year. After a more pro-European government headed by Mikuláš Dzurinda came to power in 1998, Slovakia did eventually join other Central and East European states in the 2004 EU enlargement. However, after 1998, Slovakia would only return to the ESC in 2009, thereby being another example of a state in which the ESC has been more appropriated in cultural diplomacy under an authoritarian government than a liberal one.

Although the 1990s were marked by the increasing number of Central and East European entries in the ESC, the decade was also characterized by the success of one small state that would in the late 1990s be a model of economic growth, European integration and nation branding for Central and East European states: Ireland. It succeeded in winning the ESC four times in 1992, 1993, 1994 and 1996, during a period in which Irish cultural exports were growing in international popularity, with the opening act of the 1994 ESC featuring dancing caricatures of internationally famous Irish artists such as Bono, Bob Geldof and Sinéad O'Connor. The peace process in Northern Ireland had also received momentum in 1993 with the issue of a joint declaration between the governments of Ireland and the UK, culminating in the Good Friday Agreement of 1998; the peace process was also referred to by host Mary Kennedy in her introduction to the 1995 ESC. Three of the Irish ESC victories in the 1990s came just before the Celtic Tiger period that began in the mid-1990s, when Ireland experienced rapid economic growth that was partly attributed to its EU membership and which saw it go from one of the poorest to one of the richest per capita states in the EU. Ireland won the ESC each time in the 1990s with a ballad, and its folk dancing and music were also promoted in the contest by the troupe Riverdance that featured as the interval act in the 1994 ESC, which was a springboard for the group's international success and also marked the beginning of a repopularization of folk styles in ESC entries. Ireland's winning of the 1996 ESC had a political symbolism as it came just before Ireland's presidency of the Council of the EU in the second half of 1996.[28] The success of Ireland at the ESC was a model for states of Central and East Europe in transforming their international images. Indeed, for those small states in which nationalist critics predicted that EU membership would threaten national identity, Ireland was the best example that Europeanists could point to – except, perhaps, when it came to linguistic diversity. Ireland's success at the ESC in the 1990s, together with the victory of the UK in 1997, meant that most of the winners in the ESC from 1990 to 1998 came from English-speaking states (and the winning Norwegian entry in the 1995 ESC, 'Nocturne', performed by the group Secret Garden, had hardly any lyrics). This prompted the abrogation of the language rule in 1999, allowing all entries to be performed in any language, with most thereafter being in English.

It was after 2000 that the connection between the Europeanist aspirations of states and their victories in the ESC became most apparent, as from 2000 to 2009 five Central and East European states won the contest, as well as Denmark, Greece, Finland, Norway and Turkey. The first two Central and East European states to win the ESC after 1989 were Estonia and Latvia, which were victorious in 2001 and 2002 respectively and were the only Central and East European states that were engaged in EU accession negotiations at the time of their ESC victories. Both states won the ESC with English-language pop songs and artists who epitomized social diversity: Estonia's was a duet between an Estonian, Tanel Padar, and a Dutch citizen, Dave Benton, who is black and originally from Aruba; Latvia had a female singer, Marie N, who is of Russian descent and whose performance in the ESC had a drag element as she wore a mannish suit for part of it.[29] When the ESC was held in Estonia and Latvia, their national broadcasting organizations initially struggled to finance the organization of the contest due to their limited budgets. However, realizing the opportunity that the ESC provided for their states' international promotion, especially in the context of their EU accession negotiations, their governments provided some financial assistance.[30] In the 2002 ESC in Tallinn, there were also allusions to Estonia's independence movement in the postcards – the one for the Russian entry was titled 'Freedom' and showed a goldfish being liberated from an aquarium – and in the interval act, which was a dance performance called 'Rebirth'.

The Europeanist symbolism of the ESC gained further weight with the victory of Turkey in the 2003 ESC with 'Everyway That I Can', sung by Sertab Erener, which also represented the first victory in the contest by a Muslim-majority state. That Turkey had applied for membership of the EC already in 1987 yet had by 2003 not begun negotiations for this, whereas eight Central and East European states were about to join the EU, was due to its economic development, human rights situation and relations with Cyprus and Greece; public opinion in other European states was also sceptical of having such a populous Muslim-majority state in the EU. 'Everyway That I Can' was itself suggestive of Turkey's relationship with the EU: it was about trying to get someone's love in any way possible; it combined Turkish folk dancing and music with Europop and also included dancers from West Europe. When 'Everyway That I Can' was internally selected by TRT, there was some criticism from journalists and politicians in Turkey regarding the eroticism and orientalism in the song's music video and onstage performance and the fact that the song was in English. Such criticism, however, quietened as Erener's victory was celebrated as a sign of Turkey being accepted into the European mainstream, at a time when it was winning other international competitions and, like many West European states, also opposing the US-led invasion of Iraq.[31] Recep Tayyip Erdoğan, the then prime minister, even predicted that the ESC victory would 'speed up Turkey's EU process'.[32] 'Everyway That I Can' was also symbolic for the votes that it received from Cyprus, one of only two occasions that it has awarded a Turkish entry in the ESC points, and the song even topped the music charts in Greece. This period was generally one in which Turkey's political relations with Cyprus and Greece were improving, and Cyprus' points for 'Everyway That I Can' were noted by a Turkish diplomat in a meeting at the CoE in which the situation in Cyprus was discussed:

> There are very recent examples of the peoples' endorsement of the good-will measures and the optimism and hope generated by them. One of these is the Eurovision Song Contest where, for the first time in the history of this European-scale organisation, the Greek Cypriots voted for the Turkish song. This optimism and constructive attitude of the peoples of the Island should also be adopted by everybody.[33]

Erener was also chosen by the European Commission to perform at a concert marking the EU enlargement of 1 May 2004 alongside artists from the acceding states, including some others who had performed in the ESC, the Cypriot singer Michalis Hadjiyiannis and the Latvian group Brainstorm.[34] Two weeks later, the 2004 ESC was staged in Istanbul at a time when the EU was debating the opening of accession negotiations with Turkey, which it approved in December. Turkey finally began its negotiations for accession into the EU in 2005, at the same time that Croatia did.

With the enlargement of the EU in 2004 and to Bulgaria and Romania in 2007, the Europeanist symbolism of the contest waned in the cultural diplomacies of the EU's new members. Yet, a new realm was opened up as the ESC expanded to include more members from the former USSR, some of which were also seeking closer ties with the EU. Foremost among them was Ukraine, which had first entered the ESC in 2003 and already in its second year of participation in 2004 achieved victory in the contest with Ruslana singing 'Wild Dances'. The song was significant for its costumes, lyrics and music that had influences from Transcarpathia, the western-most region of Ukraine.[35] This was also symbolically occidentalist: as was the case with Eastern Europe during the Cold War, not every state in post-Cold War Europe has shared the same reference points for 'East' or 'West' – Poland, for example, is Ukraine's 'West' but Germany's 'East'. In 2004, Ukrainian citizens were caught between political options that advocated a more Russian orientation versus those supporting a more EU one. Just six months after Ruslana's victory, the Orange Revolution began in Ukraine, prompted by allegations of vote rigging in the presidential election that had been won by the pro-Russian Viktor Yanukovych. The supporters of the Orange Revolution advocated the pro-

Western platform of Viktor Yushchenko, who won a rerun of the election in December.

When the ESC was held in Kiev in 2005 under the motto 'Awakening', it gave the new government an opportunity to promote a fresh international image for Ukraine in the context of its democratization efforts and Europeanist aspirations. A lasting legacy of the 2005 ESC has been that visas for EU citizens visiting Ukraine were abolished because of the contest.[36] The entry publicly selected to represent Ukraine that year was a protest song from the Orange Revolution, 'Razom nas bahato' (Together We Are Many); references to Yushchenko in the original version had to be removed for the ESC performance, though, and the EBU consequently made a ban on political references in performances more explicit in the contest's rules. Yushchenko did, however, come onstage to present the prize to the winner of the 2005 ESC, and Prime Minister Yulia Tymoshenko was also filmed in the audience. The Klitschko brothers, two champion boxers, also appeared onstage to open the voting; one of them, Vitali, would later lead a pro-European political party, the Ukrainian Democratic Alliance for Reform, and he became mayor of Kiev in 2014. Ruslana had herself been a spokesperson of the pro-European forces in the Orange Revolution, and she served as a member of the Ukrainian parliament from 2006 to 2007. Klitschko and Ruslana were also leading figures in the Euromaidan Revolution of 2013 and 2014, when demonstrations opposed the pro-Russian policies of Yanukovych, who had been elected president in 2010 and suspended the signing of an Association Agreement with the EU. In 2014, Ruslana received the International Women of Courage Award from the American Department of State, and was presented it by the first lady of the United States, Michelle Obama. In the same year, Ruslana spoke about EU–Ukraine relations at a meeting of the EU's consultative European Economic and Social Committee.[37]

Ruslana's political engagement also reflected the development of another aspect in the Europeanist narrative of the ESC: the involvement of artists who had performed in the contest in national and European politics. Modugno had been the first of them. Then there was Kleveland, who served as Norway's minister of culture in a Labour Party government from 1990 to 1996. Nana Mouskouri, who had performed for Luxembourg in the 1963 ESC, was a Member of the European Parliament (MEP) from 1994 to 1999 for Greece's centre-right New Democracy party. Iva Zanicchi,

Italy's representative in the 1969 ESC, was an MEP from 1999 to 2009 for the centre-right Forward Italy and People of Freedom parties led by Silvio Berlusconi. Dana Rosemary Scallon, Ireland's 1970 ESC winner, served as an independent MEP from 1999 to 2004 advocating Eurosceptic and socially conservative policies; she also unsuccessfully ran for the Irish presidency in 1997 and 2011. Dervoz was a member of the national parliament of Bosnia and Herzegovina from 2010 to 2014 for the centre-right Union for a Better Future of Bosnia and Herzegovina, and she also served in the parliamentary delegation to the CoE. In 2011, Jaana Pelkonen, a host of the 2007 ESC, became a member of the Finnish parliament representing the centre-right National Coalition Party. Claudette Buttigieg, who performed for Malta in the 2000 ESC, became a member of the Maltese parliament in 2013 for the centre-right Nationalist Party. And Zlata Ognevich, who represented Ukraine in the 2013 ESC, entered the Ukrainian parliament in 2014 on the list of the Radical Party. It is, expectedly, Portugal that has had the most politicians with a record of participation in the ESC. The most prominent among them has been Manuel Alegre, a poet whose patriotic ode 'Uma flor de verde pinho' (A Green-Pine Flower) was the text for Portugal's 1976 ESC entry. A member of the Socialist Party, he came second in the Portuguese presidential elections in 2006 and 2011. As politicians, all of these figures have represented different political persuasions with varying policies towards European integration that have depended on national political contexts. However, the ESC did not play a decisive role in their political careers or their attitudes towards Europe: it was just one of their artistic achievements that contributed to the development of their public profiles which were in turn foundational for their political careers.

Although there were MEPs who had performed in the ESC, the CoE remained more connected than the EU to the ESC after the Cold War, as the reference to the CoE that was incorporated into the EBU's statutes in 2004 demonstrated. This was unsurprising considering the role that the CoE had played in facilitating the cultural cooperation that had assisted the development of the Eurovision Network in its early years. The importance of the CoE for the ESC was acknowledged in the contest in 1989, when the host Jacques Deschenaux noted that the CoE – 'the oldest and biggest European organization' – was celebrating its fortieth anniversary and underlined its contribution to European broadcasting. After the Cold War, the CoE expanded to include all European states with the exception of Belarus and Vatican City, the first being excluded because of its continued use of the death penalty and other human rights issues, and the second because it is a theocracy. Non-membership of the CoE has not, of course, precluded Vatican City from continuing its membership in the EBU, or Belarus from joining the EBU in 1993 and the ESC in 2004. In the 1996 ESC, when diplomats, ministers and heads of government and state introduced their state's entries at the end of each postcard, all of the figures represented member states of the CoE except those from Bosnia and Herzegovina and Croatia. The CoE also co-opted ESC artists in its public diplomacy by employing them to perform at its official events: for example, the winner of the 2009 ESC, Norway's Alexander Rybak, performed at the ceremony marking the sixtieth anniversary of the CoE.[38] The ESC was thus continuing to associate itself with the European organization that was most inclusive and which promoted cultural and political cooperation on an intergovernmental and not a supranational level. Yet, it was not the CoE that was the leading organization for European states after the Cold War, but rather the EU, whose more exclusive membership standards and supranationalist aims also gave it a greater economic and political influence in international affairs. However, the EC and the EU were hardly explicitly referred to in the contest after the 1990 ESC. With all of the contest's Europeanist symbolism, the actor that was actually missing most from the ESC picture was the elephant in the arena: the EU itself.

Euroscepticism

With the transformation of the EC into the EU in 1993, more was done by the organization to promote a European identity through common cultural references and symbols. A stand promoting the European Year of Equal Opportunities for All was set up as part of the public events accompanying the 2007 ESC in Helsinki. It was there that Vladimír Špidla, a former Czech prime minister who was then European Commissioner for Employment, Social Affairs and Equal Opportunities, declared that the ESC and the EU 'share a rich history' and that the ESC is 'itself a celebration of European cultural and musical diversity'.[39] Yet, there was otherwise no direct cooperation between the ESC and the EU after 1990, even as the EBU and the European Commission were jointly engaged in other matters.[40] There were hardly even any discussions in the EP on the ESC and its integrative potential: on the contrary, two Greek MEPs – including the composer Stavros Xarchakos from New Democracy – complained about the credibility of televoting, dominance of the English language and lack of musical diversity in the ESC, but they were told by the European Commission that it could not intervene as the ESC was not in the EU's competence.[41] When it came to their shared European symbols, especially the circle of twelve stars, there was also a distancing on the EBU's part from this symbol that it had pioneered but which had become more synonymous with the EU. The last time that the logo based on the circle of twelve stars was used to introduce the ESC was in 1993. After that, a new logo comprising three blue arrowheads that formed a star on a golden circle was adopted for the Eurovision Network. Golden stars were in the 1990s also usually included in the logos for each individual contest, but only for the ones held in EU member states. However, golden stars never appeared again in any of the logos thereafter, nor did any of the contests after the 1998 one ever again coincide with a Europe Day. In 2012, the Eurovision Network's logo was again changed to merely consist of the word 'Eurovision' in an upper case, blue or white font, with the first 'O' being stylized to look like an eye,[42] the emphasis becoming more on the 'vision' rather than the 'European.'

Although the ESC had a Europeanist meaning in many of the states that participated in it, it was again generally not taken as seriously by EU officials as it was by some politicians in Central and East Europe. The Maastricht Treaty became the first of the EU's treaties to institutionalize a cultural policy for the organization, but debates continued within the EU over how far cultural integration or the promotion of a European identity should go. Divisions persisted in member states between politicians who thought that there should be more supranational cultural integration and those who believed that culture should remain overwhelmingly a national matter. For some critics, the ESC was itself an example not of the strengths of European cultural integration, but of what could go wrong in trying to produce a common culture for Europeans: a lowest-common-denominator, mishmash, vulgar form of culture, too forced, ridiculous and simple. Indeed, although the ESC has been typically viewed as a stage upon which states can affirm their belonging to Europe, because it has figured in the battles between Europeanist and Eurosceptic political factions it has also prompted reactions from the Eurosceptic side. This has reflected the polysemy of the ESC, its different meanings for different states at different times: from an ideal forum for nation fashioning and European identity construction, to an expression of cultural homogenization at the expense of national diversity.

Although it is intuitive to associate a Euroscepticism directed at the EU with criticism of the ESC, the correlation is not so simple. There have also been states in which there has been more popular enthusiasm for European integration than the ESC, and vice versa. For Switzerland, which has always been outside of the EU, its successes in the contest during the Cold War demonstrated this. Norway, which won the ESC in 1995, did so after a referendum on EU membership was rejected in 1994, and this despite the engagement of Kleveland on the side in favour of EU accession. As all of the states of Central and East Europe entered the ESC in the 1990s and the 2000s, one of the states that was for a long time missing was Špidla's own Czech Republic. It was a Central European forerunner for NATO and EU membership in 1999 and 2004 respectively, but it only debuted in the ESC in 2007. Despite the Czech Republic's relative economic success in comparison to other Central and East European states, in 2003 the Czech national broadcasting organization, Czech Television (ČT), explained that its non-participation in the ESC was due to financial constraints.[43] Yet, there was also not so much public interest in the Czech Republic for the contest. The ESC had even declined in popularity there after the Velvet Revolution: in 1989, 29 per cent of Czechs watched the ESC, but in 1991 that figure was 14 per cent.[44] Perhaps this was due to the fact that Czechs in the early 1990s had more viewing options or to the public fashion for rock over pop. Like some other central and northern Europeans, such as the Estonians and Finns, the Czechs self-identify more as a rock culture, which was also reflected in the important role that rock music had in bringing down the communist government. Havel, the first president of post-communist Czechoslovakia and then of the Czech Republic from 1993, who had rallied the Charter 77 movement around the case of the Plastic People of the Universe, was renowned as a fan of rock. When the Czech Republic first entered the ESC in 2007, the national selection resulted in the public choosing the hard rock group Kabát (Coat), whose denim outfits and rocker screams were glaringly out of place on the ESC stage. Kabát came last in the semi-final of the 2007 ESC, scoring only one point from Estonia. The group had perhaps assumed that musical diversity had been affirmed in the ESC by the hard rock band Lordi, which in 2006 scored Finland's first ever victory in the ESC with 'Hard Rock Hallelujah' – but its members were also more memorably dressed as monsters and, unlike Kabát, sang in English.

The explaining of the Czech Republic's failure in the 2007 ESC by the Czech public's musical tastes morphed into a broader discussion on the relationship between the Czech Republic and the EU as the state's subsequent entries also fared poorly in the ESC. In 2008, the Czech public voted in the national selection to send Tereza Kerndlová and the English-language bubblegum pop song 'Have Some Fun' to the ESC; it came second last in its semi-final. The Czech Republic finished last again in its semi-final in the 2009 ESC with the group Gipsy.cz and its song 'Aven Romale', which incorporated Romani musical styles and was internally selected by ČT. Having tried various musical genres and selection methods, ČT subsequently did not return to the ESC until 2015 because of the poor results and continued disinterest in the contest from the Czech public. Czech media commentators wondered why the Czech Republic had fared so poorly in the contest, especially as the state had since the end of the Cold War fared relatively well with its international image: it had an internationally admired former president in Havel, a major international tourist destination in Prague, and several internationally prominent artistic and sporting figures, like Kundera and the tennis player Martina Navrátilová. However, from 2003 to 2013, it also had a president, Václav Klaus, who was outspokenly Eurosceptic, denied climate change and opposed the legal recognition of same-sex partnerships. Even after its entry into the EU, the Czech Republic was also still being criticized for the human rights situation of its Roma minority, which Gipsy.cz presented a more positive image of. For the media commentator Jiří Pehe, a former adviser to Havel, the sending of Kabát to the ESC was a metaphor for how the Czech Republic's political establishment was egotistically and parochially out of touch with EU trends.[45] Some Czech journalists considered the Czech Republic's poor showing in the ESC to be due to national exceptionalism for other reasons: they explained it in terms of the

Czechs being culturally superior to other Europeans and rising above such a 'decadent' manifestation.[46] Such commentaries conveniently forgot the success of Gott or Vondráčková or the Czechs' pioneering role in the ISC.

Something that the Czech Republic did lack in the ESC was strong cultural affinities with other national audiences that would be inclined to vote for it. It had this with Slovakia, with which it shared the history of a common state and linguistic similarities that made them a common cultural market. However, because of their irregular participation in the ESC – after 1998, Slovakia was only represented in the ESC from 2009 to 2012 – the two states have only once been represented in the same ESC, in 2009; yet, as they were placed in separate semi-finals, their national juries and publics did not get a chance to demonstrate how they would vote for each other. Through the Czech Republic and Slovakia we arrive, then, at one of the paradoxes of the ESC: that, while neighbourly voting has been a phenomenon in the contest, the states that are located most centrally in Europe and which share borders with several other states have actually benefitted the least from bloc voting. The examples of the Czech Republic and Slovakia demonstrate that allegations made in the West European media regarding Central and Eastern European voting blocs were often exaggerated and even a legacy of Cold War-era prejudices. These claims especially arose at major turning points in European integration, such as the waves of EU enlargement in 2004 and 2007, and they reflected an angst in West European states that was motivated by concerns about the economic, political and social impact that the EU enlargements would have, especially regarding migration from East to West. This was particularly the case in the UK which has, of all the EU member states, seen the biggest influx of migrants from Central and East Europe since 2004, and which has also historically had the strongest Eurosceptic political movements of any EU member state. This, combined with the national popularity of one of the ESC's longest-reigning national commentators, Wogan, makes the UK an ideal case study for the relationship between the ESC and Euroscepticism. In the post-Cold War era, Wogan remained infamous for his derisive humour – which often perpetuated negative stereotypes about other Europeans – that was directed at the ESC and its contestants. Apparently unaware of the historical hybridization of genres as well as the international importance of Italian popular music, including for the

ESC, or the multipolarity of the global popular music industry, he wrote in 1998 that popular music was

> an Anglophone thing. It has its roots in America, whence came jazz, blues, rhythm and blues, rock 'n' roll and country. It just doesn't sound right if it isn't sung in English. French pop? German? Italian pop's never left Napoli. Spain can't lose the flamenco, ditto the Portuguese with the fado. Dutch doesn't sound right, the Scandinavians and the Slavs even more so, and if those singing in Greek didn't vote for each other, who would?'[47]

Although he had criticized bloc voting among West European states – but less so when it occurred between Ireland and the UK – the string of wins by Central and East European states between 2001 and 2008, when British entries finished lowly in the contest, prompted him to most condemn the bloc voting among Central and East European states and demand the reform of the voting system. In 2008, he ultimately resigned from his commentator's position over this issue.[48]

Wogan was, however, just one example – albeit the most prominent one – of a wider British phenomenon of mocking the ESC and other examples of cultural production that were dubbed 'Eurotrash', which the ESC was often considered to be the epitome of. In 1996, the BBC produced the television film *The Tony Ferrino Phenomenon*, a comedy about a fictitious Portuguese crooner who had once won the ESC. Then there was the programme *Eurotrash* that was broadcast in the UK on Channel 4 from 1993 to 2007. It was hosted by two Frenchmen: the fashion designer Jean Paul Gaultier and Antoine de Caunes, an actor whose mother Jacqueline Joubert had hosted the ESC in 1959 and 1961. The show featured reports about popular culture, with an emphasis on the bizarre and comical, from around Europe, and one of its special episodes in 1998, 'A Song for Eurotrash', from which a namesake album was also released, was dedicated to the ESC with famous contemporary artists doing covers of ESC entries. The term 'Eurotrash' had actually been coined in the United States in the early 1980s: Americans came up with their own response to European anti-Americanism to refer to vacuous European popular cultural imports and prosperous Europeans obsessed with fashion.[49] Each side of the northern Atlantic, then, was in some way mocking the other for constructing a national or supranational identity through popular culture. The term 'Eurotrash' found its way to Europe across an Anglo-American bridge via the UK. That the prefix 'Euro-' was increasingly gaining a pejorative connotation in the UK, especially as it was becoming more synonymous with the EU, was also due to the development of Euro-English variants of the English language, which were foreshadowed in the ESC during the Cold War in the use of the basic English vocabulary that was used to pepper songs when they had to be performed in national languages. Euro-English is also notable for its grammatical and lexical errors relative to standard English, such as the omission of articles or the use of non-English forms. These also became more common in ESC entries after the language rule was abrogated, and they have also been spread by the bureaucracy of the EU in which English is the functioning lingua franca.[50]

At a time when the EU bureaucracy was broadly being criticized by Eurosceptic journalists and politicians in the UK for what they portrayed as ridiculous decision-making (the standardized sizes of fruits and vegetables being the classic example), the concurrent mocking of the ESC, especially in major British newspapers that habitually employed Eurosceptic sensationalism in their reporting on EU affairs, further fuelled Eurosceptic sentiment in the UK.[51] Indeed, from 1990 to 2016, British attitudes to the ESC were more politically connected to public opinion on the EU than they had been during the Cold War, when the UK had generally done well in the contest. The victory of Katrina and the Waves for the UK at the 1997 ESC came just days after the Labour Party, under the leadership of Tony Blair, won national elections based on a centrist platform that was more pro-European than the programme of its rival Conservative Party. It also came at the height of the 'Cool Britannia' wave which from the mid-1990s saw a resurgence in the global popularity of British popular culture, especially popular music. After 2000, a string of low placings for UK entries in the ESC were attributed not only to the contest's changing geopolitics, language rule and voting system, but also to publicly unpopular policies of the Blair government. In the 2003 ESC, after the UK was one the few EU member states to participate in the American-led invasion of Iraq, Wogan claimed that the UK was awarded no points for its song 'Cry Baby' because of its internationally unpopular foreign policy.[52] However, the UK's linguistic imperialism and its farcical readings of the ESC had also made it a victim of its own success: other states could send their most famous artists to sing in English, but the UK's biggest stars were reluctant to participate in the contest because its stigma in the UK could hamper their careers. When the

BBC sent two established, older artists, Engelbert Humperdinck and Bonnie Tyler, to perform in the 2012 and 2013 contests after having sent a succession of internationally lesser-known performers, it seemed that the UK had really gone out of fashion at the ESC as the two entries placed lowly. In 2014, Nigel Farage, the leader of the UK Independence Party (UKIP) that campaigned for the UK's withdrawal from the EU, said about the ESC that 'I absolutely hate it' and that it was prejudiced against the UK.[53] Polls conducted in Denmark, Finland, France, Germany, Norway, Sweden and the UK by the market research firm YouGov in 2013 showed that Britons and Swedes were the keenest to leave the EU, but while Britons were most in favour of leaving the ESC as well, the Swedes were the most enthusiastic for their state to stay in the contest. A majority of respondents in all seven states did not believe that the ESC brought Europeans closer together. However, it was only in the UK that a majority – and 75 per cent at that – thought that the contest was unfair because of political voting, although there were more respondents in Denmark, Finland, France and Germany agreeing that this was the case compared to those who did not.[54]

The YouGov poll demonstrated that the number of wins by Central and East European states in the ESC from 2001 also prompted much criticism in other West European states of the voting system based only on public televoting. This had been first tested in the contest by five states – Austria, Germany, Sweden, Switzerland and the UK – in 1997 and then introduced for all participating states in 1998. There was a sentiment in many states of West Europe that they were marginalised in this new, post-Cold War order in the ESC. There had already been dissatisfaction in Germany with the experiments made to accommodate more states in the contest without extending the length of the show, when its failure to qualify for the 1996 ESC through a preselection resulted in it not participating in the ESC for the first and only time in the history of the contest – although Denmark, Hungary, Israel, Macedonia, Romania and Russia also failed to qualify that year. To avoid the potential absence of the most populous West European states in the finals and a consequent reduction in viewing figures and commercial revenues, the entries of the biggest financial contributors to the ESC – France, Germany, Spain and the UK, known as the 'Big Four', and then the 'Big Five' when Italy joined them after returning to the contest in 2011 – were from 2000 given automatic qualification for the finals. For Eurosceptics from other parts of Europe, it then became easy to point to the favouritism in the ESC towards the large Western European states as an example of the inequality of states in European organizations. Subsequent German criticisms of bloc voting also stemmed from a frustration that Germany was not benefitting from this, even though it had the most neighbouring states participating in the ESC of any state in Europe. ORF was also frustrated with the voting system after a string of low placings for its entries, including some which even failed to pass the semi-finals that had been introduced in 2004 to accommodate more participants in the contest. After Serbia won the 2007 ESC, ORF withdrew from the contest from 2008 to 2010 because its officials considered that the contest had become a politicized event.[55] France was additionally marginalized in the ESC because its language was no longer so dominant: some French-speaking states were no longer represented in the contest, such as Luxembourg after 1993 and Monaco from 1980 to 2003 and then from 2007. Belgium and Switzerland were also mostly represented by English-language entries after the abrogation of the language rule. Among the Central and East European states that were traditionally Francophile and members of the Francophonie – Albania, Bulgaria, Macedonia, Moldova and Romania – the entries that they did not submit in their official languages were otherwise usually in English. For Italy, which did not participate in the ESC from 1994 to 1996 and from 1998 to 2010, the controversies over bloc voting did not help to promote a show that, despite or because of the national attachment to the Sanremo Italian Song Festival, was not so popular among Italian viewers. RAI justified its decision to withdraw from the contest on the basis that none of its channels wanted to broadcast a show in primetime, and in foreign languages to boot, that did not promise high ratings: only 2 per cent of the Italian audience had watched the 1993 ESC.[56]

In the discussions on bloc voting in the ESC from 1998 – as well as the booing heard from the live audience in the show in response to examples of this – Central and East European states were painted as the leading culprits of politically biased voting. The implication was that the Central and East Europeans were still not thinking like 'Europeans', that they did not understand democracy, meritocracy and objectivity and were conniving, corrupt and suspicious, especially because of their communist past.[57] Although Wogan had welcomed the debut of Central and East European states in his commentary for the 1994 ESC and had spoken diplomatically when he co-hosted the 1998 ESC, he commented on neighbourly voting during the 2007 ESC with phrases such as 'we're back to the Cold War, really' and 'we're going to have to build a wall'. He called for 'a Western alliance' to be formed: 'Where's NATO when we really need it?', he asked, even though, by then, NATO had several members from the former Eastern Bloc. As the examples of the Czech Republic and Slovakia demonstrated, the allegations about bloc voting in Central and East Europe were exaggerated: there was never one Central and East European voting bloc, not all Central European states benefitted from neighbourly voting, nor did East European states always win the contest. Only four of the eleven winners from 1998 to 2008, when the voting system was principally based on televoting, came from states that had been in the Eastern Bloc. None of the other winners came from any of the Big Four, but some of them were from states that had historically been somehow peripheral in the contest and had never previously won it, such as Finland, Greece and Turkey. The claims about Central and East European bloc voting also misunderstood the motivations behind bloc voting and the success of East European entries. The Central and East European entries themselves often had more resources invested into them as the ESC was regarded in their states as more important for cultural diplomacy than it was in West European ones. Research has also shown that the voting relationships in the ESC are influenced less by political and more by cultural factors, especially linguistic connections that underlie a regional popular music market.[58] And voting blocs did not only exist in Central and East Europe but also in West Europe, as they had during the Cold War. For example, a scientific study by the geneticist Derek Gatherer concluded that 'collusive voting patterns [in the ESC] have been spreading throughout Europe since the early/mid 1990s'. In the contests from 2002 to 2006, he identified such blocs among the Baltic and Nordic states – what he called 'the Viking Empire' – and between Belgium and the Netherlands as well as Ireland and the UK. Gatherer also identified a 'Warsaw Pact' bloc comprised of other states from the former USSR plus Poland and Romania, and a Balkan bloc based on the states of southeastern Europe.[59] There was no voting bloc among other states in Central Europe that were founding members of the Intervision Network: ČT and STV were not participating in the ESC in the period covered by Gatherer, and Hungary was also not represented in the contest from 1999 to 2004 and in 2006; that they were not even one cultural bloc during the Cold War was demonstrated by the fleetingness of the two series of the ISC. Where bloc voting in Central and East Europe was strongest, namely in the former USSR and the former Yugoslavia, this was more motivated by cultural affinities and a common popular music industry rather than any political motivations. In the states of the former Yugoslavia, where multinational teams from the region's states have even produced different national entries in the ESC, the bloc voting should have been lauded as a sign of reconciliation after the wars of the 1990s and despite continuing political tensions between these states.

In response to the complaints from West European national broadcasting organizations, the EBU decided to again amend the voting system in 2009, so that the voting would be determined half by a public vote and half by a jury vote, with the jury being comprised of five music industry professionals. These changes prompted a strong response from Turkey, which also complained about the Big Five rule considering that it has had a population that is bigger than that of each of the Big Five with the exception of Germany. If Turkey were to enter the EU in the 2020s, it would by then likely have the biggest population of any EU member state, which would also mean that it would acquire proportionate voting power and would therefore have one of the leading voices in that organization. Despite its 2003 win, the hosting of the ESC in Istanbul in 2004 and the beginning of EU accession negotiations in 2005, Turkey continued to feel politically marginalized within the ESC and by the EU. Such sentiment found expression in its ESC entries which often had a theme of wanting to be loved, as 'Everyway That I Can' expressed. The Turkish rock group maNga also suggested this in the 2010 ESC, when it sang 'We Could Be the Same' and finished in second place. The motto of the 2004 ESC had similarly been 'Under the Same Sky'. Despite some high placings for its entries in the ESC from 2003, in 2012 TRT withdrew from the ESC due to its criticisms of the voting system: it argued that the Big Five system and the reintroduction of jury voting were both unfair[60] – from a Turkish perspective, the latter diminished the impact of the Turkish diaspora vote, which was especially strong in West European states. TRT's withdrawal from the ESC occurred at a time when Turkey's relations with the EU were deteriorating: EU accession negotiations were stalled amid the increasing authoritarianism of Erdoğan, under whose prime ministership the negotiations had begun and who became president of Turkey in 2014.

Turkey's human rights situation and its relations with Cyprus remained stumbling blocks in the negotiations, while public opinion in many West European states was also increasingly against Turkey's membership in the EU and to the enlargement of the organization more generally.

However, Turkey's growing economic power was accompanied by increasing political clout on the international stage as the Erdoğan government reoriented its foreign policy towards expanding Turkey's influence in regions that had been part of the Ottoman Empire, especially the Caucasus, Middle East, northern Africa and southeastern Europe. One cultural expression of this has been the Turkvision Song Contest (TSC), which was established in 2013 after Turkey's withdrawal from the ESC. The TSC was created by Türksoy (literally meaning 'Turkic ancestry'), the International Organization of Turkic Culture which was set up in 1993 and headquartered in Ankara, in cooperation with the Turkish Music Box television station and with the support of the Turkish government. The TSC has accordingly been aimed at Turkic regions and states from eastern and southeastern Europe, Central Asia and the Middle East – that is, Eurasia – that are members of Türksoy; it has usually been held annually in the city that is designated by Türksoy as the Cultural Capital of the Turkic World, an equivalent to the EU's European Capital of Culture. However, the TSC differs from the ESC in that entries in the former are submitted by both public and private broadcasting organizations, including the Türkshow channel based in Germany which caters to the Turkish diaspora in West Europe. The TSC was started as a cultural expression of Turkey's geopolitical aspirations as the state sought to affirm itself as a major power on the global stage: Turkey appropriated the European models that it had aspired to and become disillusioned with and refashioned them to promote its other geopolitical identities, especially a neo-Ottomanist one, at a time when its relations with the EU regressed. Although the TSC was not presented by its creators as a competitor to the ESC, the fact that TRT has still not returned to the ESC suggests otherwise. There are other states that have been represented in both contests, namely Albania, Azerbaijan, Bosnia and Herzegovina, Bulgaria and Romania, from which Turkish entries also usually received high scores in the ESC and with which Turkey has close economic and political relations. There are other examples of the TSC reflecting Turkish foreign policy interests: Kosovo and the TRNC both appeared in the TSC when it was held in the Turkish cities of Eskişehir and Istanbul in 2013 and 2015 respectively, making the TSC an exceptional international event for these entities that have been supported by Turkey but otherwise have had limited international recognition which has prevented them from participating in other international mega events.

After 1989, the ESC served as a symbol of both the attractiveness and shortcomings of European integration. Europeanists could point to the EBU as a European organization that, like the CoE, pioneered the integration of Central and East European states with West Europe and to the ESC as an ongoing and popular example of pan-European cultural and technical cooperation. Eurosceptics, meanwhile, could use the ESC as an example of the problems posed in arranging a system that could reconcile the inequalities between populous, prosperous states and more numerous smaller ones, especially when it came to voting in the contest. The ESC also highlighted the question of what could be produced through a common European popular culture. If the songs came down to a lot of 'la la la' with clichés about love and peace in Euro-English, could this produce any consciousness of what it meant to be European? The EU bureaucracy was also criticized by Eurosceptics for speaking in platitudes about identity, peace and values at the same time that wars were taking place in some European states and as the EU faced an economic crisis from 2009. The EU evolved from the EEC without maintaining 'economic' in its name, but even the ESC showed that it was still unclear which different measurements of culture, economics and politics should go into unifying Europe. Nonetheless, from 1990 to 2016 there were also politically and socially engaged songs in the ESC which showed that the contest could function as a forum for shaping the 'European values' that the EU sought to forge. The irony was, however, that such engaged songs usually represented states that were not EU members.

Figure 7 Yohanna, 2009 ESC

5

The Values of Eurovision

It was a moment of national pride for Iceland at a time of economic shame. Just after the beginning in September 2008 of a financial crisis in the state that saw the collapse of some of its major banks, Iceland's Yohanna finished in second place at the 2009 ESC in Moscow singing 'Is It True?' A slow ballad, 'Is It True?' lamented the end of a relationship and had the singer wondering whether she had squandered it. The song was chosen through a national selection and it reflected the economic and political mood of an Iceland that was suffering the consequences of excessive consumer spending based on large household debt; it was even used as the soundtrack of a video on the global financial crisis that was made by the *NATO Review*, a publication of NATO.[1] The first ever Icelandic entry in the ESC in 1986, sung by the group Icy, had been about happiness coming from 'Gleðibankinn' (The Bank of Joy), but it finished sixteenth out of twenty entries (the first line of the song also referred to satellites, with Iceland's entry into the ESC being made possible by the live broadcast of the contest via a satellite connection). In May 2008, Iceland had been represented in the ESC by the duo Eurobandið (Euroband) with the vigorous dance song 'This Is My Life', which was about how happy they were with their life and how they did not want to change it; the song finished fourteenth in the ESC final. Yohanna's second place was the best ever result for Iceland in the ESC, together with the same result that had been achieved by Selma in 1999 with 'All Out of Luck'. Yohanna's success was, however, the luckiest result that Iceland could have achieved considering its economic downturn: it was enough to boost national spirits with something other than a shot of Brennivín, yet by avoiding victory Iceland did not have to face hosting the contest just after Russia had set the record for the most expensive ESC ever staged. Indeed, national broadcasting organizations have often considered second place to be the best result in the ESC for the reason of not having to finance the organization of the contest the following year.

The beginning of Iceland's financial crisis came just before the start of the European debt crisis, during which several national governments in the EU, namely those of Cyprus, Greece, Ireland, Portugal and Spain, could not service their financial credits. Some of the national broadcasting organizations of these states consequently economized their participation in the ESC or temporarily withdrew from it. During this, the EU's worst ever economic crisis, member states debated how much economic assistance should be given to the indebted states in order to maintain them within the Eurozone, the grouping of states that had adopted the euro currency in 2002. Despite the EU's efforts to promote a European identity, the debates over the European debt crisis demonstrated that, as the beginnings of the EU in the 1950s had shown, the organization was still motivated more by economic values than the cultural and social diversity and solidarity that it now also tried to legitimize itself through. Iceland applied to join the EU in 2009 just months after Yohanna's ESC performance, with its then leftist government seeing EU accession as a way to forestall a future financial crisis, but in 2013 a new centrist government stopped accession negotiations as the Icelandic economy improved. Fears over the impact of EU membership were stoked by Iceland's relations with the UK, with which it had a banking dispute connected to its financial crisis. Iceland's all-important fishing industry also had a history of conflicts with the UK over fishing rights in the North Atlantic, as the Cod Wars between the two states during the Cold War had exemplified.

Yet, when it came to the political and social values required for EU accession, especially democratic standards and fundamental rights, Iceland was so advanced that some EU member states were willing to fast-track its negotiations. Although one of the world's most nationally homogenous states, Iceland had become increasingly open to immigration as a result of its integration into the European Economic Area (EEA) that was established between the EU and EFTA in 1994, and Iceland's Central and East European immigrant communities also influenced its televoting in the ESC. However, it was Iceland's policies towards sexual minorities that made it stand out the most: its gay pride also brought it national pride. In 1997, Iceland was represented in the ESC by Paul Oscar, the first openly gay artist ever to perform in the contest. His sexually risqué performance of the song 'Minn hinsti dans' (My Last Dance) did not finish highly placed but proved publicly popular as it received points mostly from the states that were using televoting at the time.[2] Yohanna performed at the ESC some three months after her namesake Jóhanna Sigurðardóttir became the world's first openly lesbian head of government, a development which branded Iceland as one of the world's most gay-friendly states. As the ESC was increasingly being publicly perceived as a stage for the promotion of the rights of sexual minorities, especially due to its large following in the gay community, Iceland sent the group Pollapönk (Rascals' Punk) to the 2014 ESC. A group of heterosexual males who wore dresses to the opening ceremony of the contest a week before the final, Pollapönk regularly performed for children with songs about diversity and tolerance. The group was accompanied in the 2014 ESC by the backing singer Óttarr Proppé, who at the time was a member of the Icelandic parliament as the leader of the centrist Bright Future party. Pollapönk appeared in the ESC when Conchita Wurst, the bearded drag queen from Austria, won with 'Rise Like a Phoenix', which prompted debates across Europe over whether the contest should be used as a stage for promoting queer issues.

The controversies over the visibility of sexual minorities in the ESC highlighted divisions in Europe that allegedly symbolized a divide between East and West Europe that echoed the Cold War, but which actually reflected the political conflicts between conservatives and liberals in all European states. These controversies also highlighted issues of democratic development, as the states which tended to be most hostile towards gay rights were also those in which the development of liberal democratic institutions was stalled or undermined. This especially applied to Azerbaijan and Russia, where issues of both authoritarian government and gay rights were spotlighted by their hosting of the ESC, into which they each invested record amounts of money. However, as the EBU reformed the ESC's voting system from the late 2000s in order to address concerns about the fairness of televoting as well as corruption within the juries, it grappled with issues of democratic representation that the EU was also addressing – and not only in the EU's relations with authoritarian governments, but within its own institutions too. As Icelanders reconsidered how much of a voice they would have in the EU as potentially its smallest member, they still turned out en masse to watch and vote in the ESC, proportionately representing the largest national audience to do so. And they demonstrated that they did not need to be in the EU in order to embrace and promote certain values at the ESC.

Diversity

The EU adopted 'United in Diversity' as its motto in 2000, which was the first of its symbols – that is, apart from its anthem and flag – that was not taken from the CoE.[3] While the EU used the ESC to promote its European Year of Equal Opportunities for All, the ESC rules themselves never mentioned the word 'diversity' in the contest's aims, but this was implied in the reference to 'international comparison' in the rules from the contest's beginning. Although it was also initially inspired by cultural diversity based on national differences, the term 'diversity' increasingly came to be used by the EU to refer to other social categories, especially as the EU expanded its legal remit over fundamental – and particularly minority – rights and as its economic policies resulted in more intra-European migration. While migration patterns were always reflected in the ESC through the biographies of artists who had transnational careers, after the end of the Cold War the contest more consciously acknowledged migration waves. European societies and their national broadcasting organizations became more cognizant of diversity issues, especially as many European states that had historically been sources of emigrants had, due to these states' rising prosperity, become host to more immigrants. As was the case during the Cold War, artists of immigrant backgrounds continued to be used strategically in ESC entries to present a cosmopolitan and tolerant image of their states, often when the international image of a state had been politically damaged and needed to be refashioned. However, such choices were also sometimes controversial in the context of broader debates in European societies on the issues of immigration and multiculturalism.

The issue of racial diversity already had a history in the ESC during the Cold War, with non-white artists having usually represented states with a colonialist past. After 1989 they featured more prominently in the entries of France, the Netherlands, Portugal and the UK; the Portuguese entries of 1995, 1996 and 1998, 'Baunilha e chocolate' (Vanilla and Chocolate), 'O meu coração não tem cor' (My Heart Has No Colour) and 'Se eu te pudesse abraçar' (If I Could Embrace You) respectively, even alluded to the Portuguese empire. However, despite the prominence of black artists in the global popular music industry, there had not been a solo performance by a black artist in the ESC since Nascimento had represented Portugal in 1967 until the 1990 ESC, when France's Joëlle Ursull sang about racial equality with 'White and Black

Blues', which was written by Gainsbourg. French entries in the 1990s that were internally selected by the national broadcasting organization Antenne 2 (Antenna 2) – which was renamed France 2 in 1992 – emphasized ethnic minorities, especially those originating from the Caribbean and the Maghreb, and regional languages, which reflected the multiculturalist turn in French cultural policies that was spearheaded by minister of culture Lang in the 1980s and early 1990s.[4] In subsequent years, however, the representation of states without a colonialist past by black artists reflected newer patterns of migration. At the 1999 ESC in Jerusalem, Israel was represented by the group Eden which included Eddie and Gabriel Butler, two Black Hebrews, that is, African Americans who consider themselves to be descendants of the ancient Israelites. Eden's song 'Happy Birthday' had a political symbolism in the context of the thirtieth anniversary of the immigration of the first Black Hebrews to Israel and the celebration of the fiftieth anniversary of the founding of the State of Israel that had taken place in 1998. Eden reflected the increasing multiracialism of Israeli Jewish society and, as Haza had done for Mizrahi Jews in the 1983 ESC, the cultural affirmation of a group which had historically faced prejudice in an Israel that was politically dominated by Ashkenazi Jews. Eddie Butler also represented Israel at the 2006 ESC with the song 'Together We Are One'.

It was Benton, however, who was the first black artist to win the ESC when he represented Estonia in 2001. He personified various migration trajectories: he had settled in Estonia with his Estonian wife in 1997, having originally come from the Dutch Caribbean territory of Aruba and lived in the Netherlands. Aruba's colonial past made Benton a citizen of the EU before Estonians were. However, while Benton promoted an image of a multicultural Estonia, there was no reference in the show of the 2002 ESC in Tallinn to the Russian minority that comprised a quarter of the Estonian population and which had been the subject of political tensions in Estonia amid complaints that the minority was discriminated against in the post-Soviet state.[5] The biographies of other black artists in the ESC reflected how Eastern European states had drawn immigrants from African states during the Cold War. These immigrants usually migrated for educational or professional reasons in the context of the ties that Eastern European states developed with African ones, such ties being also demonstrated by the OIRT's cooperation with African national broadcasting organizations. For example, Viktoras Diawara, who was born to Lithuanian and Malian parents, sang in the group Skamp for Lithuania in the 2001 ESC.[6]

Gaitana, who sang 'Be My Guest' for Ukraine in the 2012 ESC, is of Congolese–Ukrainian background and was born in the USSR.[7] Although her representation of Ukraine at the ESC drew racist criticisms from some extreme nationalist politicians, Gaitana had won Ukraine's national selection for the 2012 ESC by coming second in the televote and first in the jury vote. She was also one of the official artists for the 2012 Union of European Football Associations' (UEFA) European Championship that was held in Poland and Ukraine in that year, and for which she composed the song 'Viva, Europe!' In the 2010 ESC, the French-Congolese singer Jessy Matador represented France with the song 'Allez olla olé' (Go, Olla Olé) that alluded to the upcoming 2010 World Cup in South Africa.

In the 2000 ESC, Austria was represented by two black artists, Kim Cooper and Lynne Kieran, who with Tini Kainrath formed the group the Rounder Girls. This was a political statement by ORF at a time when the Austrian government faced diplomatic sanctions from other EU member states due to the inclusion of the right-wing populist Freedom Party of Austria (FPÖ) in a coalition government. The Rounder Girls had themselves participated in public demonstrations against the formation of the coalition government and the anti-immigration policies of the FPÖ.[8] The Austrian example demonstrated how West European states were also still strategically being presented in the ESC as cosmopolitan, multicultural and tolerant for political reasons. Germany continued to best typify this as it struggled with the integration of immigrant communities which had been established during the Cold War, especially from Turkey, yet also sought to refashion its national identity in the wake of German reunification. In 1999, Germany was represented by its most cosmopolitan entry ever in the ESC: the group Sürpriz (Surprise) comprised six German Turks who sang 'Journey to Jerusalem – Kudüs'e seyahat' with lyrics in English, German, Hebrew and Turkish. Finishing in third place, it also demonstrated how multicultural entries could draw diasporic votes as the song received high scores from states with large Turkish immigrant communities, such as Austria, Belgium, France and the Netherlands. The song was also one of only two German entries that received any points from Israel between 1990 and 2016, and twelve points at that.[9]

The expansion of the EU to Central and East Europe also saw a growth in Central and East European immigrant communities in West Europe as a result of intra-EU migration, and these also had an impact on the televoting results in some states. This was seen in the high points from Italy, Portugal and Spain to Romanian entries, and from Italy to Albanian ones as well: although it was not a member of the EU, Albania was from 1990 the source of hundreds of thousands of immigrants to Italy, one of whom, Hersi, represented Albania in the 2014 ESC. The televoting in Iceland, which was also not a member of the EU but saw the growth of Central and East European immigrant communities by being a part of the EEA, became more favourable towards entries from Poland, from where the largest Central and East European immigrant community in Iceland originates (although Iceland has historically given its highest scores in the ESC to Denmark, its former colonial power with which it remained culturally, economically and politically closely connected). In Ireland and the UK, the televoting results for Lithuanian and Polish entries also reflected the growth of Lithuanian and Polish immigrant communities in these states since 2004. In the 2010 ESC, Ireland and the UK awarded high scores to the Lithuanian entry 'Eastern European Funk', whose lyrics explicitly addressed the prejudices against Central and East European immigrants. The Polish entry in the 2014 ESC, 'My Słowianie – We Are Slavic', also poked fun at Western stereotypes of Slavs as backward, communist and folkish – as well as unchaste, being particularly notable for its sexual innuendo. The song placed first in the televoting in Ireland and the UK and second in Iceland, but it ranked at the bottom in the jury results from all of these states. Such self-parody in the ESC has usually been the mark of a state that is confident in its national identity: the Swedes excelled at this in the opening and interval acts that they produced when they hosted the ESC, from the first contest staged in Sweden in 1975 to the 'Swedish Smörgasbord' interval act in the 2013 ESC. In the Polish case it also underlined Poland's economic success in spite of the EU's financial crisis – when it was one of the few European states not to experience an economic recession – and its international political standing on the tenth anniversary of its EU accession, with the former Polish prime minister, Donald Tusk, becoming president of the EU's European Council later in 2014.

Whereas these Lithuanian and Polish songs highlighted the prejudices faced by Central and East European immigrants in West European states, the branding of the contests often presented an idealized vision of West European multiculturalism. After Lena won the 2010 ESC for Germany with the song 'Satellite', the 2011 ESC was staged in Düsseldorf, where each entry was introduced with a postcard featuring residents of or visitors to Germany from the entry's state. However, in 2010 and 2015, Chancellor Angela Merkel asserted that multiculturalism in Germany had 'utterly failed' as immigrants were not sufficiently integrated but lived in parallel societies, and her opinion was shared by some other West European political leaders regarding their own states.[10] The 2013 ESC in Malmö was branded with the motto 'We Are One'; the show included interval acts that parodied Swedish culture, including with a film appearance by Prime Minister Fredrik Reinfeldt, but also presented Swedes as tolerant of minorities, including immigrants, with the Kurdish-Swedish singer Darin and the Bosnian-Swedish soccer player Zlatan Ibrahimović making guest appearances. Loreen, the Swedish winner of the 2012 ESC, is also the daughter of Moroccan immigrants. Still, Sweden's self-confidence in presenting such a politically correct image of itself concealed its own problems with the integration of immigrants. These came to the fore in some Swedish cities a day after the final of the 2013 ESC, with the beginning of riots that were attributed to the discontent of some immigrants with economic inequality and social exclusion.[11] Sweden's immigration policies were thus not without their social shortcomings, something that was also seen in the rising support for its anti-immigrant, right-wing populist party, the Sweden Democrats.

One ethnic group that was commonly accused by right-wing populist parties across Europe of failing to integrate into mainstream societies is the Roma, many of whom also immigrated from Central and East European to West European states upon the enlargement of the EU. The Roma have historically been not only political scapegoats but also prominent musicians and singers, especially in Central and East Europe as well as in Spain, where they were particularly associated with the development of flamenco music. The first ever Romani artist in the ESC was Peret, who represented Spain in 1974 with 'Canta y sé feliz' (Sing and Be Happy), which referred to Europe and the pleasures – namely drinking and sunbathing – of living in it. Although Romani artists who participated in the ESC promoted the mainstream visibility of Roma in European societies, some of them also supported right-wing nationalist parties in their states. Šerifović was the artist of Roma descent who was most successful in the ESC, but while she was at the time of her victory interpreted in West European media commentaries as being symbolic of an inclusive and tolerant post-Milošević Serbia, she later stoked controversy for her engagement in the election campaign of the extreme nationalist Serbian Radical Party. Esma Redžepova, who represented Macedonia in the 2013 ESC in a duet in which she also sang some Romani lyrics, was the most famous Roma artist from southeastern Europe and nicknamed 'Queen of the Gypsies'. She was also a politician from the right-wing Internal Macedonian Revolutionary Organisation – Democratic Party for Macedonian National Unity (VMRO-DPMNE) and became a member of the city council of Skopje in 2009. The song that she had initially intended to perform at the ESC, 'Imperija' (Empire), was replaced with 'Pred da se razdeni' (Before the Dawn) following criticism that the former promoted the nationalist programme of the VMRO-DPMNE.[12] The ESC entry that took the most activist stance on Romani issues was the Czech Republic's Gipsy.cz in the 2009 ESC. The group's song 'Aven Romale' (Come On, Roma) had the ESC's first Romani lyrics, and it tried to redress the Czech Republic's low placings in the contest in the previous two years as well as the state's international image regarding Roma rights. Despite the colourful performance, 'Aven Romale' still came last in its semi-final with zero points, which showed that, unlike other groups, the Roma had not yet affirmed themselves as a transnational voting bloc in the ESC.

One transnational community that certainly did become well represented in the ESC was the gay one. The EBU was reluctant to acknowledge the contest's special appeal among gays until the late 1990s. The gay outing of the ESC came at a time when the ESC was changing as the show became staged in bigger venues, thereby allowing its gay fans to become more visible on-screen, and televoting was introduced. Most importantly, it also occurred in the context of political advancements across European states in terms of gay rights. The EU actively promoted gay rights from the late 1990s, especially with the adoption of anti-discrimination provisions in the Treaty of Amsterdam in 1999, which were also invoked in the negotiations for the accession of Central and East European states. However, it was actually states that were never members of the EU that did more to promote queer visibility in the ESC, beginning with the Norwegian entry 'Romeo' in 1986 and Oscar's performance for Iceland in 1997. The major turning point for the visibility of sexual minorities in the ESC came in 1998, when the transsexual Dana International – a play on the name of Dana, the Irish winner of the 1970 ESC – won for Israel. Her song 'Diva' had a feminist theme that focused on powerful women, and it referred to two ancient goddesses and a pharaoh, Aphrodite, Victoria and Cleopatra. The song caused controversy in Israel as it was condemned by some conservative politicians who considered Dana International an inappropriate representative for Israel and religious leaders who considered homosexuality and transsexuality an abomination; on the other hand, Dana International was supported by secular Israelis and the gay community who applauded her for internationally promoting an image of Israel as diverse and tolerant. Dana International underlined Israel's Western credentials as a liberal democracy different from its neighbouring Arab states, in which homosexuality was illegal or at least less publicly tolerated. The victory of Dana International advanced the visibility of the gay community not only in Israel but also in the ESC: as it was the first year in which televoting was widely used, her win was widely interpreted as reflecting the large gay fan base of the contest.[13] Israel also gave the ESC its first gay kiss – albeit a peck on the lips between two men – in the song 'Sameach' (Happy) in 2000. The Israeli government appropriated the ESC to promote Israel to the international gay community: at the official Israeli party during the 2012 ESC, leaflets published by the government's Ministry of Public Diplomacy and Diaspora Affairs presented Israel as a place welcoming of sexual minorities.[14] Critics of the Israeli government have, however, attacked its appropriation of sexual minorities as drawing attention away from – or 'pinkwashing' – Israel's human rights record regarding Israeli Arabs and Palestinians.[15]

After Israel fully opened up the gates to gays in the ESC, it was Central and East European entries that took up queer themes – and much more so than West European ones did. The only West European entry that in the 2000s explicitly depicted sexual minorities was Denmark's drag act 'Drama Queen' in 2007, which was hardly controversial in Denmark considering that it was the first state in the world to legally recognize same-sex unions in 1989. Although the EU did not adopt a common position on same-sex unions, it increasingly expected aspiring members to advance gay rights. This was demonstrated by the case of Slovenia in the 2002 ESC, when the drag trio Sestre (Sisters) won the national selection by the jury and not the public vote. Protests ensued against the group, with some politicians arguing in parliament that they did not want Slovenia to be represented by gay men and transvestites. MEPs also became involved in the debate and indicated that Slovenia should not enter the EU if the human rights of its sexual minorities were not respected.[16] In the end, Sestre did perform in the 2002 ESC and Slovenia entered the EU in 2004, and in 2006 it became one of the first Central and East European states to legally recognize same-sex unions. Russia sent the female duo t.A.T.u. to the 2003 ESC with the song 'Ne ver', ne boisia (Don't Believe, Don't Fear)', after the singers had become famous internationally by being promoted as a teenage lesbian couple. It was hoped that, with their international popularity and shock factor – which they amplified by threatening to perform naked onstage in the ESC – they would secure Russia's first ESC win; however, they came second. That their faux homosexuality was a deliberate marketing strategy conceived to appeal to a West European audience, especially as social attitudes towards homosexuality were less tolerant in Russia, was later admitted by t.A.T.u. in media interviews when they stated that they were really 'normal Russian girls' and that they considered homosexuality a 'sickness'.[17]

t.A.T.u. was the first shot in an international battle over gay issues that would include Russia and be waged through the ESC. The second came at the 2007 ESC when Ukraine was represented – despite protests from some Ukrainian conservative politicians because of her transvestitism – by the drag queen Verka Serduchka. During her ESC performance she wore a silver star on her head that appeared to mock the USSR. The last two words of her song's title, 'Dancing Lasha Tumbai', were a made-up phrase that when sung sounded very much like 'Russia, goodbye' and was easily interpreted as an allusion to the Orange Revolution. A reference in the original version of the song to Kiev's Independence Square that was the major site of the Orange Revolution protests was, however, replaced with 'Europe' in the ESC performance.[18] Serduchka came second in the ESC to Šerifović, whose performance of 'Molitva' was, as the writer Germaine Greer described it, 'lesbian chic',[19] with Šerifović dressed up in a mannish suit and accompanied by five female backing singers who went on to form the group Beauty Queens. While Greer lauded Šerifović as a representative of Roma and lesbians, Šerifović never publicly declared herself to be the latter until she did so in 2013 in a documentary film about her. Considering the high level of homophobia in Serbian society – the first gay pride parade in Belgrade had been brutally attacked by protesters in 2001 and there was not a repeat attempt until 2010, when it was held under high police security – such a declaration could have harmed her career prospects. The queer aspects of 'Molitva' were not at all acknowledged by Serbian politicians, who only praised her win on patriotic grounds. However, the producers of 'Molitva' knew what they were doing: they deliberately made it a queer act in order to attract more attention and votes from the ESC's international audience.[20]

The queer entries in the ESC from Central and East European states thus strategically presented these states as being more gay-friendly than political and social attitudes within them actually were; it was West European states that had been more progressive in institutionalizing gay rights after 1989. However, West Europe also has its own mixed records on gay rights; unlike the Central and East European states, West European ones that acceded to the EU until 1995 did not have to achieve standards on gay rights in order to do so. Northern Europe has generally been more advanced in this regard than the south, where states such as Italy and Greece lagged in the legal recognition of same-sex unions, although Portugal and Spain allowed same-sex marriage from 2010 and 2005 respectively. And there were also exceptions in northern Europe. In the 2013 ESC, Krista Siegfrids brought up the issue of same-sex marriage in her song 'Marry Me', which represented Finland. Although its music video featured Siegfrids marrying a man, in the ESC act she was shown marrying a woman and kissing her at the end of the song – something that Siegfrids said demonstrated her support for same-sex marriage in Finland, which was the only Nordic state not to yet allow it in 2013, although the Finnish parliament ultimately did approve it in 2014.[21] The 2013 ESC was also the first edition of the contest in which positive references to its gay fans were made by the host, and there was also a kiss between two men in the interval act 'Swedish Smörgåsbord'. In the 2014 ESC in Copenhagen, further references were made by the hosts to the ESC's gay audience, and the Danish entry 'Cliche Love Song' referred to a girl kissing a girl.

The controversies over gay rights at the ESC even reached as far as the states where one could not even find a gay bar in a tourist guide. When the ESC was staged in Baku in 2012, a gay bar was opened briefly and likely not closed by the authorities for fear of criticism from the international media, but it did not survive after the media and tourists went back home. The security of gay fans at the ESC in Baku had been emphasized by the EBU and, considering the extent of security generally at the 2012 ESC, it was heeded by the Azerbaijani organizers. Azerbaijan had decriminalized homosexuality in 2000 in order to enter the CoE, but accusations of homosexuality were thereafter still used to smear critics of the government of Ilham Aliyev. Yet, the 'gayness' of the ESC also figured in Azerbaijan's diplomatic relations with states outside of the EBA. Azerbaijan's ties with Iran, its southern neighbour in which more ethnic Azeris live than in Azerbaijan itself, were strained because of territorial disputes and different attitudes towards the role of Islam in government. The Islamic Republic of Iran is more religiously conservative than secular Azerbaijan, and it also has the death penalty for homosexual acts. In addition, Azerbaijan was one of the few Muslim-majority states that developed close ties with Israel, with the two engaging in military cooperation that Iranian political leaders perceived as being directed against their state. Iranian officials stated that the ESC went against Islamic values and falsely accused the Azerbaijani authorities of hosting a gay pride parade during the week of the 2012 ESC, which prompted a public protest outside of the Iranian embassy in Baku and the mutual recall of the two states' ambassadors; there were also similar criticisms of the contest made by the Islamic Party of Azerbaijan.[22] The motto of this contest was 'Light Your Fire': Iran was fuming that Azerbaijan was flaming. In news that was only released after the contest, during the week of the 2012 ESC Azerbaijani authorities arrested Islamist terrorists who had planned to target the contest. This was presented by the Azerbaijani government as a justification for the extensive security measures that it had employed, including police protection of visitors and a venue that was not only guarded with metal detectors and policeman in official and plain uniforms, but also by boats of the Azerbaijani coast guard that were stationed on the Caspian Sea.

Still, the biggest controversies over gay issues in the ESC involved Russia and reflected not only how gay rights was becoming a more debated issue in international relations, but also increasing political tensions between Russia and Western states. A demonstration in Moscow was held under the banner of 'Slavic Pride' on the same day that the 2009 ESC final was held in the city. The demonstration was stopped by police and some of its participants were detained because mayor Yuri Luzhkov had banned gay pride parades, for which he was criticized by members of the EP.[23] In 2013, Russia adopted a law banning the promotion of homosexuality to minors, which prompted international concern over whether gay athletes would be discriminated against in the upcoming 2014 Winter Olympic Games in Sochi – as well as whether another gay kiss in the ESC could be broadcast in Russia or even if the ESC could be staged in Russia again. Such a law was not unique to Russia: the UK had, after all, had one prohibiting the promotion of homosexuality by local authorities or in schools from 1988 to 2003, and one was also adopted by the Lithuanian parliament in 2008 but was watered down in 2009 following criticism from the EP. There was also opposition in Russia to such laws: an open letter signed by some three hundred celebrities, including Philipp Kirkorov and Dima Bilan who had represented Russia in the ESC, protested against the adoption of one by the city council of St. Petersburg.[24] However, in the context of the other causes for political tensions in the West's relations with Moscow, it was the Russian national law that stoked the most international controversy. A particular reaction came from Austria, where ORF decided, without holding a national selection, to send the bearded drag queen singer Wurst as its representative to the 2014 ESC. Wurst had previously come second in the national selection for the ESC in Baku – had she won then, she would have been an easy target for the Islamist critics of Azerbaijan's staging of the ESC. In bringing Wurst to the 2014 ESC, ORF directly challenged those European states that that had anti-gay laws, but it also drew criticism from conservative politicians in Austria, especially ones from the FPÖ. While Pollapönk also had an act that promoted diversity, the group did not receive as much media attention as the strikingly bearded drag queen, whose marketing strategy promoted her as a symbol of tolerance against Russian president Putin. Upon her win, Wurst dedicated her victory to those who believed 'in a future of peace and freedom' and exclaimed 'we are unity and we are unstoppable.' Wurst's performance in the ESC was loudly cheered by the live audience while there was booing for the Russian representatives, the Tolmachevy Sisters. Her victory consequently had a political symbolism in the context of tensions between Russia and the West over the war in Ukraine, and it was criticized by Russian politicians such as Putin and the extreme nationalist Vladimir Zhirinovsky. However, the voting results for Wurst did not follow a strict East–West line – she even received five points from Russia after placing third in its televote.[25]

Despite the ESC's greater emphasis on sexual diversity from the late 1990s, there was one aspect in which it became less diverse: language. With the abrogation of the language rule in 1999, most entries were thereafter performed in English: the original emphasis in the ESC rules on promoting national diversity in the contest was thus lost, as most artists considered their chances for success in the contest greater if they sang completely or mostly in English. Non-English words were sometimes added to give songs a national flavour, but even this became a dwindling phenomenon; if other languages were used in entries they were usually French, Italian or Spanish. There was even a tendency in France's entries for English-language words to be incorporated into their lyrics: the French entry in the 2007 ESC, 'L'amour à la française' (Love the French Way), mocked Franglais and French stereotypes, but when the 2008 French entry 'Divine' was sung by Sébastien Tellier mostly in English, it drew criticism from some French politicians.[26] That this was happening to world languages such as French and Spanish, which were both supported by large, transnational popular music industries, was the ultimate victory of Anglicization in the ESC. In the 2014

ESC, the group Twin Twin represented France with the song 'Moustache', which was mostly in French but used the French loanword from the title in some lines in English to express a critique of a materialist society and how all the group wanted was a moustache. Yet, the hegemony of the English language in the ESC otherwise reflected the personal ambitions of artists, composers and lyricists to achieve international success with their entries, which also underlined the increasing commercialization of the contest from the 1990s.

Commercialism

When it came to national broadcasting organizations withdrawing from the ESC during the Cold War, the commercialization of the contest or the cost of participating in it was usually cited as the major reason, even if other political or programming issues were at play. During the Cold War, there were five occasions when the winning national broadcasting organization declined to host the contest the subsequent year – after this became a tradition but not a rule from the 1958 ESC – due to the financial cost. The smaller national broadcasting organizations of Luxembourg and Monaco did so for the 1974 and 1972 contests respectively, but so did the larger national broadcasting organizations of France, Israel and the Netherlands for the 1963, 1980 and 1960 contests. In four of the cases the BBC instead took on the role of host broadcaster; the Dutch national broadcasting organization, the Dutch Broadcasting Foundation, hosted in 1980 after the IBA declined to do so. Participation fees based on the economic wealth and population size of each national broadcasting organization's state were introduced from the 1976 ESC in order to reduce the financial burden on the host national broadcasting organization. In 1974, it was estimated that the ESC cost a minimum of 40,000 British pounds to stage, which was the equivalent of approximately 500,000 American dollars in 2016.[27] Beginning in 1983, there were also discussions within the EBU about how the financing of the contest could be aided through commercial cooperation with record companies,[28] at a time when national media markets in Western Europe were being deregulated and commercial television broadcasters were being increasingly established. The moves towards seeking commercial sponsorship for the ESC were also motivated by concerns that national broadcasting organizations from smaller states would be prevented from hosting the contest due to its financial cost. RTÉ set a precedent in this regard when it included the airline Ryanair as a commercial sponsor for the 1988 ESC, with images of the company's planes being shown during the show.

By 1991, the EBU noted that sponsorship of the ESC 'was now a tradition borne of necessity',[29] although it has never permitted the entries themselves to contain commercial messages. After the ESC opened up to commercial sponsorship – as well as to that from the EC – in the late 1980s, one of the major issues that the newly formed Reference Group dealt with in the late 1990s was how to make the ESC a more commercially viable and less financially burdensome event for the host broadcasting organization through advertising, branding and televoting. Marketing firms were engaged to consult the EBU on how it could overcome the contest's image problems – including it seeming old-fashioned, being commonly mocked and prone to allegations of vote rigging – to attract more commercial sponsors. The EBU looked to other international mega events, like the UEFA Champions League and Olympic Games, for inspiration.[30] Merchandising also became a feature of the contest: the first official compact disk compilation with all the entries from an ESC was released in 2000 by the commercial labels EMI Records and CMC International. From 2001, accounting firms, starting with Deloitte and Touche, were brought in to audit the voting results, and in 2004 the German company Digame Mobile became responsible for the centralized televoting. A generic logo for the contest featuring the name 'Eurovision Song Contest' with a heart in place of the 'v' that could be filled with the flag of the host state was also introduced in 2004. That the ESC was being increasingly commercialized also reflected the pressure on national broadcasting organizations to become more financially viable, as many of them introduced commercials in the 1990s and were more intensely competing with commercial television broadcasters.

The move towards the greater commercialization of the ESC in the late 1990s came after Ireland had to host the contest four times in the 1990s at a time when it was still not experiencing its economic boom; RTÉ accordingly had to seek commercial sponsorship in order to finance its multiple hostings. An Irish MEP from the centre-right Fianna Fáil party, Gene Fitzgerald, even requested that the European Commission provide Ireland with financial support to host the 1995 ESC, but this was rejected by the president of the EP as not being a matter for that institution.[31] While Irish political leaders such as Prime Minister Albert Reynolds and Minister of Culture Michael D. Higgins acknowledged the importance of the ESC for the international promotion of Ireland, the contests staged in Ireland in the 1990s also demonstrated the commercial potential of the ESC. Although Irish folk music had been promoted in earlier contests staged in Ireland, the example of Riverdance after its performance in the 1994 ESC showed how the contest could be used to launch an internationally successful commercial product.[32] In synergy with a growing international popularity of Irish folk and popular music, the contests held in Ireland in the 1990s also underlined how the popular music industry of a small state could become a significant global player, with Ireland offering the best example of this after Sweden – although between 1956 and 2016 Ireland won the ESC one more time than Sweden did. However, after the advent of the Celtic Tiger period, Ireland's success in the ESC waned, possibly because the ESC was no longer considered as important in Ireland for the state's international image now that Ireland could promote itself through its economic success. Ireland also no longer profited from the image of a poor, small underdog in the ESC as the contest's expansion in the 1990s brought in new underdogs from Central and East Europe, many of which were the sources of immigrants to a more prosperous Ireland. The decline in Ireland's success in the ESC also accompanied an increase in Euroscepticism in the state: despite having economically benefitted from EU membership, Irish citizens initially rejected in referenda in 2001 and 2008 the treaties of Nice and Lisbon respectively that would reform the EU. Although the Irish entry in the 2007 ESC, 'They Can't Stop the Spring', had been about European unity, to the 2008 ESC the Irish public decided in the national selection to send a puppet, Dustin the Turkey, whose song 'Irelande Douze Pointe' (Ireland, Twelve Points) mocked both Europe and the ESC.[33]

In the 1995 ESC, which was won by Norway, Fionnuala Sherry, one of the members of the victorious group Secret Garden, was also Irish. Although Norway, unlike Ireland, had since the 1970s been experiencing an economic boom based on its energy industry – which was portrayed in the interval act and postcards of the 1996 ESC – NRK still drew on commercial sponsorship when it staged the contest in 1996. That ESC was pioneering as it was the first time that the contest was held in a high-capacity arena, the Oslo Spektrum, which it also was in 1998 when Birmingham's National Indoor Arena was the venue.

Sweden topped both of these in 2000 by hosting the ESC in the Stockholm Globe Arena which, with a capacity of 16,000 spectators, was the biggest venue until then that the contest had ever been staged in. This was superseded by Denmark in 2001, when the contest was held in Copenhagen's Parken Stadium with 38,000 spectators. These venues differed from the conference centres, concert houses or television studios that had usually been the venues for the contest previously. The change in the type of venue used to host the ESC signified a new focus in the contest on the participation of both businesses and the public, such as in the introduction of televoting which brought profits for telephone companies as well as the sale of relatively expensive tickets for the live event. It was ironic that Nordic states were at the forefront of the ESC's commercialization after the Cold War, considering that they had been among the most vocal critics in the EBU of the commercialization of the ESC in the 1970s and that they still did not allow advertising in their broadcasts after 1989. Yet, in the 1990s, the Nordic states were themselves also seeing their social democracies transformed by neo-liberalism. Following an economic crisis in the early 1990s which prompted such reforms, the Swedish export industry boomed and became especially renowned for its consumer goods. These included popular music, and as the Swedish popular music industry also developed through the success of Swedish entries in the ESC, the Swedish popular music industry provided a model for the further commercialization of the contest. From the 1990s, Swedish composers and songwriters increasingly featured in the production of ESC entries for other states, while the Swedish national broadcasting organization, Sweden's Television (SVT), provided technical assistance to the national broadcasting organizations in East Europe and Turkey that hosted the ESC.[34] Svante Stockselius, a former SVT official, also served as the ESC's executive supervisor – the leading EBU official responsible for overseeing the organisation of the contest – from 2004 to 2010.

It was at the 2002 ESC in Tallinn that the branding of each contest further developed with the adoption of a motto, alongside a logo that had already been created for each contest by the host national broadcasting organizations since the ESC's beginning. However, while the Estonian national broadcasting organization, Estonian Television, struggled with its financing of the 2002 ESC, two other states from the former USSR set records for the amount of money invested into hosting the ESC. The first was Russia: after Dima Bilan won the

2008 ESC with the song 'Believe', the Russian national broadcasting organization, Channel One, invested approximately forty-two million American dollars into hosting the ESC in Moscow in 2009.[35] An elaborate stage was built that broke the world record for the amount of LED lighting used in a single event, and the final of the 2009 ESC also had exclusive acts by the international performing troupes Cirque de Soleil and Fuerza Bruta. This ESC was viewed by the Russian government as a prestige project, and then prime minister Putin personally visited the show's venue to view the preparations for it.[36] Although it was held against the background of a brief recession that hit Russia after the 2008 ESC, the 2009 ESC was a showcase for the economic growth that Russia had experienced in the previous decade as well as its revived political power on the world stage. The combination of Russia's economic and military might was epitomized by the joint performance of t.A.T.u. and the Alexandrov Ensemble, an official choir of the Russian army that is also known as the Red Army Choir, in the interval act of the first semi-final and accompanied onstage by a mock blue fighter jet and pink military tank. The 2009 ESC was the first international mega event that Russia hosted after the Cold War, and it was in this regard a prelude to the 2014 Winter Olympic Games in Sochi that Russia had been awarded in 2007, which would be the most expensive Olympic Games ever staged, and the 2018 World Cup that Russia submitted its successful bid for in 2009.

The next record breaker for the hosting of an ESC was Azerbaijan, which in 2012 invested the largest amount of money ever into the contest: estimates put the figure for the 2012 ESC at approximately seventy-six million American dollars, with additional indirect expenses mostly related to associated construction projects at approximately 645 million American dollars.[37] The 2012 ESC's motto 'Light Your Fire' was a reference to Azerbaijan being dubbed the 'land of fire' partly because of the presence on its landscape of naturally occurring flames caused by natural gas and oil deposits, but one could also interpret it as a reference to the energy industry that fuelled Azerbaijan's economic growth from 2005. Yet, in hindsight, the 'fire' also came to symbolize the fact that the 2012 ESC was one of the most politically controversial contests in the history of the ESC. A whole area of Baku was redeveloped for the 2012 ESC with some of its residents being forcibly evicted, drawing criticisms from international human rights organizations; money that was intended to be invested in a water distribution improvement project was also instead diverted to the contest.[38]

A brand new arena, the Baku Crystal Hall, was constructed especially for the contest, with its facade being lit up before each entry in the colours of the flag of the entry's state. Next to it stood National Flag Square, which had until the year before been the world's tallest flagpole. Other lavish construction projects, such as a new building for the Azerbaijan Carpet Museum and the Flame Towers skyscrapers, were also underway during the 2012 ESC. The Heydar Aliyev Centre, a cultural centre designed by architect Zaha Hadid and named after the first president of Azerbaijan, was officially opened just before the 2012 ESC by his son Ilham, who succeeded his father as president in 2003.

Also benefitting from Azerbaijan's economic boom were Austrian, British, German and Swiss firms that were involved in the construction of the Baku Crystal Hall or the technical production of the 2012 ESC. International composers and lyricists, especially ones from Sweden, had also been employed to produce Azerbaijan's entries for the ESC after its debut in the contest in 2008, including for its winning song 'Running Scared' in the 2011 ESC. A major sponsor of the 2012 ESC was the telecommunications company Azercell, which was owned by Sweden's TeliaSonera, in which the Swedish government held the largest ownership stake. A month before the 2012 ESC, SVT produced a documentary in which TeliaSonera was alleged to have cooperated with the Azerbaijani secret service in the surveillance of citizens – including those who had voted for Armenia in the 2009 ESC – and in 2014 the company became embroiled in a corruption scandal involving it and the family of President Aliyev.[39] The Azerbaijani government saw the ESC in Baku as an opportunity to demonstrate that it could organize other international mega events as well. These included the 2020 Olympic Games, although Baku's application for that was rejected by the International Olympic Committee during the week of the 2012 ESC; the city was, however, later in 2012 awarded the European Olympic Committees' 2015 European Games, for which the Baku Crystal Hall would be one of the venues.

In between the contests in Moscow and Baku, the EU faced its financial crisis. The economically most powerful state in the EU, Germany, which would bear the greatest cost for bailing out the indebted states, won the 2010 ESC at a time when the financial crisis was generating political tensions within the EU. This was Germany's second ever win in the ESC, despite it having participated in all but one of the contests since 1956. Germany spent the second highest amount until then to stage an ESC: the 2011 ESC in Düsseldorf cost approximately thirty-seven million American dollars.[40] Germany had hosted the World Cup in 2006, an event which was viewed in the international media as promoting an unthreatening German patriotism that underlined the state's contemporary cultural, economic and social achievements. Amid criticism that Germany was becoming too dominant in the EU because of its economic power, which some Europeans continued to be apprehensive about because of its militaristic past, Germany was also promoted as multicultural and tolerant in the 2011 ESC. This was most obvious in the postcards that were used to introduce the entries, which included citizens from other European states working in Germany who highlighted the fact that the state was a major destination for intra-European economic immigrants. As the German government was facing criticism from other EU members for being too strict in dictating EU policies in the financial crisis, the message that was sent from the ESC 2011 was that Germany was an accepting and generous place for all Europeans.

Such criticism of the German government especially came from Greece, which was the state that was most affected by the debt crisis. Some Greek media reports equated Merkel and her ministers with Nazis, even as Greece's far right Golden Dawn party – which had its own neo-Nazi tendencies – was growing in popularity.[41] The Greek economy had experienced continued economic growth from the early 1990s to 2007. However, a combination of factors, including excessive government spending, the impact of Eurozone membership and structural weaknesses – the Greek entry in the 1993 ESC, 'Ellada, hora tou fotos' (Greece, Country of Light), had already called for Greece to modernize and reform – fostered the debt crisis, which also saw an increase in the emigration of Greek citizens. Greece won the 2005 ESC with the Swedish-Greek artist Elena Paparizou singing 'My Number One'; she had previously represented Greece as part of the duo Antique in the 2001 ESC. Paparizou personified the migration networks typical of ESC artists, having been born and raised in Sweden by Greek immigrant parents, as well as the international influence of the Swedish popular music industry through which she began her career.[42] Before Athens hosted the 2006 ESC, it had staged the 2004 Summer Olympic Games whose high cost contributed to Greece's debt crisis. The 2006 ESC was itself held in the Olympic Indoor Hall in Athens that was renovated for the Olympic Games, and one of the hosts of the 2006 ESC, Sakis Rouvas, had during the Olympic Games carried the Olympic torch and – like Vissi, who represented Greece in the 2006 ESC –

performed in the closing ceremony. The 2006 ESC did not contribute to Greece's indebtedness, though, with the Greek national broadcasting organization, the Hellenic Broadcasting Corporation (ERT), making a net profit from it.[43]

However, the debt crisis would have an impact on Greece's continued participation in the ESC. This was even brought into question in the first years of the crisis, although in the end Greece managed to participate every year by economizing on its entries. As with other entries from states that were hard hit by the financial crisis, costs were cut by involving commercial or private sponsors, not staging a national selection or spending less on the promotion and staging of entries. The music video for Greece's entry 'Aphrodisiac' in the 2012 ESC, for example, was simply filmed in a shopping mall. ERT was closed down by the centre-right Greek government in 2013 for two years due to what the government considered to be ERT's excessive operating costs, although it continued to do limited broadcasts with the support of the EBU. From 2013, the commercial television broadcaster MAD TV, a music channel, collaborated with ERT and then the interim national broadcasting organization, New Hellenic Radio, Internet and Television (NERIT), in organizing and producing the Greek entries for the ESC. Although NERIT joined the EBU just days before the 2014 ESC began, the EBU wanted to maintain Greece in the contest due to the state's track record in the ESC and the popularity of the contest there.[44] Even during the financial crisis, Greek entries placed relatively well in the ESC, including 'OPA!', 'Watch My Dance' and 'Alcohol Is Free', all of which had lyrics that alluded to the state's economic problems.

Other southern European states that suffered from the debt crisis, however, withdrew from the ESC in some years. Cyprus, which was especially affected by the debt crisis because of its connections with the Greek economy, did not participate in 2014 for financial reasons; the close connections between Cyprus and Greece were in this case not beneficial to the former in the contest. Then there was Portugal, which did not compete in the 2013 ESC for financial reasons. However, in the 2011 ESC Portugal had been represented by the group Homens da Luta (Men of the Struggle), a comedy group whose songs were based on ones from the revolutionary period in the years just after the Carnation Revolution. The group's ESC entry also echoed the politically engaged Portuguese entries in the contest from the mid-1970s: 'A luta é alegria' (The Struggle is Joy) called for people to get together and demonstrate and was a reference to the public protests against the austerity measures taken by the Portuguese government. Two of the group's members wore red carnations onstage, and one of them was also in an army uniform. The entry itself had democratic legitimacy as it had won the national selection based on the televote, which judged it the best song, whereas it only came sixth in the jury vote.

The most explicit statement on the EU's financial crisis came from a non-member state, Montenegro, which began its negotiations for EU accession in 2012 just over a month after the ESC was staged in Baku. Montenegro had already adopted the euro as its official currency in 2002, after having used the Deutschmark in the late 1990s due to the economic crisis in Yugoslavia that had resulted in the hyperinflation of the local currency, the dinar. Although the European Central Bank did not initially oppose Montenegro's adoption of the euro as its official currency, the issue became problematic in Montenegro's EU accession negotiations considering that EU accession has normally been a prerequisite for Eurozone membership. RTCG withdrew from the ESC in 2010 and 2011 for financial reasons. However, for the 2012 ESC RTCG internally selected one of Montenegro's most politically engaged artists, Rambo Amadeus, who had even been referred to in the lyrics of the Yugoslav entry in the 1991 ESC, 'Brazil'. At the 2012 ESC he performed 'Euro Neuro', which placed lowly in its semi-final. The satirical song was critical of the EU's handling of the financial crisis yet also of the economic dominance of northern European states over southern ones. Its music video depicted a Montenegro that was taken over by West European tourists, contrasting poor locals against a 'Miss Sweden' sunbathing on a yacht – the irony being that Sweden was an EU member that had not adopted the euro, while Montenegro had the opposite situation.

A similar message could be read less directly from the Croatian entry in the 2013 ESC, 'Mižerja' (Misery), which was sung by Klapa s mora (Klapa from the Sea) and internally selected by HTV. The song was performed in the style of Dalmatian folk *klapa* (group a cappella singing) and its themes were also influenced by the Adriatic coast, the centre of Croatia's burgeoning tourist industry. However, the lyrics focused on the fact that the singers were poor and had nothing else to offer except faith and love. It was a discordant message from a Croatia that would just months later enter the EU as one of its poorest states, but it was also a metaphor for the fatigue with EU enlargement that was felt in Croatia due to the length of its accession negotiations, and in the EU more widely because of the financial crisis. HTV withdrew from the ESC in 2014 for financial reasons, as did national broadcasting organizations from other southeastern European states that were not in the Eurozone, namely Bulgaria and Serbia. That of Bosnia and Herzegovina had already done so in 2013: even after the Bosnian and Herzegovinian band Dubioza kolektiv released the song 'Euro Song' in which the group criticized West Europe's political leaders, anti-immigration policies and the EP and proclaimed that they did not just want to be European only at the ESC, from 2013 to 2015 Bosnians and Herzegovinians could not even affirm their belonging to Europe through the contest. The national broadcasting organizations of Hungary, Poland and Slovakia also cited financial issues as the reason for their withdrawals from the contest between 2010 and 2014, with the Polish one additionally being financially constrained in 2012 because of Poland's hosting of the UEFA European Championship. The financial cost of participating in the ESC was a major reason why the small national broadcasting organizations from Andorra, Luxembourg and Monaco each only participated in the ESC a few times after 1989; Luxembourg, for example, was not at all represented in the ESC after 1993.

At the northern end of Europe were the national broadcasting organizations of its wealthiest states, where there was no question of them not participating in the ESC because of financial issues and which continued to stage extravagant national selections, such as the Melody Festival in Sweden. They could also afford to invest into the elaborate staging of entries in the ESC; indeed, one could usually measure the economic health of a state by the effects and props, and especially fireworks, that its entries could afford to use on the ESC stage. Nonetheless, after the record spending on the ESC 2012 in Baku, SVT decided to stage a less expensive ESC in Malmö in 2013, with that contest costing approximately twenty-six million American dollars.[45] Compared to other EU members, Sweden had fared relatively well economically during the European debt crisis, partly because it was not a member of the Eurozone. However, SVT's modest budget for the 2013 ESC was a message of fiscal responsibility in a time of European economic crisis and a rejection of one-upmanship in contest spending: after all, how would smaller states represented in the ESC be able to afford – or even want – to host the contest if its cost kept on increasing? That, however, was not the message that was sent from the 2014 ESC in Copenhagen, which ended up costing approximately fifty-four million American dollars.[46] That figure made it the second most expensive ESC ever staged. The 2014 ESC went three times over budget, especially because DR decided to stage it in an old shipyard, the B&W Hallerne, that needed to be completely refurbished and to transform the island on which it was situated into 'Eurovision Island'.[47] The economic legacy of the ESC could thus also be burdensome for a host city.

The ESC was established in the context of the Eurovision Network's original aim of reducing production costs for public service broadcasters through international cooperation. Sixty years later, it was widely criticized for costing national broadcasting organizations too much. Despite the increasing commercialization of the contest after 1989, its commercial impact was also arguable. When it came to launching international superstars, the contest had not been so successful in this since the victory of Dion in 1988. That the ESC did not necessarily bring the winning artist major commercial success was a reason why established stars often shunned the contest, and after 2000 the ESC instead became more of a next step for the victorious artists from the reality television talent shows that were blooming all over Europe. For national broadcasting organizations, the financial benefits of hosting the ESC were varied: for some, like DR in 2014 and RTÉ in the 1990s, it drained resources; for others, like ERT in 2006 and SVT in 2013, it was a profitable enterprise. Yet, for all of them it was an opportunity to gain experience in producing an international mega event and boost their profiles in the international television industry. The commercial benefit for cities that hosted the contest was also mixed: for cities that were already well-established international tourist destinations, like Istanbul and Moscow, the contest brought extra visitors but not a drastic change to the tourism industry; for lesser-known destinations, such as Baku or Belgrade, the contest gave them an opportunity to brand themselves to an international market. The biggest benefit of the ESC came for states that found themselves at a historical juncture and used the contest to promote refashioned cultural and political identities, especially in the cases of the East European states that hosted the ESC from 2002, although for some of them it also put their political problems – such as their democratic development – into the international spotlight.

While national broadcasting organizations had during the Cold War often struggled to reconcile their public service missions with the commercial interests of record companies in the ESC, their engagement with commercial sponsorship in the contest from the 1990s posed new dilemmas regarding their public service aims. This figured in public debates on how far national broadcasting organizations should be allowed to supplement their budgets – most of which were largely financed by public fees or taxes – with commercial revenues. In 2010, the Norwegian Media Authority, the Norwegian government agency responsible for media regulation, criticized NRK for generating revenues from televoting in the ESC, believing that this went against NRK's non-commercial, public service remit.[48] The national broadcasting organizations were often caught between, on the one hand, political pressure not to squander public money for an event that was widely considered to be excessively costly and, on the other hand, to take into consideration the public interest in selecting an ESC entry that was nationally representative as well as to deliver a show that was widely popular. In the end, whoever was selected to represent a state in the ESC could have been representing a commercial interest, the interest of the national broadcasting organization, the public interest or some combination of each of these. The national trademark that the artist performed under was therefore questionable: even though the EBU had decided to have entries in the ESC appear under the names of states because these were recognizable to the international audience, those names were often just labels that masked personal and commercial ambitions and had little to do with national or public interests. Indeed, just as the Icelandic government opposed its state's name being trademarked in the EU by the British supermarket chain Iceland in 2014,[49] the continued commercialization of the ESC also begged the question: what or who was actually being represented in the contest in the name of the state?

Democracy

The increasing commercialization of the ESC and the social diversity promoted through the contest's entries after 1989 both highlighted the ESC's fraught relationship with democratic values. Throughout its history, the ESC also grappled with issues of democracy through its voting system, especially the inclusion of public voting in the national selections and the final itself. Public voting in the ESC had been discussed by the EBU as early as 1969, when the Luxembourgian Broadcasting Company suggested that the voting in each state should be half determined by a jury composed of record industry professionals and half by the public which would vote through a hit parade.[50] In 1991, the emphasis on the public representativeness of the juries was diminished when these were required to be half composed of music industry professionals, again reflecting the commercial reorientation of the ESC in the 1990s. With the introduction of public voting by telephone for some participants in 1997, which became compulsory for all of them from 2003, a new era of public voting in the ESC began, although a jury was still used in the case of technical problems or if there were not enough people voting in a state, especially in the cases of Andorra, Monaco and San Marino. SMS voting was also introduced in 2002. Debates over public voting in the ESC that occurred in liberal democracies after 1989 highlighted problems concerning the democratic deficits in these states as well as within the EU. They posed questions regarding the political influence on and public involvement in the decision-making processes of national broadcasting organizations, which in liberal democratic states were ideally meant to be an expression and instrument of public democracy. The ESC was a concentrated forum for such debates because it was a rare example of direct democracy in cultural diplomacy. No other international mega event has employed public participation in the selection of its participants and winners like the ESC has: sporting events like the Olympic Games and the UEFA European Championship rely on sportspeople who prove themselves through scientifically measurable physical achievements, an aspect which is also absent in the Venice Biennale, but for which national representatives are chosen through varying processes that usually involve culture ministries and professional experts.

The national publics' willingness to participate in the selection process for the ESC and to decide on the representation of their state was legitimized by their financial payments to the national broadcasting organizations, and also because popular music – as its name highlights – is itself based on mass desires that produce a commercial affirmation of a song's success; as a report on the 1958 ESC by NTS put it: 'Light music, after all, exists by the grace of the public taste'.[51] Although voting results in the ESC after 1989 were still deceivingly perceived as representing a homogenous national public opinion as they continued to be presented under the names of the states that they came from, in liberal democratic states they were determined by the decisions of the national broadcasting organizations, juries and publics, and not by the government. With their public service missions, the national broadcasting organizations that were members of the EBU were meant to be independent from government interference as well as the commercial motivations of private television broadcasters. As a result, liberal democratic governments were not directly involved in the national selections for the ESC. However, there was also another issue at play in this regard: because the ESC was often publicly disparaged for being decadent, unserious or wasteful, especially if a state's entries had not done well in the contest in the recent past, liberal democratic governments also did not want to compromise themselves by being involved in the national selections. Their approaches to the contest usually changed if their state won the ESC, as the organization of the event then required financial or logistical support from local or national governments, which also saw the potential for appropriating the contest in their cultural diplomacies and place branding.

As the rules for the ESC left the method of choosing the entry that would represent a state up to the national broadcasting organization, this meant that various alternatives continued to be used after 1989, including ones based on a jury or public vote, a combination of the two, or a decision made internally by officials from the national broadcasting organization who sometimes also considered the opinions of music industry professionals. In the cases in which entries were selected by a jury or internally within the national broadcasting organization, this often drew public criticism: when the Ukrainian national broadcasting organization, the National Television Company of Ukraine, internally selected an entry for the 2010 ESC, it came under pressure to reverse this decision and stage a national selection with a jury and public voting. A national broadcasting organization usually decided not to involve the public in the national selection for the ESC if entries from its state had not placed highly in the contest in recent years and the national public had lost interest in the event, with the cost of staging a national selection that could achieve acceptable viewership ratings usually being cited as the reason – and the most compelling one in times of the economic crises that most European states faced in the sixth decade of the ESC. Sometimes, however, the national broadcasting organization took full control of the selection process for the ESC entry with the aim of doing well in the final, such as if its officials considered public tastes too parochial to be able to choose an internationally competitive entry, as had also been the case during the Cold War. When this technocratic way of selection took place, the cultural, economic and political connections, interests and preferences of the officials from the national broadcasting organization were internally decisive but not always publicly transparent. Officials from ORF were politically activist when they internally selected the Rounder Girls and Wurst – as well as Brauer, Corren and Gott during the Cold War – to represent Austria in the ESC. Yet, the opportunity to make such political statements lay not only at the stage of an entry's selection: even after a public vote, a national broadcasting organization could also change the message of a song through interventions in the original performance, such as by changing the language or the staging, as was seen in the queering of Šerifović's performance.

In other states, however, allegations of vote rigging in the national selection were symptomatic of wider corruption that hampered these states' transitions to liberal democracy. The Moldovan authorities, for example, blocked a protest by the non-governmental organization Hyde Park against the non-transparent process of the Moldovan national selection for the ESC in 2006, which had also allegedly occurred in the national selection in 2005 when Moldova debuted in the ESC. This was one of the reasons why Hyde Park won a case that it had brought against the Republic of Moldova in the CoE's European Court of Human Rights, which judged that the Moldovan authorities had violated the group's right to freedom of assembly as per the European Convention on Human Rights.[52] There were also allegations of vote rigging in Moldova in the final of the 2005 ESC, when its televote was replaced by a jury vote and the final results favoured the Russian entry over the Romanian one. National media that was critical of the government of the Party of Communists – the only communist party in Central and East Europe that after 1989 held a majority in a government, which it did from 2001 to 2009 – alleged that there had been political interference so that the results would reflect the party's policy of maintaining a distinct Moldovan national identity in contrast to those political parties who considered Moldovans to be part of the Romanian nation.[53] After 2005, Moldova and Romania usually awarded twelve points to each other in their ESC voting. Expert juries were reintroduced in the ESC in 2009 with the expectation being that the music industry professionals in them would provide an objective counterweight to the televoting, and the national broadcasting organizations freely chose the jury members in accordance with rules set by the EBU. The identities of the jurors and how each of them ranked the entries before they were combined into a final result were kept confidential until 2014, following allegations that İTV had attempted to buy votes in several states in order to produce a favourable result for Azerbaijan. Although the EBU did not find proof of the allegations against İTV, it adopted a rule that banned national broadcasting organizations from the contest for three years if they were found guilty of vote rigging.[54] However, this rule was not applied in 2014 after members of the Georgian jury were found to have each allocated their points in almost exactly the same way, after which its results were invalidated and only the Georgian televoting ones were counted.[55] Yet, the public release of the identities of the jurors and detailed breakdowns of their voting possibly had the effect of self-censorship among some jury members, for they might have chosen not to vote for entries which for political reasons could be unpopular in the states of the jurors: if, for example, an Azerbaijani jury member voted for an Armenian entry, or if a juror from a state with a high level of social homophobia voted for a queer act. Indeed, in the 2014 ESC, when the voting was most controversial regarding Wurst, there was a wide gap in several Central and East European states – including Armenia, Azerbaijan, Belarus, Macedonia, Montenegro and Poland – between a favourable public vote for her and a low placing by their juries. It was likely that jury members were cautious of giving their vote to her because of what they considered to be high levels of homophobia in their societies and the negative impact that they thought their support for Wurst could have on their professional opportunities and public image.

The discussions on the voting system in the ESC after 1989 echoed broader debates in the EU concerning its own democratic deficit, from the direct role of citizens in decision making to how much the voting in EU institutions should be based on the representation of populations or states. The EU tried to make itself more democratically legitimate by increasing the powers of the popularly elected EP through the successive treaties that were adopted to reform the EU and by making the bureaucratic workings of EU institutions more transparent. The EBU similarly did this in the ESC by introducing public voting and making voting results transparent. Still, the issue of technocratic government remained an issue in the EU, especially during the financial crisis when such governments were installed in Italy and Greece under the prime ministerships of Mario Monti and Lucas Papademos respectively. Eurosceptics continued to criticise the EU for being too distant, elitist and technocratic. Eurofederalists, on the other hand, distrusted national electorates for being too parochial in their interests and of lacking altruism for the Europeanist project. Similar tensions existed in the ESC between those who sought a complete return to public voting and those who argued that the expert intervention of music industry professionals was an objective counterweight to public voting. However, the major difference between the voting systems in the ESC and the EU was how they addressed the different population sizes of states. Whereas decision making in the EU always had some element of qualified majority voting that took this into account, and seats in the EP were also accordingly apportioned among states by population, the ESC was based on the principle of each state having the same voting power. The Big Five principle became an exception in this regard, as it ensured that some of the most populous states represented in the ESC had entries in and could vote in the finals, and it also allowed their national audiences to vote in the semi-finals. In 2008, the ESC was expanded to include two semi-finals, with the Big Five each being allowed to vote in one of these. The placement of entries in these semi-finals was determined by a complex system of lot drawing that limited the number of states with close cultural affinities in the same semi-final. The concept of the Big Five was, however, not new in the EBU: it had already been an organizational principle in the EBU during the Cold War;[56] the idea of having semi-finals had also first been discussed in the Programme Committee in 1961, but not along the lines of dividing big states and smaller ones.[57] Still, all of the changes to the ESC's voting system from 2000 did not translate into high results for entries from the Big Five which, with the exception of Italy, had never fared as poorly in the contest as they did from 2000. This was perhaps due to the fact that their entries were, unlike the others, not performed twice onstage in a semi-final and the final, or because national audiences from other states resented the privileging of the Big Five and protested accordingly in their voting.

It was ironic that TRT became the biggest critic of the Big Five system and the staunchest advocate of public voting in the ESC, considering the increasing authoritarianism of prime minister-cum-president Erdoğan and his government's suppression of media freedom. The 2004 ESC was staged in Istanbul's Abdi İpekçi Arena, which was named after a left-wing journalist who was assassinated in 1979, with one of his assassins having been Mehmet Ali Ağca, who later shot Pope John Paul II in 1981. The 2004 ESC ended with the hosts farewelling viewers with the famous quotation from Atatürk that was considered a tenet of Turkish government policies: 'Peace in the world, peace in the country', better translated as 'Peace at home, peace in the world'. Yet, in 2014, Turkish journalists who were critical of the Erdoğan government could hardly live in peace, with the non-governmental organisation Freedom House downgrading the Turkish media's status to 'not free' and Turkey having the highest number of imprisoned journalists in the world.[58] That TRT favoured the 'voice of the people' in the ESC over that of experts or states was also a metaphor for the divisions within Turkish society between those who believed that its secular system should be upheld by the judicial and military establishment and those like Erdoğan who presented themselves as governing by the 'will of the people'.

Like Turkey, Russia was also excluded from the Big Five even though it was by far the most populous state participating in the ESC, and the television host Yana Churikova reminded viewers that Russia was the biggest state in the contest when she presented the Russian voting results in the 2004 ESC. Media freedom in Russia also suffered under the authoritarianism of Putin, who served as either the president or prime minister of Russia from 1999. During the Soviet era, Putin had worked as an intelligence officer for the Committee for State Security, or KGB, and he was stationed in East Germany from 1985 to 1990. In the final of the 2009 ESC, a parodical film was shown during the interval that sought to dispel myths about Russia: it insisted that Russians were no longer living in the USSR under the control of the KGB. In 2014, Freedom House also rated the national media in Russia as being 'not free', noting the government's control over national broadcasting organizations such as Channel One and Russia 1, which were responsible for organizing Russia's ESC entries.[59] While the Putin government avidly appropriated the ESC in its cultural diplomacy, some Russian politicians also alleged that the voting results in the contest were rigged against Russia. After the 2013 ESC, in which the Russian entry unusually did not receive any points from Azerbaijan, the Russian minister of foreign affairs, Sergei Lavrov, stated at a press conference with his Azerbaijani counterpart Elmar Mammadyarov that the votes had been 'stolen' and 'the outrageous action at Eurovision regarding the Russian contestant will not go unanswered'; Mammadyarov responded that his government would launch an investigation into the matter.[60] With the increase in political tensions between Russia and the West that was made obvious at the 2014 ESC, some Russian politicians called for the ISC to be revived for participants from the former USSR and Asian states from the Shanghai Cooperation Organisation as an expression of Russia's geopolitical power and Eurasian economic aspirations, and as a way of combating the 'pro-gay' and 'pro-Ukrainian' politics of the ESC.[61] However, the ISC was only revived once when it was held in Sochi in 2008, and then for states from the Commonwealth of Independent as well as Latvia. Calling that ISC 'revived' was a misconception, of course, because the ISC was during the Cold War never a Russian-led event or just for parts of the USSR.

While liberal democracies represented in the EBU grappled with issues of representation and transparency in their national broadcasting organizations, government control over the media thus remained an issue in authoritarian states whose national broadcasting organizations were members of the EBU. As with the fall of the right-wing dictatorships and the transitions to liberal democracy in Portugal and Spain in the 1970s, the ESC had a symbolic role in the democratization movements in some East European states after the fall of communism, especially those from the former USSR in which the transition was thwarted by authoritarianism, like Ukraine. However, together with Russia, other states from the former USSR continued to have authoritarian governments, such as Azerbaijan. Azerbaijan entered the CoE in 2001, but its membership in this organization remained controversial due to the authoritarian government of Aliyev; ironically, membership in an organization that promoted democracy, human rights, the rule of law and media freedom allowed Azerbaijan to join the EBU. After the state-controlled national broadcasting organization AzTV was rejected for EBU membership for not having a public service character, İTV was admitted into the EBU in 2007 as the Azerbaijani member, and in 2008 Azerbaijan and San Marino became the last members of the CoE to join the ESC. Yet, despite its professed public service aim, İTV remained effectively controlled by the Azerbaijani government.

From the beginning of Azerbaijan's participation in the ESC in 2008, its government saw the contest as an important stage for the state's international promotion in the context of an economic boom based on its energy industry. The winners of the 2011 ESC, Ell & Nikki, or Eldar Gasimov and Nigar Jamal, were received by Aliyev and the first lady, Mehriban Aliyeva, upon their return to Azerbaijan after their ESC victory. Aliyeva would also head the organizing committee of the 2012 ESC and her son-in-law, the billionaire businessman and singer Emin Agalarov, performed the interval act in the final. The concentration of power in Azerbaijan's first family undermined its government's Western aspirations. However, participation in the ESC was also an expression of the pro-Western foreign policy that the Aliyev government pursued because of economic interests – especially those related to the Azerbaijani energy industry – as well as to attract Western political support in the face of conflicts with Armenia and Iran. That Azerbaijan should define itself as 'European' – its official tourism slogan at the time of the 2012 ESC was 'European Charm of the Orient', and Gasimov referred to it when he co-hosted the 2012 ESC as 'the easternmost part of Europe' – was politically surprising for many European journalists covering the 2012 ESC, but the Azerbaijani definition of 'Europe' was also self-referential. It was defined by historical ties to Russia and Turkey, two European powers that had a strong cultural, economic and political impact on Azerbaijan. It was also defined against Azerbaijan's southern neighbour Iran.

The participation of Azerbaijan in the ESC thus reflected the realpolitik towards Baku of Western states, which tolerated Aliyev's authoritarianism because of economic and geopolitical interests. Still, there was widespread international media and political attention given to Azerbaijan as it prepared for the 2012 ESC. Both the CoE and the EP had their biggest ever discussions on the ESC because of its hosting in Azerbaijan: the imprisonment of artists and journalists critical of the government, suppression of opposition protests and forced evictions of residents to make way for construction projects were the focuses of the organizations' attention. The EP adopted two resolutions on Azerbaijan that referred to the ESC.[62] Herman Van Rompuy, the first president of the EU's European Council, José Manuel Barroso, the president of the European Commission, and Catherine Ashton, the high representative of the EU for Foreign Affairs and Security Policy, all congratulated Azerbaijani officials whom they met on Azerbaijan's ESC win and urged them to use the ESC to improve the state's human rights record and international image. Barroso said in a statement after meeting Aliyev:

> I look forward to continuing our cooperation and to bringing Azerbaijan and the EU even closer together. I think we can be inspired by Azerbaijan's impressive victory in the Eurovision Song Contest last month, which was a first step in that regard. The fact that a majority of the Europeans voted for

> Azerbaijan in this European contest showed the sincere good will there is in Europe regarding Azerbaijan. I know that this will be a year in which the international spotlight will be in your country, and I am sure that you will use this time to show commitment to the modernisation of your country and also how committed you are on our European common values.[63]

Germany's minister of foreign affairs, Guido Westerwelle, also declared that he hoped that the 2012 ESC would be an opportunity to 'promote our democratic values'.[64] The actress Anke Engelke, who co-hosted the 2011 ESC, made a similar statement on-air when she presented Germany's voting results in the 2012 ESC: 'Tonight nobody could vote for their own country. But it is good to be able to vote. And it is good to have a choice. Good luck on your journey, Azerbaijan. Europe is watching you.' Loreen also met with human rights campaigners in Azerbaijan during the week of the ESC.[65] Yet, despite all of these calls, as well as the EBU's attempts to address criticism of itself by instituting initiatives to democratize the Azerbaijani media,[66] the ESC did not bring democratic change to Azerbaijan. When Azerbaijan took over the rotating chairmanship of the CoE's Committee of Ministers in 2014, its government was still being criticized for its authoritarianism. For the 2012 ESC, the local Sing for Democracy campaign had been formed and its members staged protests in Baku to draw international media attention to Azerbaijan's human rights record.[67] However, leaders of the campaign were subsequently monitored by the Azerbaijani authorities and in 2014 one of them, Rasul Jafarov, was jailed as he sought to establish a similar campaign for the European Games.[68] According to Freedom House, the level of media freedom in Azerbaijan not only remained 'not free' but even declined after 2012.[69]

Another example of an authoritarian state whose national broadcasting organization joined the ESC between 1990 and 2016 was Belarus. Due to its human rights record, especially its extant death penalty, Belarus was not a member of the CoE, and it also had tense relations with the EU because of the policies of its President Aleksandar Lukashenko, who ruled Belarus from 1994 and whom the international media dubbed 'Europe's last dictator'. Lukashenko himself also slurred Western politicians who criticized his way of rule: his infamous barb against Westerwelle, who was openly gay, was that it was 'better to be a dictator than gay'.[70] In the era of European unification, Belarus was Europe's last internal outsider. The national broadcasting organization of Belarus, the

Belarusian Television and Radio Company (BTRC), joined the EBU in 1993; it debuted in the ESC in 2004 and participated in it every year thereafter. Unlike its neighbours Latvia, Russia and Ukraine, Belarus never won the ESC and its entries mostly did not even qualify for the final. However, the Belarusian-born Rybak, who emigrated to Norway as a child, won the 2009 ESC for Norway. Belarusian entries also did win the Junior ESC (JESC) – which was started in 2003 as a children's version of the ESC – in 2005 and 2007, and Minsk hosted the JESC in 2010. Despite Belarus' poor track record in the ESC, Lukashenko was an avid follower of the contest and made several public statements about it. The Belarusian entry in the 2011 ESC, 'I Love Belarus' (I Love Belarus), was a statement of national pride in the face of criticism of Lukashenko's authoritarianism by Western governments and organizations. That song replaced 'Born in Byelorussia', which had originally been internally selected by BTRC for the 2011 ESC and had lyrics that expressed nostalgia for the USSR, which was also a mark of Lukashenko's rule. However, 'Born in Byelorussia' had been performed before the release date allowed for ESC entries and so had to be replaced. Lukashenko also accused Western states of rigging the vote at the ESC, even as he himself was criticized by Western governments and organizations for not allowing fair and free elections.[71] Yet, when it appeared in 2012 that the voting in the national selection had been rigged in favour of Alyona Lanskaya, Lukashenko ordered an investigation into the result which confirmed that the rock band Litesound was the legitimate winner; Litesound also included an Italian member, Jacopo Massa, who made the group appear more cosmopolitan. Lukashenko publicly declared his support for Lanskaya when she went on to represent Belarus at the 2013 ESC, and before which he reiterated to a group of university students in Minsk that the voting results in the ESC were in any case biased against Belarus:

> Maybe, I take this contest too close to heart, though I understand very well what is going on there, the things that you might not be aware of. I know that this contest is not objective at all. Any state, if needed, can give you any number of points, and what you see on the screen, these points and so on – everything is fake, a show.[72]

The concept of 'European values' was a contested one in Europe after the end of the Cold War, both in terms of defining 'Europe' as well as its 'values', and this was also reflected in the ESC. Although the EU attempted to define these values in terms of cultural and social diversity, human rights and liberal democracy, the national broadcasting organizations of its member states were not necessarily at the vanguard of championing these in the ESC, and these values were often strategically used in the contest to improve the international images of states in the context of political controversies. Like the EU, the ESC had to grapple with issues of democracy, especially as its voting system was reformed in response to enlargement in Central and Eastern Europe. However, even though more than two decades had passed since the fall of the Berlin Wall – so much so that one of the hosts of the 2011 ESC, Stefan Raab, could jokingly declare 'tear down this wall' during the show – Europe was still divided along economic and political lines, old and new. The increasing commercialization of the contest and its excessive financial cost for some national broadcasting organizations highlighted economic disparities within Europe, especially during the financial crisis; rather than being a stage for the promotion of European values, the ESC seemed more motivated by economic concerns. As had been the case during the Cold War, authoritarian governments that suppressed media freedom continued to use the ESC to whitewash their international images. The ESC could not bring democratic change to Europe, and while it continued to be interpreted as a symbol of European values, it still really functioned according to a combination of commercial motivations and the realpolitik of Europe's international relations.

Figure 8 Jamala, 2016 ESC

Conclusion: Bridges, Diamonds and Fires

When Wurst met Ban Ki-moon at the headquarters of the UN in Vienna in November 2014, it was a rare encounter between a winner of the ESC and a secretary-general of the UN. However, Ban, or at least a photo of him, had appeared in the music video for the '12 Point Song' that was shown during the interval of the final of the 2014 ESC, while António Guterres, who was elected Ban's successor as secretary-general in 2016, had even appeared as Portugal's prime minister in the postcard that introduced the Portuguese entry in the 1996 ESC.[1] Yet, the meeting between Ban and Wurst could also be interpreted as Austria's participation in the ESC having come full circle. For although the ESC has been a quintessentially European event, the participation of Austria and other states in it depended first of all on them being members of a UN specialized agency, the ITU. In 2015, at the same time that it hosted the sixtieth edition of the ESC, Austria marked seventy years since the end of the Second World War, the sixtieth anniversary of its entry into the UN and the twentieth anniversary of its accession to the EU; there were also ongoing commemorations for the centenary of the First World War. In a year of so many round anniversaries, it was time to reflect on how the ESC was not just one of the longest-running television shows in the world, but also the result of an even lengthier history of international cooperation in telecommunications. Austria was also the birthplace of international organizations as it was at the Congress of Vienna in 1815 that these were first created, meaning that there was also the 200th anniversary of that to commemorate in 2015.

The majority of discussions at the Congress of Vienna took place in the building that became the Federal Chancellery of the Austrian government, where Austria's chancellor Werner Faymann held a reception for Wurst to celebrate her victory upon her return from the 2014 ESC. Although the content of the 2015 ESC that referred to Austrian history focused largely on apolitical aspects, such as Austria's artists, inventors and sportspeople and classical music heritage, ORF alluded to Austria's position as a centre of international diplomacy in Europe's geographical centre when it adopted 'Building Bridges' as the motto for the diamond edition of the ESC in 2015. Wurst's trans identity was itself a metaphor for Austria's historically bridging role in international relations. The 'Queen of Austria', the nickname that she had been given during the 2014 ESC, was not only a reference to a drag queen but also an allusion to Austria's imperial past, and her winning song in the ESC, 'Rise Like a Phoenix', could have easily been read as a hymn to Austria's postwar reconstruction as a neutral state as much as an affirmation of sexual pride. While Wurst's win was Austria's first victory in the ESC since 1966 and brought the contest to Vienna for a second time, it was also a lost opportunity for sexual minorities in Austria. The international attention that Wurst brought Austria increased awareness of the issues of sexual minorities in the state and prompted national political leaders to declare that it was time for Austria to adopt same-sex marriage.[2] A proposal for that had been introduced in the Austrian parliament by the Greens party in November 2013, but it was rejected in June 2015 a month after Vienna hosted the ESC. Nonetheless, Wurst's promotion of the rights of sexual minorities was praised by not only Ban but also the secretary-general of the CoE, Thorbjørn Jagland, and Wurst also performed at the EP.[3]

While the stage for the 2015 ESC emphasized 'vision' as it was designed to appear like an eye, it was the metaphor of the bridge that was still needed in Europe and the ESC in 2015, as the EU continued to face its economic crisis – bridges are, after all, used as symbols on euro notes – and wars were occurring at the extremities of the borders of the EBA. Europe's fires, both extant and memorialized, continued to burn. The 2015 ESC had two entries dealing with war that connected ongoing commemorations of the world wars with contemporary conflicts. France's Lisa Angell sang 'N'oubliez pas' (Don't Forget) and Hungary's Boggie performed 'Wars for Nothing', but neither of them scored highly, respectively finishing third last and twentieth out of twenty-seven entries in the final. The war between Armenia and Azerbaijan – where the 2012 ESC had been branded with 'Light Your Fire' – continued to be played out at the 2015 and 2016 contests. In 2015, Azerbaijan protested against Armenia submitting the song 'Don't Deny', as the entry alluded to the massacres of Armenians committed by Ottoman forces during the First

World War, which Azerbaijan and Turkey officially denied was a genocide.[4] The Armenian genocide had previously also been alluded to in the 2010 Armenian ESC entry 'Apricot Stone', and both songs had the same composer, Armen Martirosyan. The group Genealogy which performed 'Don't Deny' included six members, with five of them representing the Armenian diaspora from different continents. Armenia was commemorating the centenary of the genocide in 2015, and the issue was furthermore controversial as some national parliaments in the EU were debating whether it should be recognized as a genocide; the German parliament did so in April just some weeks before the 2015 ESC. Following protests from İTV about the political message of the song, the Reference Group made Genealogy change the name of the entry to 'Face the Shadow', although the former title of the song remained in its refrain.

During the first semi-final of the 2016 ESC that was staged in Stockholm, the Armenian artist Iveta Mukuchyan waved the flag of Nagorno-Karabakh while being filmed in the greenroom, just over a month after the worst clashes in Nagorno-Karabakh occurred between Armenian and Azerbaijani forces since the 1994 ceasefire. A spokesperson for Azerbaijan's Ministry of Foreign Affairs called Mukuchyan's flag-waving 'provocative'.[5] The EBU issued a warning to Armenia at the 2016 ESC that it could be disqualified from the contest if such political statements continued. In order to prevent the display of controversial flags, potentially also those of the Islamic State and terrorist organizations, the EBU tried to ban the waving by the live audience of flags that were not of states represented in the EBU, or of the EU or UN member states, or the rainbow flag used by sexual minorities. However, the Reference Group was pressured to change this decision following protests from regions in the EU, such as the Basque Country and Wales, as well as from the governments of Palestine and the TRNC.[6] As was the case since the beginning of the ESC, the contest remained an attractive stage for the promotion of ethnic, regional and state identities. Yet, the EBU continued to present the ESC as an apolitical emperor, only for the international media and national governments to tell it that the contest was just as naked as Ivan, the Belarusian singer in the 2016 ESC whose performance included a video that showed him naked with a wolf.

The attempt by the Reference Group to ban certain flags at the ESC was part of its aim to depoliticize the atmosphere among the live audience, and from the 2014 ESC the organizers also urged the live audience not to boo any entries – which usually meant the Russian ones. When she co-hosted the 2015 ESC, Wurst even criticized the live audience for booing the Russian representative, Polina Gagarina, who eventually finished in second place with the peace song 'A Million Voices' that was produced by a Russian and Swedish team. However, there was still the potential for political statements to be made in the national selections, which the EBU never directly controlled. This was seen in the Slovenian national selection, the Eurovision Melody, in 2016, in which the host, comedian Klemen Slakonja, was shown impersonating Putin in a satirical music video called 'Putin, Putout' that afterwards went viral.[7] The Slovenian government, though, continued to court warm relations with Russia, particularly regarding economic ties, and it was critical of the sanctions that the EU had imposed on Russia in 2014 because of Moscow's role in the war in Ukraine. Putin paid an official visit to Slovenia in July 2016, attending a centenary commemoration for Russian prisoners of war who died in Slovenia during the First World War. Indeed, even though Wurst was cast as a symbol against Putin, that did not stop him from also paying an official visit to Vienna in June 2014, when he called Austria an 'important and reliable' partner and the Austrian president Heinz Fischer criticized the EU's sanctions against Moscow.[8]

Ukraine was not represented in the 2015 ESC because of its wartime economic and political situation, but in 2016 it waged its biggest ever battle in the ESC with Russia, when the two states vied for victory in the final. The Ukrainian entry '1944', which was composed, performed and written by Jamala, referred to the expulsion of Crimean Muslim Tartars by Soviet forces in 1944, part of the national deportations that were ordered by Stalin and condemned by Khrushchev in his speech in 1956. The song was unlike any other that had so far been performed in the ESC: mostly in English, but with some lyrics in Crimean Tartar, it described soldiers killing innocent people while addressing the listener in the second person. It was easily interpreted as a statement on Russia's annexation of Crimea, which had brought a new wave of political pressure on the Crimean Tartars. The Reference Group concluded that the song did not contain a political message and allowed it to remain: it would have in any case been unethical for the Reference Group to ban a song about a historical example of ethnic cleansing. For months before the

2016 ESC, international betting agencies' top prediction for the winning song was the Russian entry 'You Are the Only One', which was performed by one of Russia's leading pop stars, Sergey Lazarev, produced by an international group that included lyricists from Sweden and had the most elaborate staging of any entry that year. In a suspenseful finish that came down to the declaration of the very last results of the public voting – Ukraine won. Jamala's victory was praised by Ukraine's political leaders – she received a national honour because of it from President Petro Poroshenko – but some media commentators and politicians in Russia condemned it as a sign of the contest's politicization. The Russian international broadcasting organization Russia Today even issued an obituary of the ESC in response, claiming that politics had killed the ESC.[9]

Stockholm came to host the 2016 ESC after Måns Zelmerlöw won the 2015 contest for Sweden with the song 'Heroes'. It was apt that the state that had produced 'Waterloo' won the 2015 ESC in Vienna, two centuries after the Congress of Vienna and the Napoleonic Wars when Sweden gained control of Norway from Denmark, after Sweden had lost Finland to Russia. Sweden fought its last war in 1814, something that the comedian Petra Mede reminded viewers of during her hosting of the ESC in 2013. Ever since 1814, Sweden has in principle been a neutral state, and in the postwar era its governments strived to develop an international image of Sweden as a peaceful and stable state whose international prestige was measured by its economic success and social harmony. It was particularly open to accepting refugees, such as those who fled the war in Bosnia and Herzegovina, like the subject of Fazla's song. During the crisis that began in 2015 that saw a massive influx of migrants and refugees into Europe, especially from war-ravaged Syria, Afghanistan and Iraq, Sweden accepted proportionately to its population the highest number of refugees of any European state. The migrant and refugee crisis accordingly inspired the motto for the 2016 ESC, 'Come Together', as well as the interval act in the first semi-final, a dance performance called 'The Grey People'.

Still, it was also ironic that 'Waterloo', a song referring to a military battle, had helped to launch neutral Sweden's export popular music industry, which after the Cold War became the third largest in the world after those of the United States and the UK. Sweden's cultural diplomacy made much of the international success of its popular music industry, whose historical role in fashioning Sweden's international image was also the subject of the comical film

'The Nerd Nation' that was shown during the 2016 ESC and which highlighted the Swedes as being one of the most enthusiastic national audiences for the ESC.[10] Yet, while Sweden in 2016 topped an international ranking of states with the best reputations,[11] what was not much publicly discussed behind the well-designed international image of Sweden was the fact that it was also one of the world's top arms exporters per capita – controversially even selling them to authoritarian governments. In 2013, Sweden ranked third among the world's arms exporters per capita after two states, Israel and Russia, which featured significantly in the wars that were symbolically played out on the ESC stage. In 2011, Sweden earned five times as much from its export of arms than of popular music: 150 million American dollars for popular music versus 1.6 billion American dollars for arms.[12] Yet, arms were not an export industry that the Swedish government wanted the international public to associate with Sweden through nation branding – ABBA, H&M and Ikea, yes, but not Bofors and Gripen. These two brand names from the Swedish arms industry were also not mentioned among the Swedish icons that were listed in the interval act 'Swedish Smörgåsbord' in the final of the 2013 ESC, nor did a mock fighter jet appear then as a prop onstage as in the 2009 ESC in Moscow. That ABBA had managed to trivialize the Battle of Waterloo through a love song said something about the attitude towards consumption and war of a neutral and prosperous state. That a real song about war and its consequences won the 2016 ESC demonstrated also that there were many Europeans who did not think that the ESC should just be about Russian or Swedish soft power projected through a well-crafted but politically innocuous pop song (the typical elements of an ESC entry were also highlighted by the hosts of the 2016 ESC, Mede and Zelmerlöw, in their performance of the song 'Love Love Peace Peace' in the interval act in the final). Rather, the ESC could also be a stage upon which the continuing, grim realities of war – and in one of Europe's poorest states at that – and the dubiousness of nation branding could be reflected upon. Crimea and Sweden also had a particular historical connection: the Swedish arms industry itself developed through the Crimean War of the mid-nineteenth century, when Alfred Nobel, the Swede who would later seek to promote peace in the world by establishing the Nobel Prize – which was often referred to as a symbol of Sweden in interval acts and postcards in the ESC – profited from that war through his father's arms manufacturing company in Russia.[13]

The 2014 ESC had 'Join Us' as its motto and its logo had a diamond; although not as loaded with the political symbolism of the 2015 ESC, the diamond nonetheless suggested another dimension of international relations and national politics that was highlighted by the ESC: economic inequalities and financial crises. The biggest controversy in this regard occurred in the 2016 ESC when the Romanian national broadcasting organization, Romanian Television (TVR), was forced by the EBU to withdraw from the ESC just weeks before the contest was held. TVR had outstanding debts to the EBU of some 16 million Swiss francs, and the EBU issued an ultimatum to the Romanian government to repay the debt or be excluded from the contest, which is what ultimately occurred after the debt was not paid off.[14] This was the first time that the EBU itself had ever expelled a national broadcasting organization from the ESC. The issue of economic migration had been the topic of Romania's 2015 ESC entry, 'De la capăt (All Over Again)' (From the Beginning (All Over Again)), performed by the band Voltaj (Voltage), whose lyrics were about the children left behind in Romania by parents who were economic immigrants to West Europe. The song scored highly in the televoting in France, Italy, Portugal and Spain, which have large Romanian immigrant communities. Although the three hosts of the 2015 ESC – Arabella Kiesbauer, Alice Tumler and Mirjam Weichselbraun – were chosen by ORF partly because of their multicultural backgrounds, the national broadcasting organizations of the states which were the origins of some of Austria's biggest immigrant communities, such as Bosnia and Herzegovina, Croatia, and Slovakia, did not participate in the 2015 ESC mostly for financial reasons. It was surprising that ORF could 'build a bridge' between Australia and Europe as an Australian entry debuted in the 2015 ESC, yet not between Bratislava and Vienna, the two geographically closest capital cities in Europe. In 2016, Bosnia and Herzegovina's national broadcasting organization, Radio and Television of Bosnia and Herzegovina (BHRT), continued to be in a precarious financial situation that also made it unable to pay its debts to the EBU. BHRT was even under threat of being shut down as its state's national divisions thwarted its national parliament from adopting the required reforms for BHRT's financing, and the EBU sought to cooperate with the EU in assisting the Bosnian and Herzegovinian government to find a solution to maintain BHRT.[15] Still, that there were other states of southern Europe whose economic standing was among the poorest on the continent, but which continued to stage national selections and send entries to the ESC final, as in the cases of Albania and Moldova, demonstrated that there remained something particularly attractive about the ESC for some smaller states in which it continued to be regarded as a unique opportunity for the international promotion of these states and their artists.

In Scotland, the governing Scottish National Party had hoped that a Scottish national broadcasting organization would enter the EBU and ESC by 2016 if the referendum on Scotland's independence from the UK would have passed in September 2014.[16] British entries otherwise continued to place lowly in the ESC in 2015 and 2016. 'You're Not Alone' came third last in the 2016 ESC, with both its placing and title being symbolic in the context of the campaign for the referendum on whether the UK should remain a member of the EU, during which the economic and social impact of migration from Central and East Europe on the UK was much debated. The Brexit referendum in June resulted in a vote for the UK to leave the EU, and a survey conducted in April had also shown that more Britons wanted the UK to leave the ESC than remain in it.[17] Nevertheless, in response to a parliamentary question, British prime minister David Cameron had explained that the UK would still be able to perform in the ESC even if it were to withdraw from the EU, thereby highlighting the persistence of a popular misconception that the ESC and EU were officially connected.[18] The EBU, however, made an innovative contribution to a collective European consciousness – as it had similarly done with the adoption of the circle of twelve stars as the first symbol of the Eurovision Network – when it introduced a major change to the voting system in the ESC in 2016 that was inspired by the method used in the Melody Festival for presenting the televoting results. For the first time ever in the history of the ESC, the jury votes and the televotes were no longer combined to give final national results, but the jury votes were presented on a national basis and the public televotes from each state were combined and declared by the hosts in ascending order according to the amount of total televotes that an entry had received. Although the televote was still nationally based, there was no longer a mutual dependence between the public and jury votes in determining the collective national vote. The public televotes were presented as the vote of a whole European electorate, plus Australia and Israel. The EU had since 2014 also experimented with the concept of a European electorate in EP elections through leading candidates presented by EP party groups as potential presidents of the European Commission. Still, voting in the ESC was not a predictor for the outcome of national and European elections: a fortnight after Wurst's ESC win, for example, right-wing populist parties increased their vote in the elections for the EP. Norbert Hofer, the candidate of the FPÖ, whose politicians had criticized Wurst's representation of Austria in the ESC, also reached but did not win the final round of the Austrian presidential elections in 2016.

Although the ESC had shed stars from its symbolism, in the final of the 2014 ESC 'Ode to Joy' was played for the first time ever in the contest as part of the interval act of the same name; it was also performed by the Vienna Philharmonic in the opening of the final of the 2015 ESC. In the opening of the second semi-final of the 2016 ESC, Mede and Zelmerlöw performed the song 'That's Eurovision' which highlighted the contest's historical characteristics, including its promotion of European unity and linguistic diversity. However, the 2016 ESC had only a few entries that were not in English, with the Spanish entry 'Say Yay!' being the first ever entry in the ESC from Spain that had no Spanish lyrics. Mede and Zelmerlöw also emphasized the ESC's power to unite Europe a few other times during their hosting of the contest. In 2016, the ESC received the Charlemagne Medal for European Media, which is one of the honours given in the context of the Charlemagne Prize that is awarded annually by the German city of Aachen for contributions to European unification. Setting aside the fact that the ESC was always a more complex phenomenon as both a metaphor for European unity but also a reflection of cultural, economic and political divisions within Europe, the question of how 'European' the ESC was still going to be was prompted by the EBU's global ambitions for the contest. In 2011, the ESC's new executive supervisor, Jon Ola Sand, stated that a Worldvision Song Contest was not being planned by the EBU but could be a possibility in the future.[19] This was, of course, not a new idea, as a global song contest had also been an aim of the ISC as well as an idea proposed by Sand's colleagues in NRK in the late 1980s.

A major step towards making the ESC more of a global event occurred in 2015, when an Australian entry debuted in the ESC under the auspices of SBS. This was the first time that participation in the ESC was expanded beyond Europe and the Mediterranean rim: the EBU bent its own rules by exceptionally allowing a national broadcasting organization that was not an active member of the EBU and not located within the EBA to take part. It was not, however, the first time that SBS expressed an interest in being more involved in the ESC. In 1995, SBS had even proposed to the EBU that it host the 1997 ESC in Melbourne and that a Global Song Contest be held in 1998, with both ideas being supported by the federal government of Australia and the state government of Victoria. However, the EBU rejected the offer because of the time difference between Australia and Europe and the EBU's unwillingness to move a traditionally European event from Europe.[20] Indeed, after SBS entered the ESC in 2015, the EBU planned that should an Australian entry win the contest, SBS would co-host it the following year with another national broadcasting organization in Europe. In 2009, SBS became more directly involved with the ESC when it began regularly fielding its own commentators to the contest. SBS's participation in and live broadcasting of the ESC (it had historically broadcast the contest on Sunday in primetime due to the time difference with Europe, which was continued in 2015 and 2016 together with a live broadcast) was intended to boost ratings for a television station that had always ranked as the least-watched among Australia's five national free-to-air networks. SBS had also often been threatened with funding cuts, especially as some right-wing politicians did not support the multicultural concept behind it. Although the ESC did significantly increase ratings for SBS, and despite the media hype surrounding Australia's participation in the contest, the final of the ESC was still not the most-watched programme in Australia on the weekends when it was broadcast in 2015 and 2016, being beaten by programmes mostly offered by Australia's three commercial free-to-air networks.[21] The costs for SBS's participation in the ESC, which was put at one million Australian dollars in 2015 in addition to production costs, were mostly borne by commercial sponsors.[22] It was, then, ironic that Australia debuted in the ESC in Austria, the state whose 1977 ESC entry 'Boom Boom Boomerang' had many Australian words in its lyrics yet was not an ode to Australia, but rather a critique of the commercialism of the popular music industry and the innocuousness of ESC entries.

The involvement of Australia in the ESC was a springboard for the contest to expand into bigger markets in Asia, The original local fan base for the ESC in Australia were viewers from southern European immigrant communities:

this was depicted in SBS's first ever contribution to an ESC show, a film that was produced to mark thirty years of the broadcasting of the ESC in Australia and which was shown in the first semi-final of the 2013 ESC. When SBS first experimented with its own commentary in 2001, it employed Mary Coustas performing the comical character Effie, a second-generation Greek Australian who was popularized through the situation comedy *Acropolis Now* that ran on the commercial Seven Network from 1989 to 1992 and was one of the first Australian television shows focusing on Australians with southern European backgrounds. However, when it came to sending artists to perform in the ESC, rather than choosing representatives with origins from southern European immigrant communities, SBS instead internally selected artists of Asian descent. These included the singer Jessica Mauboy (who performed in the interval act in the second semi-final of the 2014 ESC after a dance performance that presented clichéd images of Australia and joked about it entering the ESC), as well as the artists who represented Australia in the 2015 and 2016 contests, Guy Sebastian and Dami Im, and the presenter of Australia's voting results, Lee Lin Chin. The appearance of Asian Australians in the ESC also highlighted how underrepresented Europeans of Asian origin had historically been in the contest.[23] While it seemed ironic that Australia had such an Asian representation in the ESC, it was understandable considering that the growth in immigration from Asian states to Australia since the 1970s meant that Asian immigrant communities had become as large of a market for SBS as its original target audiences from southern Europe. The promotion of Australia's Asian identity in the ESC was also a political statement as it occurred amid debates in Australia about immigration, national identity and the state's geocultural orientation, in the context of ongoing issues such as the human rights of indigenous Australians, Australian governments' controversial policies towards asylum seekers and whether Australia should change its flag with the Union Jack and become a republic. Still, many European media commentators praised the expansion of the ESC not because they were cognizant of its commercial benefits for the EBU, but because they considered Australia as a modern state that shared democratic and multicultural values with Europe. Yet, Australia had also been founded on European colonialism, genocide and racism, something which the appearance of indigenous Australians in SBS's film in the 2103 ESC were a poignant reminder of, as were Mauboy, who also had indigenous Australian origins, and the onstage display of the Australian Aboriginal flag after her performance in the 2013 ESC.

A further step towards the expansion of the ESC in Asia was made in 2015 when China's second most-watched television channel, Hunan Television, began broadcasting the ESC. This had been anticipated by the 2014 ESC, in which several references to China were made by the hosts, including in the '12 Point Song'. The discovery of the Asian market was not a new phenomenon considering that the contest had first been broadcast in China in 1990 and in other parts of East Asia in the 1970s and 1980s, including Hong Kong, Japan, Malaysia and especially South Korea, where in the 1980s the ESC had a popular following. Indeed, when Ban met Wurst, he was probably already familiar with the ESC. Popular music industries in states such as China and South Korea boomed from the 1990s in the context of the rapid economic growth of these states. South Korea established itself as the 'Sweden' of East Asia as a result of the successful global export of its popular music and other popular cultural products through the 'Korean Wave'. This also made East Asian states a new market of interest for the ESC. In 2016, the EBU signed an agreement with SBS for the latter to develop the Eurovision Asia Song Contest, thereby confirming that the contest's expansion to Australia was indeed part of a strategy for the further global growth of the Eurovision brand. Australia's bridging role between Asia and Europe in the ESC could also be used to challenge a possible Russian revival of the ISC for Eurasian states that are members of the Shanghai Cooperation Organization; it furthermore partly filled a gap left in the ESC due to the absence of Turkey, which was in the 2004 ESC presented as the ESC's bridge between Asia and Europe through the host city of Istanbul. Another part of the world that the ESC reached out to in 2016 was the United States, where the ESC was broadcast for the first time since 1971 – and for the first time live – by the commercial television broadcaster Logo, whose content was otherwise aimed at sexual minorities. The American artist Justin Timberlake also performed the interval act in the final of the 2016 ESC, although he was of course just a new chapter in a tradition of American artists performing in the ESC from its very beginning. That there was a growing awareness of the ESC in the United States, where major media outlets were also giving coverage to the contest, was also demonstrated when US president Barack Obama referred to the ESC in a speech in Germany in 2016 in which he supported European unity.[24]

With the worldwide expansion of the ESC at a time when Europe was in an economic crisis, it was questionable whether the contest itself had become less interested in promoting European unity and more in pursuing global commercial growth. By 2016, there were no longer any European states that the ESC could expand to: the only European states with full international recognition that had not yet been represented in the ESC were Liechtenstein, because it did not have a national public service broadcasting organization and so could not join the EBU, and Vatican City, which was represented in the EBU but its officials did likely not see the ESC as an appropriate forum for its cultural diplomacy.[25] With a population of some 40,000, Liechtenstein, although Europe's wealthiest state per capita, did not offer a large enough market to be particularly attractive for the ESC. However, amid all of the focus on the ESC's global expansion, the European puzzle was left without another of its pieces, Kosovo, which by 2016 had still not achieved the full international recognition that could make it a member of the CoE or UN. Considering that Kosovo also had one of Europe's poorest economies, its desire to enter the ESC, and its government's insistence that it would have no problem in covering the the cost of this, demonstrated how for some states the political benefits of participating in the ESC still outweighed the financial expense. The Kosovan government viewed participation in the ESC as another affirmation of its Europeanist aspirations and international recognition. The EU had played a major role in the establishment of the Republic of Kosovo, which was reflected in the colours of and stars on the state's flag as well as its wordless anthem called 'Evropa' (Europe); Kosovo was also one of the few states in Europe in which Europe Day, May 9, was made a public holiday. In 2009, the Kosovan government launched an international campaign designed by the advertising agency Saatchi & Saatchi that branded Kosovo as the 'Young Europeans', considering that it had the most youthful population in Europe while also being the continent's youngest state.

Upon the declaration of Kosovo's independence in 2008, the Kosovan national broadcasting organization, Radio and Television of Kosovo (RTK), sought to enter the EBU and the ESC: Petrit Selimi, the Kosovan deputy minister of foreign affairs, even declared that 'nothing is more important than the Song Contest in nation-building'. However, the EBU did not admit RTK into its ranks because Kosovo was not a member of the ITU, for which membership of the UN or the support of a two-thirds majority of members of the ITU was still required.[26] In 2015, Kosovo unsuccessfully tried to enter UNESCO, which also admitted non-UN members, as it did Palestine in 2011, on the basis of the support of a two-thirds majority of its members. That Kosovo was not included in these UN specialized agencies was ironic considering that the UN's Interim Administration Mission in Kosovo had played a key role in constructing Kosovo's governmental institutions after the Kosovo War. The EBU had also assisted in the setting up of RTK. Still, when in 2016 the Reference Group proposed banning the waving of certain flags by the live audience, which would have also affected the Kosovan flag, the Kosovan government and RTK threatened to end their cooperation with the EBU unless the Kosovan flag was taken off the list of banned flags, and the Reference Group ultimately withdrew the flag policy.[27] Kosovan artists otherwise participated in the Albanian national selection for the ESC. In 2012 one of them, Rona Nishliu, even achieved Albania's best ever result in the ESC when she placed fifth in the final, and she was received by political leaders of both Albania and Kosovo after her win. Albania thus turned into Kosovo's bridge to the ESC, whereas during the Cold War the situation had been the opposite.

Although the EBU explained that it could not admit RTK because Kosovo was not a member of the ITU or UN, there had been precedents of the EBU bending its own rules in the past, such as when it accepted Morocco's and Tunisia's broadcasting organizations into the EBU in 1950 when they still were not independent states, permitted Greece to continue participating in the contest after the closure of ERT, and allowed SBS to enter the ESC even though it was an associate member of the EBU based outside of the EBA. The International Olympic Committee and UEFA also accepted into their ranks their corresponding Kosovan organizations in 2014 and 2016 respectively. The ESC as well should have included RTK in order to demonstrate that the contest's expansion was not just about commercial ambition, but also about the values of democracy and diversity that the EBU sought to promote. It was a question of solidarity with Europe's youngest state, which was also one of its poorest states and a major source of immigrants for West Europe. Having Kosovo in the ESC would have furthermore sent a positive message on European values in light of the growing tensions between the Muslim world and the West in the post-Cold War period, considering that Kosovo is the third state in Europe, after Turkey and Azerbaijan, whose population has the highest percentage of Muslims.

Indeed, by 2016 the ESC still faced a major challenge: to build bridges across the Mediterranean and attract entries from Muslim-majority Middle Eastern and northern African states that were located in the EBA, some of which had national broadcasting organizations that joined the EBU before ones of other European states did. As the ESC's commercial and cultural epicentre moved to northern Europe in the post-Cold War era, even Europe's Mediterranean region became marginalized in the ESC. This was underlined by low viewing figures in Italy and the withdrawal of Turkey: with a combined population of 140 million people in 2016, these two Mediterranean states alone offered opportunities for the ESC to increase its viewership of 200 million in that year. The Mediterranean region may have become synonymous with economic crises and migration waves, but it must also be remembered that it was there that the ESC was conceived, as an Italian invention polished with Francophone panache. It was also there that Europe was named. After its sixtieth anniversary, the ESC needs to rediscover its history of cultural diversity and social criticism, the most laudable qualities of the contest that were especially notable during the Cold War but were afterwards dumbed down by Anglicization and commercialism, and to consciously display the cultural interconnectedness that really defines European identity. It was the cultural interconnectedness among Europeans and their common experience of political and social changes that made the ESC and defined a European identity in the postwar era. These two aspects of the contest could be enhanced if the ESC were to incorporate a charity dimension, such as in the form of the revenues from televoting being donated to a pan-European social cause. The performances in the 2015 ESC by the Finnish group Pertti Kurikan Nimipäivät (Pertti Kurikka's Name Days), which was comprised of members with developmental disabilities, and the Polish artist Monika Kuszyńska, who was paralysed after a car accident and appeared onstage in a wheelchair, highlighted two causes that could benefit from a charity dimension in the ESC.

Bridges, diamonds and fires figured in the branding of the ESC around its sixtieth anniversary, but they also symbolized the cooperation, commerce and conflict that had constantly defined the history of postwar Europe and the ESC. On the map of the EBA, the political ambitions and interests of various international organizations, national governments and regional alliances harmonized and clashed to produce different associations of national public broadcasting organizations and even song contests. Yet, the ESC has outlived all of the changes in international relations in the postwar era, being held without fail every year since it was first staged in 1956. Although it was always more of a symbol rather than a catalyst for political and social changes from 1956 to 2016, the ESC's constancy has made the contest an ideal eye for taking a synonymous 'broad view' of the developments in the history of postwar Europe that magnifies the interconnectedness between its citizens, cultures and states. All of which has made the ESC the concert of Europe of the postwar era.

Notes

Introduction

1 Jean Coucrand, 'Un "tube" est né à Jérusalem: "Hallelujah"!' *Le Soir* (1 April 1979) [European Broadcasting Union Archives (EBUA), Concours Eurovision de la chanson, 1979].
2 Johan Fornäs, *Signifying Europe* (Bristol and Chicago: Intellect, 2012), 9.
3 For an explanation of the differences between active and associate membership in the EBU, see Rüdiger Zeller, *Die EBU – Union Européene de Radio-Télévision (UER) – European Broadcasting Union (EBU): Internationale Rundfunkkooperation im Wandel* (Baden-Baden: Nomos, 1999), 72–82.
4 Milan Kundera, trans. Michael Henry Heim, *The Unbearable Lightness of Being* (New York: Harper & Row, 1984), 251.
5 Mistakes about the history of the ESC have even been made in the contest's shows. For example, in the final of the 2013 ESC, the host, Petra Mede, incorrectly stated that the ESC had been founded in the UK in the early 1950s. In its attempt to deal with the history of the ESC during the Cold War, the documentary *The Secret History of Eurovision*, directed by Stephen Oliver (Australia: Brook Lapping and Electric Pictures, 2011), incorrectly asserts that the ESC was not broadcast in Eastern Europe during the Cold War. Based on this false premise, the documentary presents the contest as having been subversively desired by Eastern Europeans who perceived it as a symbol of Western freedom and prosperity.

Chapter 1

1 Katharina Thormann and Erik Schmidt, 'Lena stapft in Walters Spuren', *Mitteldeutsche Zeitung* (1 June 2010) [www.mz-web.de].
2 Elmar Kraushaar, *Freddy Quinn: Ein unwahrscheinliches Leben – Biografie* (Zurich: Atrium, 2011), 19–22.
3 Cited in Brian E. Vick, *The Congress of Vienna: Power and Politics After Napoleon* (Cambridge, MA, and London: Harvard University Press, 2014), 51.

4 Prince Heinrich's telegrams were rejected by a British land station operated by the Marconi Company because the radio equipment on the *Deutschland* was from a rival German firm. Francis Lyall, *International Communications: The International Telecommunication Union and the Universal Postal Union* (Burlington, VT, and Farnham: Ashgate Publishing, 2011), 46.

5 International Radiotelegraph Conference (Madrid, 1932), *General Radiocommunication Regulations Annexed to the International Telecommunication Convention; Final Protocol to the General Radiocommunication Regulations; Additional Radiocommunication Regulations Annexed to the International Telecommunication Convention; Additional Protocol to the Acts of the International Radiotelegraph Conference of Madrid, Signed by the Governments of the European Region* (London: His Majesty's Stationery Office, 1933), 12 [International Telecommunication Union Archives (ITUA), Administrative Regulations]. Although the northern part of Saudi Arabia – 'the parts of Arabia and Hedjaz' – were excluded from the original definition of the EBA, since 1982 it has been explicitly included. Iraq and Saudi Arabia are the only states in the EBA that have never been represented in the EBU even though their national broadcasting organizations would otherwise qualify for membership.

6 Suzanne Lommers, *Europe – On Air: Interwar Projects for Radio Broadcasting* (Amsterdam: Amsterdam University Press, 2012), 241.

7 Ibid., 81–2, 88, 93, 97.

8 Ibid., 145–7.

9 Ibid., 95–6. The broadcasting organizations from Algeria, Egypt, Morocco, Palestine, Tunisia and Turkey did join the IBU, but only the Egyptian and Turkish ones represented independent states.

10 Ernest Eugster, *Television Programming Across National Boundaries: The EBU and OIRT Experience* (Dedham, MA: Artech House, 1983), 39–40.

11 Ibid., 44–6.

12 Zeller, *Die EBU – Union Européene de Radio-Télévision (UER) – European Broadcasting Union (EBU)*, 37.

13 Wilhelm Füchsl, 'The Sound-Broadcasting Service in Austria', *E.B.U. Bulletin* 5, no. 28 (1954): 653.

14 Stuart Hull McIntyre, *Legal Effect of World War II on Treaties of the United States* (The Hague: Martinus Nijhoff, 1958), 273–4.

15 Eugster, *Television Programming Across National Boundaries*, 98–9.

16 Ibid., 96, 123–4.

17 Cited in 'A First: Pope Pius XII in Five Languages and via Eurovision', *EBU Dossiers* 2, no. 1 (2004): 15 [www.ebu.ch]. Pope Pius XII also received delegates from

the EBU after their conference in Rome in 1955, giving their activities – and so indirectly the ESC – his blessing. 'Speech by His Holiness Pope Pius XXII to EBU Delegates', *E.B.U. Bulletin* 7, no. 35 (1956): 137–8. Vatican City only started its own television services when the Vatican Television Centre was established in 1983.

18 Marcel Bezençon, 'Eurovision – The Pattern of the Future?', *E.B.U. Bulletin* 5, no. 27 (1954): 568, 572.

19 The proportion of sports programmes in the Eurovision Network ranged from 43 per cent to 87 per cent between 1954 and 1982. Eugster, *Television Programming Across National Boundaries*, 226. Current affairs were another early focus of the Eurovision Network: the Eurovision News Exchange was established in 1958 for news footage, and its first big story was the death of Pope Pius XII.

20 EBU, 'Commission des Programmes (3ème session plénière)' (Geneva, 6 September 1955), 1 [European Broadcasting Union Archives (EBUA), Concours Eurovision de la chanson, Décisions 1].

21 'Fifth Festival of Italian Song', *E.B.U. Bulletin* 6, no. 30 (1955): 146; letter from Sergio Pugliese, RAI, to Léo Wallenborn, EBU (Milan, 15 February 1955), 1 [EBUA, Concours Eurovision de la chanson, 1956-57].

22 'International Song Festival', *E.B.U. Bulletin* 6, no. 31 (1955): 271.

23 'M. Marcel Bezençon's Statement at the SSR General Assembly', *E.B.U. Bulletin* 6, no. 30 (1955): 178.

24 Alan S. Milward, *The European Rescue of the Nation-State*, 2nd edn. (London and New York: Routledge, 2000), 2–3.

25 Cited in Eugster, *Television Programming Across National Boundaries*, 123. The BBC also initially opposed the term 'Eurovision' and preferred 'Continental Television Exchange', while the French national broadcasting organization, French Radio and Television (RTF), had suggested 'European Exchanges of Television Programmes'. Jean d'Arcy, 'Eurovision', *E.B.U. Review (Part B – General and Legal)* 10, no. 56 (1959): 6.

26 'The Council of Europe and Broadcasting', *E.B.U. Bulletin* 2, no. 5 (1951), 42–4; 'The Committee of Ministers of the Council of Europe Decides on Action to Promote the Development of European Television', *E.B.U. Bulletin* 5, no. 26 (1954): 498.

27 CoE, 'European Cultural Convention' (Paris, 1954), 1–2 [Council of Europe Archives (CoEA), European Treaty Series, 18].

28 Fornäs, *Signifying Europe*, 117–8, 136.

29 CoE, 'Minutes of the Meeting Held in Paris on 22 April 1971' (Strasbourg, 30 April 1971), 6 [CoEA, Committee on Regional Planning and Local Authorities, (22)PV10]. Charpentier composed this setting for 'Te Deum', a Christian hymn, in the late seventeenth century when he was based at the Church of Saint-Louis in

Paris, and the EBU's selection of 'Te Deum' further demonstrated the significance that its officials attached to religion in the 1950s. 'Ode to Joy' was originally intended as the setting for the poem written in 1785 by Friedrich Schiller, which praises friendship, love, sex, wine and God for uniting people of different cultures. Schiller would later consider the poem artistically inferior and even of bad taste. Maynard Solomon, *Beethoven Essays* (Cambridge, MA, and London: Harvard University Press, 1988), 209. However, his text was more thematically harmonious with ESC entries than that of 'We Write the Story', which was composed and written as the anthem for the 2013 ESC – the first time that an anthem was composed for the contest – by two members of ABBA, Benny Andersson and Björn Ulvaeus, and the musician Avicii. It had lyrics that referred to conscience, enlightenment, equality, freedom, justice, liberty, peace, reason and strength.

30 Marcel Bezençon, 'Eurovision Progresses', *E.B.U. Bulletin* 8, no. 45 (1957): 543; 'European Television Interconnections', *E.B.U. Bulletin* 8, no. 41 (1957): 67.

31 Marcel Bezençon, 'Eurovision – A Simple Idea That Worked', *E.B.U. Review (Part B – General and Legal)* 10, no. 56 (1959): 3, 4.

32 Marcel Bezençon, 'The Keys of Eurovision', *E.B.U. Review (Part B – General and Legal)* 14, no. 79 (1963): 6.

33 Marcel Bezençon, 'Eurovision, or the Price of Fame', *E.B.U. Review (Part B – General and Legal)* 15, no. 85 (1964): 9.

34 EBU, 'TV Programme Committee, Berlin, April 1965' (s.l., s.d.), 26 [EBUA, Concours Eurovision de la chanson, Décisions 1]. The last time that the *E.B.U. Review* reported that it was unsure whether the ESC would be held again the following year was in 1977. C.R.B., 'Eurovision Song Contest 1977', *E.B.U. Review (Part B – General and Legal)* 28, no. 4 (1977): 69.

35 EBU, 'Eurovision Song Contest 1971 Multi-National Audience Research Report' (s.l., s,d,), 3-4 [EBUA, Concours Eurovision de la chanson, 1970-71]. In 1989, another survey showed an average of 33 per cent of the viewing audiences across fifteen states. EBU, '56th Meeting of the Television Programme Committee' (Geneva, 13 October 1989), 5 [EBUA, Concours Eurovision de la chanson, 1990].

36 EBU, 'Rules of the Grand Prix of the 1956 Eurovision Song Competition' (Geneva, 1955), 1 [EBUA, Concours Eurovision de la chanson, 1956-57]; EBU, 'Rules of the Grand Prix of the 1966 Eurovision Song Contest' (Geneva, 21 December 1965), 1 [EBUA, Concours Eurovision de la chanson, 1966].

37 Gordon Roxburgh, *Songs for Europe: The United Kingdom at the Eurovision Song Contest – Volume One: The 1950s and 1960s* (Prestatyn: Telos Publishing, 2012), 391.

38 EBU, '1973 Eurovision Song Contest' (Geneva, 1973), 2-3 [EBUA, Concours Eurovision de la chanson, 1972-73]; EBU, 'Light Entertainment' (Geneva, October 1979), 39 [EBUA, Concours Eurovision de la chanson, 1980].

39 Simon Frith, 'Euro Pop', *Cultural Studies* 3, no. 2 (1989): 168.

40 Peter-Philipp Schmitt, 'Musik für den Wiederaufbau', *Frankfurter Allgemeine Zeitung* (9 February 2009) [www.faz.net].

41 Such international references and lexical gimmicks were especially evident in the ESC entries that were composed by Ralph Siegel from Germany, who has been the most productive composer in the ESC. Thorsten Hindrichs, 'Chasing the "Magic Formula" for Success: Ralph Siegel and the Grand Prix Eurovision de la Chanson', in *A Song for Europe: Popular Music and Politics in the Eurovision Song Contest*, ed. Ivan Raykoff and Robert Deam Tobin (Aldershot, and Burlington, VT: Ashgate Publishing, 2007), 52–8.

42 Claudia Schrag Sternberg, *The Struggle for EU Legitimacy: Public Contestation, 1950-2005* (Basingstoke and New York: Palgrave Macmillan, 2013), 76–7, 90–2.

43 Ivo Schwartz, 'The Policy of the Commission of the European Communities with Respect to Broadcasting', *E.B.U. Review (Part B – General and Legal)* 36, no. 6 (1985): 21–9; Zeller, *Die EBU – Union Européene de Radio-Télévision (UER) – European Broadcasting Union (EBU)*, 52–8.

44 EP, 'European Parliament: Written Questions with Answer', *Official Journal of the European Communities: Information and Notices* 31, no. C 303 (1988): 58–9 [www.eur-lex.europa.eu]; EP, 'European Parliament: Written Questions with Answer', *Official Journal of the European Communities: Information and Notices* 34, no. C 63 (1991): 53 [www.eur-lex.europa.eu]; EP, 'European Parliament: Written Questions with Answer', *Official Journal of the European Communities: Information and Notices* 34, no. C 98 (1991): 42 [www.eur-lex.europa.eu]. Images of EC institutions in Luxembourg had, however, already been included in the introductory films to the 1973 and 1984 contests that were held in that city. The host of the 1984 ESC, Désirée Nosbusch, also referred to the ESC as a 'European summit'.

45 Cited in European Commission, 'Commission to Support the Eurovision Song Contest Again', *European Commission Press Release Database* (Brussels, 6 April 1988) [www.europa.eu/rapid].

46 Marcel Bezençon, 'Mist Veils an Immense Horizon', *E.B.U. Review (Part B – General and Legal)* 18, no. 104 (1967): 10; Marcel Bezençon, 'The EBU in the Seventies', *E.B.U. Review (Part B – General and Legal)* 22, no. 125 (1971): 8.

47 'In the Footsteps of Eurovision', *E.B.U. Bulletin* 6, no. 33 (1955): 559.

48 Bezençon, 'Eurovision, or the Price of Fame', 9.

49 Philippe Roger, *The American Enemy: The History of French Anti-Americanism*, trans. Sharon Bowman (Chicago and London: The University of Chicago Press, 2005), 1–2.

50 De Gaulle also pushed for the creation of another television programme, *Games Without Borders*, to promote Western European cooperation. In it, teams

representing Western European states competed in doing bizarre tasks in a series of physical games. The programme was broadcast through the Eurovision Network from 1965 to 1999. Jérôme Bourdon, 'Unhappy Engineers of the European Soul: The EBU and the Woes of Pan-European Television', *The International Communication Gazette* 69, no. 3 (2007): 266.

51 Michael Baumgartner, '*Chanson*, *canzone*, *Schlager*, and Song: Switzerland's Identity Struggle in the Eurovision Song Contest', in *A Song for Europe*, ed. Raykoff and Tobin, 39–42. The Swiss group Peter, Sue and Marc, however, performed in the ESC four times, each time singing in a different language: the three official languages of Switzerland, French, German and Italian, in 1971, 1979 and 1981 respectively, and English in 1976. For Luxembourg, in which the official languages are French, German and Luxembourgish, almost all of its entries in the ESC during the Cold War were sung in French, with the only exception being its 1960 entry in Luxembourgish 'So laang we's du do bast' (As Long as You Are There).

52 After the abrogation of the language rule in 1999, most Belgian entries were in English. Perhaps as a further statement on Belgium's linguistic divisions, two of its entries were performed in imaginary languages: 'Sanomi' in 2003 and 'O Julissi' in 2008.

53 EBU, 'Television Programme Committee, Planning Group' (Geneva, 16 April 1971), 4 [EBUA, Concours Eurovision de la chanson, 1970-71]. In the late 1960s, Francophone national broadcasting organizations considered setting up their own international song contest but decided that the ESC was already sufficient. Emmanuel Robert, '"Le Francophonissime" (The World Champion)', *E.B.U. Review (Part B – General and Legal)* 20, no. 117 (1969), 31.

54 Cited in Tony Allen-Mills, 'Eurosong Ban by France', *Daily Telegraph* (24 April 1982) [EBUA, Concours de la chanson, Coupures de presse, 1979].

55 EBU, 'Eurovision Song Contest, London, 6th April, 1968' (s.l., s.d.), 1 [EBUA, Concours Eurovision de la chanson, 1968]; letter from C.R. Brown, EBU, to Andre de Vekey, Billboard Publications (Geneva, 17 April 1970), 1 [EBUA, Concours Eurovision de la chanson, 1970-71].

56 Letter from Imlay Newbiggin-Watts, BBC, to Leo Wallenborn, EBU (London, 1 April 1955), 1 [EBUA, Concours Eurovision de la chanson, 1956-57]; letter from Imlay Newbiggin-Watts, BBC, to Leo Wallenborn, EBU (London, 13 April 1956), 1 [EBUA, Concours Eurovision de la chanson, 1956-57]. The UK was also not represented in the 1958 ESC because the BBC claimed that it had 'difficulties over finding adequate material', and that contest was ultimately not even broadcast by the BBC as there was a soccer match between England and Scotland scheduled for the same time. Letter from Cecil McGivern, BBC, to Leo Wallenborn, EBU

(London, 29 November 1957), 1 [EBUA, Concours Eurovision de la chanson, 1958-59]. The 1977 ESC in London was also almost cancelled due to a strike by camerapersons. C.R.B., 'Eurovision Song Contest 1977', 69.

57 Roxburgh, *Songs for Europe*, 225.

58 Ivan Raykoff, 'Camping on the Borders of Europe', in *A Song for Europe*, ed. Raykoff and Tobin, 6.

59 There still were, however, articles in the British press then that were very critical of the ESC. For example, one in *The Guardian* in 1981 compared the ESC to other 'silly' European traditions, such as the 'butter mountain' that had become symbolic of the problems of the EC's Common Agricultural Policy, which was one of the main subjects of British criticism of the EC, especially by Thatcher. Simon Hoggart, 'The Festival of Song That Grabs You by the Throat', *The Guardian* (4 April 1981) [EBUA, Concours Eurovision de la chanson, 1981].

60 Cited in Tom Hibbert, 'Margaret Thatcher v Smash Hits – A Classic Interview from the Vaults,' *The Guardian* (9 April 2013) [www.theguardian.com].

61 The only exception was the song 'Desire', performed by Claudette Pace in 2000, which had a few lines in Maltese.

62 EBU, 'Eurovision Song Contest' (Oslo, October 1966), 21 [EBUA, Concours Eurovision de la chanson, Décisions 1].

63 Radio of Italian Switzerland, 'Gran premio Eurovisione 1956: lista dei collegamenti' (Lugano, 11 May 1956), 1 [EBUA, Concours Eurovision de la chanson, 1956-57]; letter from C.R. Brown, EBU, to Bill Watson (Geneva, 16 April 1970), 1 [EBUA, Concours Eurovision de la chanson, 1970-71].

64 Ien Ang, Gay Hawkins and Lamia Dabboussy, *The SBS Story: The Challenge f Cultural Diversity* (Sydney: University of New South Wales Press, 2008), 7–9.

65 C.R.B, 'Eurovision Song Contest 1969', *E.B.U. Review (Part B – General and Legal)* 20, no. 115 (1969): 59; letter from M. Porto, Associated Dailies, to C. Brown, EBU (Rio de Janeiro, 14 April 1969), 1 [EBUA, Concours Eurovision de la chanson, 1969]. Latin American influences had, however, already been evident in the ESC: in 1959, Austria's 'Der K.u.K. Calypso aus Wien' (The Imperial and Royal Calypso from Vienna) mentioned Caracas, Ecuador, Mexico and Rio de Janeiro; the Dutch entry in 1966, 'Fernando en Filippo' (Fernando and Filippo), referred to cities in Chile and had two guitarists wearing Mexican ponchos and sombreros onstage. The first Latin American artist to participate in the ESC was Henri Salvador from French Guiana: although he had a singing career in France and was renowned for promoting Latin American styles like the bossa nova, he was not the artist but the composer for Monaco's 1962 entry 'Dis rein' (Say Nothing).

Chapter 2

1 Cited in Carlo Maria Lomartire, *Festival: L'Italia di Sanremo* (Milan: Mondadori, 2012), 289–90.

2 Maurizio Ternavasio, *La leggenda di mister Volare: Vita di Domenico Modugno* (Florence and Milan: Giunti, 2004), 116–7, 133–4.

3 Philip V. Bohlman, *Focus: Music, Nationalism, and the Making of the New Europe*, 2nd edn. (New York and Abingdon: Routledge, 2011), 4–5.

4 Oren Soffer, *Mass Communication in Israel: Nationalism, Globalization, and Segmentation*, trans. Judith Yalon (New York and Oxford: Berghahn Books, 2015), 121–5, 142–8.

5 In 1985, the ESC was broadcast for the first time via a satellite, Eutelsat, from within continental Europe.

6 Motti Regev and Edwin Seroussi, *Popular Music and National Culture in Israel* (Berkeley, Los Angeles and London: University of California Press, 2004), 121.

7 The increased security measures also prompted a discussion within the Television Programme Committee over whether a state involved in a military conflict should be excluded from the contest because of the high cost of security – but that could then have also excluded the UK considering the Troubles in Northern Ireland. EBU, 'Television Programme Committee, Executive Group' (Geneva, 2 October 1973), 6 [EBUA, Concours Eurovision de la chanson, Décisions 1].

8 Eric Silver, 'Blast in Israeli Market' *The Guardian* (28 March 1979) [EBUA, Concours Eurovision de la chanson, 1980].

9 Philipp Ther, *Center Stage: Operatic Culture and Nation Building in Nineteenth-Century Central Europe*, trans. Charlotte Hughes-Kreutzmuller (West Lafayette, IN: Purdue University Press, 2014), 1.

10 However, the New Year's Concert was rather an exception in terms of the Eurovision Network's high-culture programmes, which during the Cold War figured significantly less in the network's programme exchanges than sports, current affairs, light entertainment or religious ones. Eugster, 226.

11 Melanie Letschnig, 'Hofburg, kurze Kleider und Knabenchor: Der Grand Prix de la Chanson 1967', in *Eurovision Song Contest: Eine kleine Geschichte zwischen Körper, Geschlecht und Nation*, ed. Christine Ehardt, Georg Vogt and Florian Wagner (Wien: Zaglossus, 2015), 222–4.

12 EBU, 'Planning Group Meeting of Variety Programme Experts' (Geneva, 4 June 1964), 2 [EBUA, Concours Eurovision de la chanson, Décisions 1].

13 Philip V. Bohlman, *World Music: A Very Short Introduction* (Oxford and New York: Oxford University Press, 2002), 88.

14 Renée Winter, '"Vielleicht geschieht ein Wunder": Österreichische Beiträge beim Eurovision Song Conest 1957-1963 im Zeichen geschichtspolitischer Rehabilitierung', in *Eurovision Song Contest*, ed. Ehardt, Vogt and Wagner, 24–6.

15 Ibid., 20–3.

16 Lutgard Mutsaers, 'Fernando, Filippo, and Milly: Bringing Blackness to the Eurovision Stage', in *A Song for Europe*, ed. Raykoff and Tobin, 61–2, 66–7.

17 Ola Johansson, 'Beyond ABBA: The Globalization of Swedish Popular Music', *Focus on Geography* 53, no. 4 (2010): 134–9.

18 The most prominent figure from this group was the architect, designer and writer Poul Henningsen, or PH, who was the lyricist for the Danish entry 'For din skyld' (For Your Sake) which placed seventh out of eighteen entries in the 1965 ESC. Annemette Kirkegaard, 'The Nordic Brotherhoods: Eurovision as a Platform for Partnership and Competition', in *Empire of Song: Europe and Nation in the Eurovision Song Contest*, ed. Dafni Tragaki (Lanham, MD, and Plymouth: Scarecrow Press, 2013), 83–4. Such criticisms of the record industry were also heard in two Austrian entries in the 1970s, 'Musik' (Music) and 'Boom Boom Boomerang'. Like 'Boom Boom Boomerang', the Belgian entry in the 1980 ESC, 'Euro-Vision', performed by the group Telex, which released the album 'Neurovision' in 1980 and the compilation 'Belgium... One Point' in 1993, also parodied the ESC itself.

19 Alf Björnberg, 'Invincible Heroes: The Musical Construction of National and European Identities in Swedish Eurovision Song Contest Entries', in, *Empire of Song*, ed. Tragaki, 208–10. The complaints included that commercial interests deprived national broadcasting organizations of their independence, record companies were being promoted at the expense of the national broadcasting organizations, the songs were all similar and the original intent of the contest had been lost. EBU, 'Future Eurovision Song Contests' (s.l., October 1975 and March 1976), 1 [EBUA, Concours Eurovision de la chanson, Décisions 1]. As if acknowledging such criticisms, in her introduction to the 1975 ESC the host, Karin Falck, cited lines by an unnamed Danish poet on how popular culture needed to be taken as a serious phenomenon.

20 EBU, 'Observations from SR on their Reasons for Withdrawing from the 1976 Eurovision Song Contest' (Milan, October 1975), 1 [EBUA, Concours Eurovision de la chanson, Décisions 1]; EBU, 'Report from SR on Audience Research in Sweden for the Eurovision Song Contest 1975' (13 June 1975), 1–3 [EBUA, Concours Eurovision de la chanson, Décisions 1]; EBU, 'Light Entertainment and the ESC, Istanbul, April 1975' (s.d., s.l.), 18 [EBUA, Concours Eurovision de la chanson, Décisions 1].

21 Irving Wolther, *'Kampf der Kulturen': Der Eurovision Song Contest als Mittel national-kultureller Repräsentation* (Würzburg: Königshausen & Neumann, 2006), 147–8.

22 For example, a French court judged in 1965 that the magazine *Télé 7 Jours* (TV 7 Days) was guilty of libel after it had written that the voting in the 1965 ESC, which was won by France Gall for Luxembourg, had been rigged. Although the case had been initiated by her father, Robert Gall, the *E.B.U. Review* stated that the ESC itself was 'cleared of all suspicion' by this judgement. M.L., 'Judgment Relating to the Grand Prix of the Eurovision Song Contest, 1965', *E.B.U. Review (Part B – General and Legal)* 17, no. 96 (1966): 60.

23 EBU, 'Planning Group' (Geneva, February 1966), 2 [EBUA, Concours Eurovision de la chanson, 1966].

24 EBU, 'Eurovision Song Contest' (Geneva, 26 September 1961), 3 [EBUA, Concours Eurovision de la chanson, 1962].

25 Letter from C. R. Brown, EBU, to C. P Kines (Geneva, 16 April 1970), 1 [EBUA, Concours Eurovision de la chanson, 1970-71].

26 Sinn Féin, 'E.E.C. No!' (Dublin, 1971), 1 [EBUA, Concours Eurovision de la chanson, 1970-71]. The 1970 ESC was won by Dana, an Irish Catholic, who was herself from Northern Ireland but born in London. The British jury awarded her entry four points. Her victory was also politically symbolic as Ireland began its negotiations for entry into the EEC in June 1970. Brian Singleton, 'From Dana to Dustin: The Reputation of Old/New Ireland and the Eurovision Song Contest', in *Performing the 'New' Europe: Identities, Feelings, and Politics in the Eurovision Song Contest*, ed. Karen Fricker and Milija Gluhovic (Basingstoke and New York: Palgrave Macmillan, 2012), 144–6. The British contestant in the 1971 ESC, Clodagh Rodgers, was also deliberately chosen by the BBC because she was from Northern Ireland; she was awarded seven points by the Irish jury.

27 Wogan himself personified the Anglo-Celtic common cultural space as he had first worked in RTÉ and later moved to the BBC.

28 The title of a book by Peter Grünlich, *12 Punkte beim Eurovision Song Contest gehen an Deutschland: Was ein Österreicher nie sagen würde* (12 Points in the Eurovision Song Contest Go to Germany: What an Austrian Would Never Say) (Munich: Riva, 2014), additionally highlights this cultural distancing between Austrians and Germans.

29 Kirkegaard, 'The Nordic Brotherhoods', 93. Lill Lindfors, who represented Sweden in the 1966 ESC in a duet with Svante Thuresson, recalls that the Nordic juries deliberately voted for each other that year because they felt that the juries

from Francophone states had been regularly voting for each other's entries. Jan Feddersen, *Ein Lied kann eine Brücke sein: Die deutsche und internationale Geschichte des Grand Prix Eurovision* (Hamburg: Hoffmann und Campe, 2002), 82. When she hosted the 1986 ESC in Bergen, Åse Kleveland alluded to the controversies about Nordic bloc voting when she said that 'someone might think there's a plot going on' as the entries from Denmark, Finland and Sweden were performed together near the end of the running order, but she emphasized that this had been determined by a draw.

30 Wolther, '*Kampf der Kulturen*', 130–4.

31 Allegations were made in the 2008 documentary *1968: Yo viví el mayo español* (1968: I Lived the Spanish May), directed by Montse Fernández Villa, that Spanish officials had rigged the 1968 ESC vote by promising contracts to foreign artists or the purchase of television series from other national broadcasting organizations. However, these allegations seem false because the television presenter who made them, José María Íñigo, cited the examples of Bulgaria and Czechoslovakia, which were not represented in the ESC then. V. Ruiz, 'Massiel e Iñigo acusan a La Sexta de "urdir todo para favorecer a Chikilicuatre"', *El Mundo* (6 May 2008 [www.elmundo.es]. However, Íñigo may have been unwittingly referring to the ISC, in which TVE also participated in 1968.

32 Gad Yair, 'Unite Unite Europe: The Political and Cultural Structures of Europe as Reflected in the Eurovision Song Contest', *Social Networks* 17, no. 2 (1995): 153–9; Gad Yair and Daniel Maman, 'The Persistent Structure of Hegemony in the Eurovision Song Contest', *Acta Sociologica* 39, no. 3 (1996): 315–22.

33 Dean Vuletic, 'European Sounds, Yugoslav Visions: Performing Yugoslavia at the Eurovision Song Contest', in *Remembering Utopia: The Culture of Everyday Life in Yugoslavia*, ed. Breda Luthar and Maruša Pušnik (Washington, DC: New Academia, 2010), 144. Ireland also did not have diplomatic relations with Israel until 1975, but this did not prevent their juries from exchanging votes in 1973 and 1974. Greek–Israeli relations were rather tense during the Cold War even as the two states maintained diplomatic relations, but nonetheless there were also points awarded between them.

34 EBU, 'Light Entertainment' (Geneva, November 1976), 6 [EBUA, Concours Eurovision de la chanson, Décisions 1]; telex from Yoseph Lapid, IBA, to Regis de Kalbermatten, EBU (14 August 1979), 1 [EBUA, Councours Eurovision de la Chanson, 1980].

35 John Kennedy O'Connor, *The Eurovision Song Contest: The Official History*, revised edn. (London: Carlton Books, 2010), 74–5.

36 Letter from Michael Type, EBU, to Aly Rahim, Golden Chords Production (Geneva, 25 April 1989), 1 [EBUA, Concours Eurovision de la chanson, Correspondance 1];

telex from Aly Rahim, Golden Chords Production, to Michael Type, EBU (Cairo, 5 May 1989), 1 [EBUA, Concours Eurovision de la chanson, Correspondance 1]. The IBA had, however, tried to bring an Egyptian singer to the 1979 ESC, and it was then thought that Egypt might enter the contest in 1980. Judy Siegel, 'Sweet Taste of Victory for Gali, Milk and Honey', *Jerusalem Post* (2 April 1979) [EBUA, Concours Eurovision de la chanson, 1979].

37 O'Connor, *The Eurovision Song Contest*, 76.

38 In 1963, RTF and SR even recommended establishing separate semi-finals for northern and southern European states to reduce the length of the final. SR also suggested that entries could have the option of being in national languages or that northern European entries could also choose English and southern European entries French. EBU, 'Programme Committee' (Geneva, 29 April 1963), 8, 10–11 [EBUA, Concours Eurovision de la chanson, 1963].

39 EBU, 'Grand Prix of the 1960 Eurovision Song Contest' (Geneva, 6 November 1959), 2 [EBUA, Concours Eurovision de la chanson, 1960].

40 Dagmar Herzog, *Sexuality in Europe: A Twentieth-Century History* (Cambridge and New York: Cambridge University Press, 2011), 96.

41 In 1957, the Programme Committee even decided to hold the 1958 ESC on a Wednesday after 9.30pm CET as the ESC 'was not considered important enough to be put on at the peak hour on a Sunday night', as it had been in 1957. EBU, 'Special Programmes' (s.l., s.d.), 1 [EBUA, Concours Eurovision de la chanson, 1958-59]. The 1956 ESC had been held on a Thursday. In 1974, the start of the contest was fixed at 9.00pm CET as 9.30pm was considered too late for young viewers, and because some national broadcasts of news programmes meant that it could not begin between 7.40pm and 9.00pm. EBU, 'Executive Group of the Television Programme Committee' (Geneva, 27 June 1974), 5 [EBUA, Concours Eurovision de la chanson, 1974].

42 Susan Sontag, *Against Interpretation and Other Essays* (New York: Picador, 2001), 290.

43 Ralf Jörg Raber, *Wir sind wie wir sind: ein Jahrhundert homosexuelle Liebe auf Schallplatte und CD – Eine Dokumentation* (Hamburg: Männerschwarm Verlag, 2010), 23.

44 Elmar Kraushaar, 'Der homosexuelle Mann ...' (9 April 2013) [www.taz.de].

45 Cecília Amaral Figueiredo, *Ary dos Santos: A voz da resistência à ditadura salazarista* (Lisbon: Chiado Editora, 2014), 13.

46 Menico Caroli, *Proibitissimo!: Censori e censurati della radiotelevisione italiana* (Milan: Garzanti, 2003), 160.

47 EBU, 'Eurovision Song Contest' (Geneva, March 1974), 44 [EBUA, Concours Eurovision de la chanson, Décisions 1]; 'Gigliola Cinquetti censurata dall Tv: niente Eurofestival perché canta la canzone "Sì"', *Corriere dell Sera* (30 March 1974) [www.corriere.it]. The 1974 ESC was eventually shown on RAI on 6 June, but some northern Italian homes were able to watch the live broadcast if they could receive the signal of SRG SSR.

48 'Diskussion um die politischen Rechte der Frau', 'Keine Chance für Biggi', *Liechtensteiner Vaterland* (24 January 1976) [www.vaterland.li]. Although Liechtenstein has still never taken part in the ESC because it lacks a national public service broadcasting organization, its citizens have been able to take part in the Swiss national selection.

49 EBU, 'France's National Mourning Leads to Withdrawal from Eurovision Song Contest' (Geneva, 4 April 1974), 1 [EBUA, Concours Eurovision de la chanson, 1974-75].

50 Thomas Hilder, *Sámi Musical Performance and the Politics of Indigeneity in Northern Europe* (Lanham, MD, and London: Rowman & Littlefield, 2015), 59.

51 Luisa Pinto Teixeira and Martin Stokes, ' "And After Love …" ': Eurovision, Portuguese Popular Culture, and the Carnation Revolution', in *Empire of Song*, ed. Tragaki, 223–5. A photograph of Franco even appeared in the *E.B.U. Review* in 1970 in an article about a Spanish radio programme. Aníbal Arias Ruiz, '"Operation Plus Ultra": A Genuinely European Radio Programme from Spain', *EBU Review (Part B – General and Legal)* 21, no. 120 (1970): 30.

52 Sílvia Martínez and Amparo Sales Casanova, 'Afterword: Mediterranean Love Songs – A Conversation with Joan Manuel Serrat', in *Made in Spain: Studies in Popular Music*, ed. Sílvia Martínez and Héctor Fouce (New York and Abingdon: Routledge, 2013), 202–3. The Andorran government had expressed interest in entering the ESC in 1967 with a song in Catalan, the official language of Andorra, but it could not do so because Andorra did not have a national broadcasting organization at the time. Letter from Francesc Escudé Ferrero, General Council of Andorra, to Daniel Boada Vila (Andorra la Vella, 5 March 1967), 1 [EBUA, Concours Eurovision de la chanson, 1967]. The Andorran national broadcasting organization, Radio and Television of Andorra, was established in 1989 and participated in the ESC from 2004 to 2009.

53 Juan Francisco Gutiérrez Lozano, 'Spain Was Not Living a Celebration: TVE and the Eurovision Song Contest During the Years of Franco's Dictatorship', *View* 1, no. 2 (2012): 14–7.

54 SR, 'Press Release Issued by Sveriges Radio on February 28th, 1969', 1–2 [EBUA, Concours Eurovision de la chanson, 1969].

55 Lyall, *International Communications*, 113.
56 Pinto Teixeira and Stokes, '"And After Love ..."', 236.
57 Letter from Clifford R. Brown, EBU, to Michael Yiannakakos, EIRT (18 October 1972), 1 [EBUA, Concours Eurovision de la chanson, 1972-73].
58 Telex from Erik Jurgens and Carel Enkelaar, NOS, to Saban Karatas, TRT (Hilversum, 3 April 1976), 1 [EBUA, Concours Eurovision de la chanson, 1976-77]. Although the ESC at that time did not have any rules regarding the lyrics of entries, the rules were amended in 1978 so that a song could be disqualified if it was not in the national language or if the performance in the final departed from what had been rehearsed.
59 Letter from Özer Berkem, Bayrak Radio and Television, to Werner Rumphorst, EBU (26 November 1987), 1–2 [EBUA, Concours Eurovision de la chanson, 1988].
60 Letter from Joanna Spicer, EBU, to Edvin Risi, TRT (Geneva, 29 November 1973), 1–2 [EBUA, Concours Eurovision de la chanson, Décisions 1].
61 Thomas Solomon, 'Articulating the Historical Moment: Turkey, Europe, and Eurovision 2003', in *A Song for Europe*, ed. Raykoff and Tobin, 136.

Chapter 3

1 Mariusz Szczygieł, *Gottland: Mostly True Stories from Half of Czechoslovakia*, trans. Antonia Lloyd-Jones (New York and London: Melville House, 2014), 152–7.
2 Helena Vondráčková, *'Unter der Asche meiner Liebe ist noch Glut': Erinnerungen* (Berlin: Ullstein, 1997), 62.
3 Milan Kundera, 'The Tragedy of Central Europe', trans. Edmund White, *The New York Review of Books* 31, no. 7 (1984): 33.
4 Michael H. Kater, *Different Drummers: Jazz in the Culture of Nazi Germany* (New York: Oxford University Press, 1992), 186–7.
5 S. Frederick Starr, *Red and Hot: The Fate of Jazz in the Soviet Union 1917-1991*, 2nd edn. (New York: Limelight Editions, 1994), 37–203.
6 Timothy W. Ryback, *Rock Around the Bloc: A History of Rock Music in Eastern Europe and the Soviet Union* (New York and Oxford: Oxford University Press, 1990), 8–14.
7 Walter L. Hixson, *Parting the Curtain: Propaganda, Culture, and the Cold War, 1945-1961* (New York: St. Martin's Press, 1997), 116–7.
8 Richard H. Cummings, *Cold War Radio: The Dangerous History of American Broadcasting in Europe, 1950-1989* (Jefferson, NC, and London: McFarland & Company, 2009), 10.

9 Katalin Miklóssy, 'Competing for Popularity: Song Contests and Interactive Television in Communist Hungary', in *Competition in Socialist Society*, ed. Katalin Miklóssy and Melanie Ilic (Abingdon and New York: Routledge, 2014), 115–9.

10 Karin Taylor, *Let's Twist Again: Youth and Leisure in Socialist Bulgaria* (Vienna and Berlin: Lit, 2006), 125.

11 Alexandru Matei, 'The Golden Stag Festival in Ceausescu's Romania (1968-1971)', *View* 1, no. 2 (2012): 19–24.

12 Uta G. Poiger, *Jazz, Rock, and Rebels: Cold War Politics and American Culture in a Divided Germany* (Berkeley, Los Angeles and London: University of California Press, 2000), 31–3.

13 Eugster, *Television Programming Across National Boundaries,* 167–9.

14 Hans-Joachim Kynaß, '"Dresden '72" – Rendezvous mit Schlagern', *Neues Deutschland* (26 October 1972) [www.neues-deutschland.de].

15 Yulia Yurtaeva, 'Ein schwarzer Rabe gegen Conchita Wurst oder: Wovor hat Russland Angst?', in *Eurovision Song Contest*, ed. Ehardt, Vogt and Wagner, 116–7.

16 Eugster, *Television Programming Across National Boundaries,* 66, 167–9.

17 Christine E. Evans, *Between Truth and Time: A History of Soviet Central Television* (New Haven, CT, and London: Yale University Press, 2016), 98–114.

18 Eugster, *Television Programming Across National Boundaries,* 104–6.

19 Ibid., 59–61.

20 Ibid., 219–20, 223.

21 Mari Pajala, 'Intervision Song Contests and Finnish Television Between East and West', in *Airy Curtains in the European Ether: Broadcasting and the Cold War*, ed. Alexander Badenoch, Andreas Fickers and Christian Henrich-Franke (Baden-Baden: Nomos, 2013): 219–21.

22 ČST, 'Rozborová zpráva o činnosti OIRT, Intervize a Eurovize' (Prague, September-October 1965), 30–31 [Archives of Czech Television (ACT), Zahraniční styky, 200/1129]; EBU, 'Relations avec l'OIRT' (London, 13, 14 and 16 November 1964), 1–2 [EBUA, Concours Eurovision de la chanson, 1967]; Eugster, *Television Programming Across National Boundaries*, 188–90, 193–6.

23 OIR, 'Resolution' (Moscow, 21 May 1958), 6 [ACT, OIRT, 5/2].

24 OIR, '31st Session of the OIR Administrative Council' (Prague, August 1959)', 3–4, [ACT, OIRT, 6/2]; OIRT, '34th Session of the OIRT Administrative Council' (Prague, June 1961), 3–4 [ACT, OIRT, 7/2].

25 Jiří Pelikán, 'Předběžná zpráva o setkání s delegacemi OIRT a UER /Eurovize/ a Intervize' (Prague, 2 July 1964), 5, 8 [ACT, Zahraniční styky, 248/27]. In

1965, the EBU and OIRT also agreed to exchange the Sanremo and Sopot song festivals. ČST, 'Rozborová zpráva o činnosti OIRT, Intervize a Eurovize', 42, 44.

26 OIRT, '52nd Meeting' (Algiers, 16-19 May 1975), 56 [EBUA, Concours Eurovision de la chanson, Décisions 1].

27 ČST, 'Statut intervizní "Soutěže tanečních písní a chansonů" o "Zlatý klíč"' (Prague, 10 March 1965), 1–5 [ACT, Zahraniční styky, 30/262].

28 Ivan Szabó, *Bratislavská lýra* (Bratislava: Marenčin PT, 2010), 17.

29 Jaromír Vašta, Jiří Malásek and Josef Koliha, 'Zpráva o přípravě vysílání pořadu "Vstup volný pro písničku" Intervize – "Zlatý klíč"' (s.l., 1965), 1–2 [ACT, Zahraniční styky, 30/262]; Jiří Malásek and Ladislav Peprník, 'Národní soutěž a Zlatý klíč' (Prague, 11 July 1966), 2–3 [ACT, Zahraniční styky, 30/262]; 'Bratislavská lyra 1967' (s.l., 1967), 2–3 [ACT, Zahraniční styky, 40/331].

30 Malásek and Peprník, 'Národní soutěž a Zlatý klíč', 3.

31 'Golden Clef Festival Open for All Europe', *Billboard* (11 May 1968) [www.billboard.com].

32 Lubomir Doruzka, '4th Intervision Song Contest's Golden Clef to a Czech Singer', *Billboard* (13 July 1968) [www.billboard.com].

33 Eugster, *Television Programming Across National Boundaries,* 194.

34 'Prague's Golden Clef Contest Revived', *Billboard* (17 April 1971) [www.billboard.com].

35 OIRT, 'XXIInd Session of the OIRT General Assembly' (Prague, April 1969), 14 [ACT, OIRT, 9/2].

36 OIRT, '64. Tagung des Intervisionsrates' (Helsinki, May 1980)', 2 [ACT, OIRT, 27/2].

37 Maciej Szczepański, 'Międzynarodowy festiwal piosenky Sopot 1977' (Warsaw, 8 November 1976), 1 [Archives of Polish Television (APT), Komitet do spraw radia i telewizji 'Polskie radio i telewizja', 1716/66].

38 Letter from Maciej Szczepański, Radio and Television Committee, to Henry Kisiel, Ministry of Finance (Warsaw, 22 August 1977), 1 [APT, Komitet do spraw radia i telewizji 'Polskie radio i telewizja', 1716/66].

39 Tadeusz Kędzierski, 'Sprawozdanie z udziału w 63 Sesji Rady Interwizji' (Warsaw, 1979), 2, 4 [APT, Komitet do spraw radia i telewizji 'Polskie radio i telewizja', 1702/1].

40 Szczepański, 'Międzynarodowy festiwal piosenky Sopot 1977', 2.

41 Alla Pugacheva's winning song in the 1978 ISC, 'Vse mogut koroli' (Kings Can Do Anything), was, however, censored in the USSR, likely because its royal subject was considered an inappropriate theme by the Soviet authorities considering that the Bolsheviks had come to power after the Romanov dynasty had been deposed in the February Revolution. David MacFadyen, *Red Stars: Personality*

and the Soviet Popular Song, 1955-1991 (Montreal: McGill-Queen's University Press, 2001), 217–8. Although there was also censorship of Boney M's 'Rasputin' in the USSR because its subject was the mystic of the last Russian tsar, Nikolai II, the group performed the song at the 1979 ISC. Leslie Woodhead, *How the Beatles Rocked the Kremlin: The Untold Story of a Noisy Revolution* (London: Bloomsbury, 2013), 117.

42 Polish Radio and Television, 'Festiwal Interwizji - Sopot 1979' (Warsaw, 1979), 1–2 [APT, Badania sondażowe 1976-79, 4590/172].

43 Pajala, 'Intervision Song Contests and Finnish Television Between East and West', 225–35.

44 Steve Rosenberg, 'The Cold War Rival to Eurovision', *BBC* (14 May 2012) [www.bbc.com].

45 Cited in Agence France-Presse, 'Kein Geld für Chanson', *Frankfurter Allgemeine Zeitung* (15 August 1981) [German Broadcasting Archive, Pressearchiv, Medien, Medienveranstaltungen, Sopot].

46 Tor Paulsen and Harald Tusberg, 'Report to the EBU Programme Committee Meeting on the World Song Contest Project' (Oslo, 18 September 1987), 8 [EBUA, Concours Eurovision de la chanson, Concours mondial de la chanson].

47 OIRT, '63. Tagung des Verwaltungsrates' (Prague, August 1988), 11 [ACT, OIRT, 15/2].

48 Mary Fulbrook, *The People's State: East German Society from Hitler to Honecker* (New Haven, CT, and London: Yale University Press, 2005), 135.

49 Vuletic, 'European Sounds, Yugoslav Vision', 125–8. Yugoslav popular music was also exported to Eastern Europe states after Yugoslavia's relations with them were normalized from 1955; Yugoslav artists in Eastern Europe benefitted from an association with Western trends because of Yugoslavia's openness towards Western cultural influences. Dean Vuletic, 'Sounds like America: Yugoslavia's Soft Power in Eastern Europe', in *Divided Dreamworlds?: The Cultural Cold War in East and West*, ed. Peter Romijn, Giles Scott-Smith and Joes Segal (Amsterdam: Amsterdam University Press, 2012), 115–31. Yugoslavia also fed the Mediterraneanist fantasies of Eastern Europeans, with Yugoslavia being the most accessible part of the Mediterranean for them if they could get permission from their national authorities to travel there.

50 Vuletic, 'European Sounds, Yugoslav Vision', 128–9.

51 Ibid., 130–5; EBU, 'Minutes – 56th Meeting Administrative Council' (Geneva, 10–11 December 1976), 8 [EBUA, Concours Eurovision de la chanson, Décisions 1]. As the journalist Maroje Mihovilović wrote regarding Yugoslavia's experience in the ESC, '[w]e are a proud nation, we know that some geographical and

historical circumstances have apparently pushed us into the background of the European cultural and pseudocultural community, and that bothers us.' Cited in ibid., 131.

52 Ibid., 136.

53 Nicholas Tochka, *Audible States: Socialist Politics and Popular Music in Albania* (New York: Oxford University Press, 2016), 100–3.

54 Smoki Musaraj, 'Alternative Publics: Reflections on Marginal Collective Practices in Communist Albania', in *Albania: Family, Society and Culture in the 20th Century*, ed. Andreas Hemming, Gentiana Kera and Enriketa Pandelejmoni (Zurich and Berlin: Lit, 2012): 181–2.

55 Karel Gott, *Zwischen zwei Welten: Mein Leben* (Munich: Riva, 2014), 91–2.

56 Jonathan Bolton, *Worlds of Dissent: Charter 77, The Plastic People of the Universe, and Czech Culture Under Communism* (Cambridge, MA, and London: Harvard University Press, 2012), 115–24.

57 Cited in ibid., 178.

58 Cited in Alexei Yurchak, *Everything Was Forever, Until It Was No More: The Last Soviet Generation* (Princeton and Oxford: Princeton University Press, 2005), 214–5.

59 Cited in O'Connor, *The Eurovision Song Contest,* 119. In the 1981 ESC, when Helga Vlahović could not immediately present the voting results of the Yugoslav jury when she was called to do so, Wogan said in his live commentary '[i]t's probably a Russian plot, as you know.'

Chapter 4

1 Neven Andjelić, 'National Promotion and Eurovision: From Besieged Sarajevo to the Floodlights of Europe', *Contemporary Southeastern Europe* 2, no. 1 (2015): 103–4; Marek Kohn, 'Would You Risk Your Life for Eurovision?', *The Independent* (30 April 1993) [www.independent.co.uk].

2 Aleksandar Pavković and Christopher Kelen, *Anthems and the Making of Nation-States: Identity and Nationalism in the Balkans* (London and New York: I.B. Tauris, 2016), 187.

3 Nenad Polimac, 'Od Grlića sam preuzeo film o Sanaderu', *Globus* (21 August 2016) [www.jutarnji.hr/globus].

4 Dean Vuletic, 'The Socialist Star: Yugoslavia, Cold War Politics and the Eurovision Song Contest', in *A Song for Europe*, ed. Raykoff and Tobin, 95.

5 Ibid., 96.

6 Cited in Ana Petruseva, 'Old Foes Serenade Serbia in Istanbul', *Institute for War and Peace Reporting* (21 February 2005) [www.iwpr.net].

7 Kenneth Morrison, *Montenegro: A Modern History* (London and New York: I. B. Tauris, 2009), 215, 270. 'Moja ljubavi' referred to 'mountains' (Montenegro, also in its native form *Crna gora*,' means 'black mountain') as well as 'dawn', with the national anthem of Montenegro being 'Oj, svijetla majska zoro' (Oh, Bright Dawn of May).

8 Dejan Anastasijevic, 'Serbs Cheer a Eurovision "Conspiracy"', *Time* (15 May 2007) [www.time.com]; European Commission, 'Bring the Peoples of Europe "Together in Diversity!": Campaign Launch of the European Year of Intercultural Dialogue 2008', *European Commission Press Release Database* (Brussels, 4 December 2007) [www.europa.eu/rapid].

9 Bohlman, *Focus*, 247; Marijana Mitrović, '"New Face of Serbia" at the Eurovision Song Contest: International Media Spectacle and National Identity', *European Review of History – Revue européenne d'histoire* 17, no. 2 (2010): 175–7.

10 Apostolos Lampropoulos, 'Delimiting the Eurobody: Historicity, Politicization, Queerness', in *Empire of Song*, ed. Tragaki, 161–3. For the director behind 'Sameach', Eytan Fox, his experience in the ESC was the inspiration for his film *Cupcakes* (Israel: Abot Hameiri, Canal Plus, Chic Films, Ciné Plus, Keshet, Lorette Productions, Rabinovich Foundation and United King Films, 2013), which is about a group of friends who enter a song into an international song contest called UniverSong. There was also controversy in the 2002 ESC when the Belgian and Swedish commentators advised their national audiences not to vote for the Israeli entry. 'Swedes, Belgians Told Not to Vote for Israel in Eurovision Contest', *Haaretz* (26 May 2002) [www.haaretz.com].

11 Telex from Marie-Claire Vionnet, EBU, to Antoine Remy, TL (Geneva, 30 January 1989), 1 [EBUA, Concours Eurovision de la chanson, Correspondance 1]; 'Lebanon Withdraws from Eurovision', *BBC* (18 March 2005) [www.bbc.com].

12 Miriam Shaviv, 'Teapacks Pushes the Wrong Button for Eurovision', *The Jerusalem Post* (2 March 2007) [www.jpost.com].

13 Ethan Bronner, 'Musical Show of Unity Upsets Many in Israel', *The New York Times* (24 February 2009) [www.nytimes.com].

14 Zoi Constantine, 'Palestinians Seek Eurovision Entry', *The National* (22 May 2008) [www.thenational.ae]. A licence for the creation of an 'Arabian Vision Song Contest' was issued by the EBU in 2008, but such a contest has not yet been established. 'A Eurovision Song Contest in the Middle East and North Africa', *Eurovision.tv* (7 January 2008) [www.eurovision.tv].

15 The definition of the EBA was last modified in 2007 to include the Transcaucasian states and currently stands as follows: 'The "European Broadcasting Area" is bounded on the west by the western boundary of Region 1, on the east by the meridian 40° East of Greenwich and on the south by the parallel 30° North so as to include the northern part of Saudi Arabia and that part of those countries bordering the Mediterranean within these limits. In addition, Armenia, Azerbaijan, Georgia and those parts of the territories of Iraq, Jordan, Syrian Arab Republic, Turkey and Ukraine lying outside the above limits are included in the European Broadcasting Area.' International Telecommunication Union, *Final Acts WRC-07: World Radiocommunication Conference (Geneva, 2007)* (Geneva: International Telecommunication Union, 2008) 5 [ITUA, ITU Conferences].

16 William Lee Adams, 'How Armenia and Azerbaijan Wage War Through Eurovision', *Time* (11 March 2012) [www.time.com]; 'Azerbaijani Authorities Interrogate Music Fan over Eurovision Vote for Armenia', *Radio Free Europe/ Radio Liberty* (14 August 2009) [www.rferl.org].

17 Andrea F. Bohlman and Ioannis Polychronakis, 'Eurovision Everywhere: A Kaleidoscopic Vision of the Grand Prix, in *Empire of Song*, ed. Tragaki, 70; Olesya Vartanyan and Michael Schwirtz, 'Georgia Offers Sideburns and a Disco Beat as Payback for a War', *The New York Times* (21 February 2009) [www.nytimes.com].

18 Yana Meerzon and Dmitri Priven, 'Back to the Future: Imagining a New Russia at the Eurovision Song Contest', in *Performing the 'New' Europe*, eds. Fricker and Gluhovic, 120–3.

19 Dmitry Volchek and Claire Bigg, '"I Won't Sing for Occupiers": A Ukrainian Singer Falls out with Russia', *Radio Free Europe/Radio Liberty* (24 September 2014) [www.rferl.org].

20 Larry Wolff, *Inventing Eastern Europe: The Map of Civilization on the Mind of the Enlightenment* (Stanford, CA: Stanford University Press, 1994), 89–94.

21 Katrin Sieg, 'Conundrums of Post-Socialist Belonging at the Eurovision Song Contest', in *Performing the 'New' Europe*, ed. Fricker and Gluhovic, 223–6. Only two other entries in the ESC from 1991 to 2002 mentioned 'Europe': Italy's 'Sole d'Europa' (The Sun of Europe) in 1993 and Spain's 'Europe's Living a Celebration' in 2002.

22 Feddersen, *Ein Lied kann eine Brücke sein*, 256, 262.

23 OIRT, '66th Session of the OIRT Administrative Council' (Prague, April 1991), 1-4 [ACT, OIRT, 16/2]

24 EBU, '1993 Eurovision Song Contest (ESC)' (Geneva, 8 January 1993), 1 [EBUA, Concours Eurovision de la chanson, 1993].

25 Letter from Henri Pérez, EBU, to Tihomir Ilievski, MRT (Geneva, 16 March 1993), 1 [EBUA, Concours Eurovision de la chanson, 1993]; letter from Jean-Bernard Münch, EBU, to George Dragonas, ERT (Geneva, 19 August 1993), 1 [EBUA, Concours Eurovision de la chanson, Correspondance 2]; letter from Jean-Bernard Münch, EBU, to Slobodan Trajkovski, MRT (Geneva, 28 April 1998), 1 [EBUA, Concours Eurovision de la chanson, Correspondance 2]. However, when the 2006 ESC was staged in Athens, the longer version 'Former Yugoslav Republic of Macedonia' was pointedly used on the scoreboard.

26 EBU, '63rd Meeting of the Television Programme Committe' (Geneva, 14 April 1993), 1–3 [EBUA, Concours Eurovision de la chanson, 1993]

27 Catherine Baker, *Sounds of the Borderland: Popular Music, War and Nationalism in Croatia Since 1991* (Farnham and Burlington, VT: Ashgate Publishing, 2010), 200–1.

28 Singleton, 'From Dana to Dustin', 149–51.

29 Elaine Aston, 'Competing Femininities: A "Girl" for Eurovision', in *Performing the 'New' Europe*, ed. Fricker and Gluhovic, 168–9.

30 Paul Jordan, *The Modern Fairy Tale: Nation Branding, National Identity and the Eurovision Song Contest in Estonia* (Tartu: University of Tartu Press, 2014), 85–8, 91–5, 100–101.

31 Miyase Christensen and Christian Christensen, 'The After-Life of Eurovision 2003: Turkish and European Social Imaginaries and Ephemeral Communicative Space', *Popular Communication* 6, no. 3 (2008), 159–60, 162–8; Thomas Solomon, 'The Oriental Body on the European Stage: Producing Turkish Cultural Identity on the Margins of Europe', in *Empire of Song*, ed. Tragaki, 181–90, 192–193. The importance that Turkish politicians accorded the ESC was underlined when President Süleyman Demirel gave the video message before the Turkish entry in the 1996 ESC; he also survived an assassination attempt on the same day that that contest was held. O'Connor, *The Eurovision Song Contest*, 145.

32 Cited in Solomon, 'Articulating the Historical Moment', 144.

33 CoE, '840th Meeting, 28 May 2003'(Strasbourg, 28 May 2003), 4 [CoE, Committee of Ministers, Del/Act(2003)840]. In the final of the 2004 ESC, during the presentation of the voting results, the co-hosts Korhan Abay and Meltem Cumbul described the Greek language as 'romantic'. They also mentioned earlier in the show that Sakis Rouvas, the artist representing Greece, had participated in a concert dedicated to Greek-Turkish friendship which had been staged in 1997 on the Green Line dividing the northern and southern parts of Cyprus. However, while the flags and maps of each participating state in the 2004 ESC were shown as their spokespersons presented the voting results, no map of

Cyprus was included – although the Cypriot flag, with its map of the whole island on it, still was. A Turkish government minister also appeared onstage at the end of the contest to congratulate the winner; it was a tradition in the ESC from 2003 to 2006 for a local politician to do so, as the mayor of Riga, the Ukrainian president and a Greek minister also did.

34 European Commission, 'Biographies of the Artists Performing at the EU Enlargement Concert 30 April 2004', *European Commission Press Release Database* (Brussels, 29 April 2004), 2-3 [www.europa.eu/rapid].

35 Marko Pavlyshyn, 'Envisioning Europe: Ruslana's Rhetoric of Identity', *The Slavic and East European Journal* 50, no. 3 (2006): 477–83.

36 Jordan, *The Modern Fairytale*, 122.

37 European Economic and Social Committee, 'José Manuel Barroso and Ruslana Lyzhychko at the EESC Plenary Session', *European Commission Press Release Database* (Brussels, 17 January 2014) [www.europa.eu/rapid].

38 CoE, 'Commemorative Ceremony for the 60th Anniversary of the Council of Europe', *Council of Europe* (Strasbourg, 1 October 2009) [www.coe.int]. Since 2008, the CoE has also been the patron of the Liet International, which is modelled on the ESC but only allows entries in minority languages – and explicitly bans ones in English.

39 Vladimír Špidla, 'Partnership Between the European Year 2007 of Equal Opportunities for All and the Eurovision Song Contest', *European Commission Press Release Database* (Helsinki, 11 May 2007) [www.europa.eu/rapid]. There were 320,000 visitors to the stand. Rambøll Management, Focus Consultancy and Eurèval, *On-going Evaluation of the 2007 European Year of Equal Opportunities for All: Final Report* (Copenhagen: Rambøll Management, 2008), 55 [www.ec.europa.eu].

40 EP, 'European Parliament: Written Questions with Answer', *Official Journal of the European Communities: Information and Notices* 44, no. C 350 E (2001): 176 [www.eur-lex.europa.eu]; EP, 'Written Question by Georgios Karatzaferis (IND/DEM) to the Commission' *European Parliament* (Brussels, 15 February 2015) [www.europarl.europa.eu]; EP, 'Written Question by Georgios Karatzaferis (IND/DEM) to the Commission', *European Parliament* (Brussels, 7 June 2006) [www.europarl.europa.eu]. Xarchakos submitted a question in the EP concerning the costs and credibility of televoting in the 2003 ESC as he considered it suspicious that such high points were given from Cyprus and Greece to Turkey. The response from the commissioner for industry, entrepreneurship and SME's, Erkki Liikanen, was that the EC had no regulations concerning voting in such programmes. EP, 'European Parliament: Written Questions with Answer', *Official Journal of the European Union: Information and Notices* 47, no. C 78 E (2004): 54 [www.eur-lex.europa.eu].

41 Fornäs, *Signifying Europe*, 136–7.

42 One of the biggest issues between the EBU and the EU concerned complaints made by commercial broadcasting organisations from the late 1980s that the Eurovision Network's purchase of sports broadcasting rights violated EU competition law. In 1993 and 2000, the European Commission made two exemption decisions for the Eurovision Network regarding this issue, citing also the network's importance for the development of a single European market for broadcasting. Ben Van Rompuy and Karen Donders, 'The EBU's Eurovision System Governing the Joint Buying of Sports Broadcasting Rights: Unfinished Competition Business', *The Competition Law Review* 9, no. 1 (2013): 12–21.

43 Dean Vuletic, 'No Eurovision for the Czech Republic?!', *Radio Prague* (23 May 2003) [www.radio.cz/en].

44 SRG SSR Research Service, 'Beachtung des "Concours Eurovision de la chanson 1989" aus Lausanne (6.5.1989)' (10 August 1989), 1 [EBUA, Concours Eurovision de la chanson, Correspondance 1]; letter from Dusan Havlicek to Frank Naef, EBU (Geneva, 4 June 1992), 1 [EBUA, Concours Eurovision de la chanson, 1992].

45 Jiří Pehe, 'Unie, Eurovize, aneb z ostudy Kabát', *Literární noviny* (14 May 2007) [www.literarky.cz].

46 Václav Štětka, 'Media Events and European Visions: Czech Republic in the 2007 Eurovision Song Contest', *Communications* 34, no. 1 (2009): 32–6

47 Terry Wogan, 'Foreword', *The Complete Eurovision Song Contest Companion*, Paul Gambaccini, Tim Rice, Jonathan Rice and Tony Brown (London: Pavilion Books, 1998), 8.

48 Karen Fricker, '"It's Just Not Funny Any More": Terry Wogan, Melancholy Britain, and the Eurovision Song Contest', in *Performing the 'New' Europe*, ed. Fricker and Gluhovic, 64–71, 76.

49 Julia Chaplin, 'A New Eurofestation', *The New York Times* (8 December 2002) [www.nytimes.com].

50 Sandra Mollin, *Euro-English: Assessing Variety Status* (Tübingen: Gunter Narr, 2006), 71–4.

51 Fricker, '"It's Just Not Funny Any More"', 53–4. For an example of an article attacking the ESC – and even calling for its termination – in a Eurosceptic British broadsheet, see Sinclair McKay, 'Let's Say Bye-Bye to Boom Bang a Bang', *Daily Telegraph* (29 May 1999) [EBUA, Concours Eurovision de la chanson, Communiqués de presse, Divers].

52 Fricker, '"It's Just Not Funny Any More"', 68.

53 Cited in 'Nigel Farage Blasts Eurovision "Prejudice" Against UK', *BBC News* (9 May 2014) [www.bbc.com].

54 'Brits Think Eurovision is All Politics', *YouGov* (16 May 2013)[www.yougov.co.uk]. In two polls conducted in Finland in 2002, around four-fifths of the respondents also wanted Finland to leave the ESC, with many of them citing Central and East European bloc voting as the reason and even suggesting the establishment of a separate contest for EU member states. Mari Pajala, 'Finland, Zero Points: Nationality, Failure, and Shame in the Finnish Media', in *A Song for Europe*, ed. Raykoff and Tobin, 81.

55 'ORF verzichtet auf Teilnahme', *Wiener Zeitung* (21 November 2007) [www.wienerzeitung.at].

56 Paolo Calcagno, 'Italia, soltanto tu snobbi l'Eurofestival', *Corriere dell Sera* (20 May 1996). Thirty-three per cent of the Italian audience watched the 1991 ESC that was staged in Rome, and only 1 per cent watched it in 1992. EBU, '1991 Eurovision Song Contest: Results of Audience Figures' (Geneva, 12 June 1991), 2 [EBUA, Concours Eurovision de la chanson, 1991]; Radio Sweden Audience and Programme Research, 'Ratings and Viewers in Thousands for the 1992 Eurovision Song Contest From Malmö, Sweden' (20 May 1992), 1 [EBUA, Concours Eurovision de la chanson, 1992]; 'Highly Irregular Ratings for Song Contest', *Eurodience* 7, no. 67 (1993): 1.

57 Alf Björnberg, 'Return to Ethnicity: The Cultural Significance of Musical Change in the Eurovision Song Contest ', in *A Song for Europe*, ed. Raykoff and Tobin, 18; Pajala, 'Finland, Zero Points', 80.

58 Victor Ginsburgh and Abdul G. Noury, 'The Eurovision Song Contest: Is Voting Political or Cultural?', *European Journal of Political Economy* 24, no. 1 (2008): 50.

59 Derek Gatherer, 'Voting in Eurovision: Shared Tastes or Cultural Epidemic?', *Empirical Text and Culture Research* 3, no. 1 (2007): 73, 76–7.

60 'TRT Releases Surprising Decision to Withdraw From Eurovision', *Daily Sabah* (15 December 2012) [www.dailysabah.com].

Chapter 5

1 'Why the Financial Crisis Matters for Security: A Three-Minute Guide', *NATO Review* 57, no. 4 (2009) [www.nato.int/docu/review].

2 Lampropoulos, 'Delimiting the Eurobody', 163.

3 Fornäs, *Signifying Europe*, 104–5.

3 Christoph Oliver Mayer, 'Die deutsch-französische Freundschaft und der Grand Prix de la Chanson de l'Eurovision', in *Populärkultur und deutsch-französische Mittler: Akteure, Medien, Ausdrucksformen/Culture de masse et médiateurs*

franco-allemands: Acteurs, médias, articulations, ed. Dietmar Hüser and Ulrich Pfeil (Bielefeld: Transcript, 2015), 159-60.

5 Jordan, *The Modern Fairytale*, 79–83, 98, 103–5.

6 Bjorn Ingvoldstad, 'Lithuanian Contests and European Dreams', in *A Song for Europe*, ed. Raykoff and Tobin, 105–8.

7 William Lee Adams, 'Ukraine's Eurovision Selection Marred by Right-Wing Racism', *Time* (5 March 2012) [www.time.com]. The far-right terrorist Anders Behring Breivik, who killed seventy-seven people in two attacks in Norway on 22 June 2011, criticized in his personal diary the selection of Kenyan-Norwegian singer Stella Mwangi as Norway's representative in the 2011 ESC. Mfonobong Nsehe, 'Norwegian Killer Anders Behring Breivik Hated Kenyan Musician', *Forbes* (25 June 2011) [www.forbes.com].

8 Caitlin Gura, 'Österreichs Abschneiden beim Eurovision Song Contest zwischen 2000 und 2013: Und dessen Auswirkung auf die österreichische Identität', in *Eurovision Song Contest*, ed. Ehardt, Vogt and Wagner, 68–70.

9 Andrea F. Bohlman and Alexander Rehding, 'Doing the European Two-Step', in *Empire of Song*, ed. Tragaki, 290–2; Bohlman, *Focus*, 218.

10 Cited in Catherine Dauvergne, *The New Politics of Immigration and the End of Settler Societies* (New York: Cambridge University Press, 2016), 95–6, 111.

11 'A Blazing Surprise', *The Economist* (1 June 2013) [www.economist.com].

12 Sonja Aleksoska-Nedelkovska, 'Darko Dimitrov i Lazar Cvetkovski angažirani za novata evroviziska pesna', *Dnevnik* (8 March 2013) [www.dnevnik.com.mk]. 'Imperija' would have been politically provocative had it been performed at the ESC due to its allusions to the Republic of Macedonia's claims of historical continuity with the Macedonian Empire of Alexander the Great, an issue which, along with the state's name, stoked political tensions between Athens and Skopje. The music video for 'Imperija' depicted monuments that were built as part of the Skopje 2014 project that was spearheaded by VMRO-DPMNE and which sought to revitalize the Macedonian capital with lavish constructions that reflected controversial approaches to Macedonian history, including a massive statue of Alexander the Great. The Greek entry in the 2013 ESC, 'Alcohol is Free', briefly mentioned Alexander the Great in its lyrics.

13 Lee Walzer, *Between Sodom and Eden: A Gay Journey Through Today's Changing Israel* (New York: Columbia University Press, 2000), 171–5; Dafna Lemish, 'Gay Brotherhood: Israeli Gay Men and the Eurovision Song Contest', in *A Song for Europe*, ed. Raykoff and Tobin, 131–3.

14 Ministry of Public Diplomacy and Diaspora Affairs, 'The True Face of Israel' (Jerusalem: Ministry of Public Diplomacy and Diaspora Affairs, 2012).

15 Milija Gluhovic, 'Sing for Democracy: Human Rights and Sexuality Discourse in the Eurovision Song Contest', in *Performing the 'New' Europe*, ed. Fricker and Gluhovic, 203.

16 Robert Deam Tobin, 'Eurovision at 50: Post-Wall and Post-Stonewall', in *A Song for Europe*, ed. Raykoff and Tobin, 32.

17 Cited in Dana Heller, '"Russian Body and Soul": t.A.T.u. Performs at Eurovision 2003', in *A Song for Europe*, ed. Raykoff and Tobin, 111–2, 119.

18 Adrian Blomfield, 'Drag Queen Starts Eurovision "Cold War"', *The Telegraph* (17 March 2007) [www.telegraph.co.uk]; Helen Fawkes, 'Eurovision Act Angers Ukrainians', *BBC* (2 April 2007) [www.bbc.com].

19 Germaine Greer, 'Go, Marija! Eurovision's Triumphant Lesbian Gypsy', *The Guardian* (21 May 2007) [www.theguardian.com].

20 Mitrović, '"New Face of Serbia" at the Eurovision Song Contest', 174–5.

21 Daisy Wyatt, 'Eurovision 2013 to Feature First Lesbian Kiss in Protest Against Lack of Gay Marriage Legislation' *The Independent* (17 May 2013) [www.independent.co.uk].

22 Shahla Sultanova, 'Iran-Azerbaijan: Offence Meant, and Taken', *Institute for War and Peace Reporting* (11 June 2012) [www.iwpr.net]; ILGA-Europe, *Annual Review of the Human Rights Situation of Lesbian, Gay, Bisexual, Trans and Intersex People in Europe 2013* (Brussels: ILGA-Europe, 2013), 55 [www.ilga-europe.org].

23 EP, 'Written Question by Sophia in't Veld (ALDE), Jeanine Hennis-Plasschaert (ALDE) and Marco Cappato (ALDE) to the Commission', *European Parliament* (7 January 2009) [www.europarl.europa.eu].

24 'Russia Pop Stars Chime in on "Sodomite Propaganda"', *Sputnik* (20 December 2012) [www.sputniknews.com].

25 Cynthia Weber, *Queer International Relations: Sovereignty, Sexuality and the Will to Knowledge* (New York: Oxford University Press, 2016), 171–5.

26 Donald Morrison and Antoine Compagnon, *The Death of French Culture* (Cambridge and Malden, MA: Polity Press, 2010): 56, 94–95.

27 EBU, 'Eurovision Song Contest: Report of the Ad Hoc Co-Financing Study Group' (Geneva, 4 October 1974), 2 [EBUA, Councours Eurovision de la chanson, 1974-75].

28 Letter by M. Cazé, EBU (7 July 1983), 1–2 [EBUA, Concours Eurovision de la chanson, Correspondance 1].

29 EBU, '4th Meeting of the Ad Hoc TV Light Entertainment Group on the Revision of the Rules for the 1991 Eurovision Song Contest' (Geneva, 26 June 1990), 3 [EBUA, Concours Eurovision de la chanson, Décisions]. For

example, the San Marinese entry in the 2012 ESC, 'Facebook Uh Oh Oh', was deemed by the Reference Group to have breached the rule banning commercial messages in entries and had to have its title and lyrics changed before the contest, where it reappeared as 'The Social Network Song Oh Oh Uh Oh Oh'.

30 EBU, '15th Meeting of the TV Committee' (Geneva, 22 June 1998), 8 [EBUA, Concours Eurovision de la chanson, Décisions 3].

31 EP, 'Minutes of Proceedings of the Sitting of Monday, 2 May 1994', *Official Journal of the European Communities: Information and Notices* 37, no. C 205 (25 July 1994), 2 [www.eur-lex.europa.eu].

32 Jordan, *The Modern Fairytale*, 64–5.

33 Tony Langlois, 'The Rise and Fall of the Singing Tiger: Ireland and Eurovision', in *Empire of Song*, ed. Tragaki, 270–6; Singleton, 'From Dana to Dustin', 149–56.

34 Björnberg, 'Invincible Heroes', 217.

35 Shahla Sultanova, 'In Eurovision Spending, Azerbaijan Is a Clear Winner', *Transitions Online* (20 April 2012) [www.tol.org].

36 'Put in More Flags', *The Economist* (14 May 2009).

37 Sultanova, 'In Eurovision Spending, Azerbaijan Is a Clear Winner'.

38 Ibid. For a detailed report on the forced evictions, see Jane Buchanan, *'They Took Everything from Me': Forced Evictions, Unlawful Expropriations, and House Demolitions in Azerbaijan's Capital* (New York: Human Rights Watch, 2012).

39 Ryan Gallagher, 'Your Eurovision Song Contest Vote May Be Monitored: Mass Surveillance in Former Soviet Republics' *Slate* (30 April 2012) [www.slate.com]; Khadija Ismayilova, 'TeliaSonera's Behind-The-Scenes Connection to Azerbaijani President's Daughters', *Radio Free Europe/Radio Liberty* (15 July 2014) [www.rferl.org].

40 Sultanova, 'In Eurovision Spending, Azerbaijan Is a Clear Winner'.

41 Aya Bach, 'Merkel as Hitler?', *Deutsche Welle* (18 April 2013) [www.dw.com].

42 Alf Björnberg, 'Return to Ethnicity', 22.

43 'Eurovision 2006 Made a Net Profit, ERT Says', *New Europe* (28 May 2006) [www.neweurope.eu].

44 In 2013 and 2014 there were, however, public protests outside of the venues of the ESC against Andreas Kouris, the owner of MAD TV. He was accused of not remunerating laid-off employees from another of his businesses, the Metropolis shops, even as he had the money to sponsor Greece's ESC entries. Hanna Weiderud and Rebecka Ljung, 'Grekiska protester utanför Malmö arena', *SVT* (18 May 2013) [www.svt.se].

45 Stephen Boyle, 'The Cost of Winning the Eurovision Song Contest', *Royal Bank of Scotland* (13 May 2016) [www.rbs.com].

46 Ibid.

47 'Eurovision blev over tre gange så dyrt som planlagt', *DR* (4 August 2014) [www.dr.dk].

48 Ingvil Conradi Andersen, 'Public Consultation on the Evaluation of NRK's Existing Public Services', *Iris* 6, no. 10 (2010), 24.

49 'Legal Action over the Use of the Word "Iceland"', *Ministry for Foreign Affairs* (24 November 2016) [www.mfa.is].

50 EBU, 'Revision of Rules of the Eurovision Song Contest' (Helsinki, September 1969), 2 [EBUA, Concours Eurovision de la chanson, 1970–71].

51 NTS, 'Eurovision Song Festival' (Hilversum, June 1958) [EBUA, Concours Eurovision de la chanson, 1958-59].

52 CoE, *Regular Selective Information Flow (RSIF) for the Attention of the National Human Rights Structures (NHRSs)* no. 14 (29 April 2009), 21 [www.coe.int].

53 Julien Danero Iglesias, 'Eurovision Song Contest and Identity Crisis in Moldova', *Nationalities Papers* 43, no. 2 (2015): 237, 239–42.

54 'Eurovision Song Contest to Ban Cheats from Show', *BBC* (7 February 2014) [www.bbc.com].

55 Karin Dofs, 'Georgiens röster diskvalificerades i Eurovision-finalen', *Aftonbladet* (11 May 2014) [www.aftonbladet.se].

56 Eugster, *Television Programming Across National Boundaries,* 136–7.

57 EBU, 'Eurovision Song Contest' (Geneva, 26 September 1961), 2 [EBUA, Concours Eurovision de la chanson, 1962].

58 Freedom House, *Freedom of the Press 2014* (Freedom House: Washington, D.C, and New York, 2014), 11–12 [www.freedomhouse.org].

59 Ibid., 10.

60 Cited in Miriam Elder, 'Eurovision Song Contest: Russian Foreign Minister Wades into Voting Row', *The Guardian* (21 May 2013) [www.theguardian.com].

61 William Lee Adams, 'Following Outrage over Conchita, Russia Is Reviving Its Own Straight Eurovision', *Newsweek* (25 July 2014) [www.newsweek.com].

62 EP, 'European Parliament Resolution of 24 May 2012 on the Human Rights Situation in Azerbaijan', *Official Journal of the European Union: Information and Notices* 56, no. C 264 E (13 September 2013), 91 [www.eur-lex.europa.eu]; EP, 'Negotiations of the EU-Azerbaijan Association Agreement', *Official Journal of the European Union: Information and Notices* 56, no. C 258 E (7 September 2013), 40 [www.eur-lex.europa.eu].

63 European Commission, 'Statement of President Barroso Following His Meeting with Ilham Aliyev, President of Azerbaijan', *European Commission Press Release Database* (22 June 2011), 3 [www.europa.eu/rapid].

64 Cited in Gluhovic, 'Sing for Democracy', 207.

65 Marco Schreuder, 'Loreen engagiert sich für Menschenrechte', *Der Standard* (21 May 2012) [www.derstandard.at].

66 Stefan Niggemeier, 'Eine Imageschaden? Glaube ich null', *Der Spiegel* (9 May 2012) [www.spiegel.de].

67 Gluhovic, 'Sing for Democracy', 208–9.

68 CoE, 'Third Party Intervention by the Council of Europe Commissioner for Human Rights Under Article 36, Paragraph 3, of the European Convention on Human Rights: Application No. 69981/14 Rasul Jafarov v. Azerbaijan' (Strasbourg, 30 March 2015), 7 [www.coe.int].

69 Freedom House, *Freedom of the Press 2014*, 10.

70 'Germany Slams Lukashenko over Slur', *Der Spiegel* (5 March 2012) [www.spiegel.de].

71 Rodger Potocki, 'Belarus: A Tale of Two Elections', *Journal of Democracy* 22, no. 3 (2011): 59.

72 Cited in 'Lukashenko: Eurovision is Totally Biased', *Belarusian Telegraphic Agency* (30 April 2013) [www.belta.by].

Conclusion

1 'UN Chief Hails Eurovision Winner Conchita Wurst's "Powerful Message"', *United Nations* (3 November 2014) [www.un.org].

2 Stephan Löwenstein, 'Schwule sind ihnen nicht mehr Wurst', *Frankfurter Allgemeine Zeitung* (14 May 2014) [www.faz.net].

3 CoE, 'LGBT Rights Are Human Rights Not Special Rights', *Council of Europe* (16 May 2014) [www.coe.int]; Bernd Riegert, 'EU Parliament Goes Nuts for Conchita Wurst', *Deutsche Welle* (8 October 2014) [www.dw.com].

4 Liana Aghajanian, 'The Armenian Genocide, as Power Ballad', *Foreign Policy* (22 May 2015) [www.foreignpolicy.com].

5 Cited in Rashid Shirinov, 'Armenian Provocation Prevented at Eurovision Song Contest', *AzerNews* (11 May 2016) [www.azernews.az].

6 Public Information Office, 'Primitive Ban from Eurovision', *Ministry of Foreign Affairs of the TRNC* (2 May 2016) [www.mfa.gov.ct.tr]; 'Erekat Slams Eurovision

Contest's Palestinian Flag Ban', *Ma'an News Agency* (30 April 2016) [www.maannews.com].

7 Helena Peternel Pečauer, 'Klemen Slakonja: Skoraj prepričan sem, da bi se Putin videospotu smejal', *Delo* (1 March 2016) [www.delo.si].

8 Cited in 'Austria Defies US, EU over South Stream During Putin Visit', *Deutsche Welle* (24 June 2014)[www.dw.com].

9 Neil Clark, 'RIP Eurovision, 1956-2016', *Russia Today* (15 May 2016) [www.rt.com].

10 Iceland and Sweden had the highest viewing figures of any European state for the finals of the 2015 and 2016 contests: 96 per cent and 86 per cent of television viewers respectively for the 2015 ESC, when the average across Europe was 40 per cent, and 95 per cent and 85 per cent for the 2016 ESC, when the European average was 36 per cent. Simon Storvik-Green, 'Nearly 200 Million People Watch Eurovision 2015', *Eurovision.tv* (3 June 2015) [www.eurovision.tv]; 'Eurovision Song Contest Attracts 204 Million Viewers!'. *Eurovision.tv* (24 May 2016) [www.eurovision.tv].

11 Reputation Institute, *2016 Country RepTrak: The Most Reputable Countries in the World* (23 June 2016), 9 [www.reputationinstitute.com].

12 Government of Sweden, 'Government Communication 2011/12:114: Strategic Export Control in 2011 – Military Equipment and Dual-Use Products', (Stockholm, 15 March 2012), 6 [www.government.se]; Ludovic Hunter-Tilney, 'How Sweden Became a Pop Music Powerhouse', *Financial Times* (1 November 2013) [www.ft.com]; Tom Sullivan, 'Sweden's Dirty Secret: It Arms Dictators', *Business Insider* (20 May 2014) [www.businessinsider.com].

13 Kenne Fant, *Alfred Nobel: A Biography*, trans. Marianne Ruuth (New York: Arcade, 1993), 35. Nobel was also a subject of controversy in the 1978 ESC, for which Vissi was meant to perform the song 'O kyrios Nobel' (Mr. Nobel) which had lyrics that were critical of him. However, ERT replaced it with the entry 'Charlie Chaplin' as ERT thought that Vissi's song could cause diplomatic problems with Sweden. Wolther, *'Kampf der Kulturen'*, 124. Unlike like the other Nobel Prizes for chemistry, literature, medicine and physics, the one for peace is awarded by the Norwegian Nobel Committee and not the Swedish one and is presented in Oslo. The Nobel Peace Prize Concert that has been staged annually since 1994 to honour the prize winners was originally held in the Oslo Spektrum that hosted the 1996 ESC, and in 1998 it was hosted by Kleveland, while Rybak performed in it in 2009.

14 'EBU Withdraws Member Services from Televiziunea Română (TVR) Following Repeated Non-Payment of Debt', *EBU* (22 April 2016) [www.ebu.ch].

15 'EBU Appeals to Prime Minister to "Rescue" BHRT', *EBU* (6 July 2016) [www.ebu.ch].

16 Scottish Government, *Scotland's Future: Your Guide to an Independent Scotland* (Edinburgh: Scottish Government, 2013), 532.

17 Will Dahlgreen, 'Eurovision Referendum: Leave Lead at 20', *YouGov* (2 May 2016) [www.yougov.co.uk]. Of the six other states – Denmark, Finland, France, Germany, Norway and Sweden – which were included in the survey, only in France were there also more respondents who wanted their state to leave rather than remain in the ESC, although there were less of them than in the UK. The Swedish respondents were the most enthusiastic about their state participating in the ESC.

18 Christopher Hooton, 'Brexit: David Cameron Addresses the Important EU Question at PMQs – Would Leaving Disqualify Us from Eurovision?', *The Independent* (20 April 2016) [www.independent.co.uk].

19 Erik Kirschbaum, 'Eurovision Head Says Global Contest a "Challenge"', *Reuters* (16 May 2011) [www.reuters.com].

20 EBU, 'Eurovision Song Contest' (Geneva, 20 June 1995), 1 [EBUA, Concours Eurovision de la chanson, Communiqués de presse, Divers]; letter from Alan Sherratt, Globe Management Services, to Gaetano Stucchi, EBU (Melbourne, 17 August 1995), 1 [EBUA, Concours mondial de la chanson]; letter from Gaetano Stucchi, EBU, to Alan Sherratt, Globe Events Management (Geneva, 21 March 1997), 1 [EBUA, Concours mondial de la chanson].

21 Michael Bodey, 'Eurovision Audience Down on 2015', *The Australian* (16 May 2016) [www.theaustralian.com.au].

22 Shannon Molloy, 'It Costs a Fortune to Compete and We're 14,000 km Away ... So Why Do We Bother with Eurovision?', *News.com.au* (15 May 2016) [www.news.com.au].

23 Considering the growth of large Asian immigrant communities across Europe during the postwar era, it is surprising that there were so few artists of Asian descent in the ESC. During the Cold War, Dutch entries set the precedent in this regard: the first artist of Asian origin in the ESC was Anneke Grönloh, who represented the Netherlands in the 1964 ESC. Other Dutch artists with mixed Asian and European backgrounds originating from the Netherlands' former colony, Indonesia, and who participated in the ESC during the Cold War were Bianca Maessen, Patricia Maessen, Stella Maessen, Sandra Reemer and Dries Holten. The only artists to perform in the ESC after having established careers in Asian states was Anggun, who immigrated from Indonesia to France in 1994 and represented the latter in the 2012 ESC, and Stephanie Topalian from Japan who was a member of Genealogy.

24 'Remarks by President Obama in Address to the People of Europe', *The White House* (25 April 2016). As was the case during the Cold War, several American artists who had immigrated to Europe also performed in the ESC after 1989, including Katrina Leskanich, the singer from Katrina and the Waves which won the 1997 ESC for the UK, Isis Gee, who represented Poland in the 2008 ESC, Hannah Mancini, who sang for Slovenia in the 2013 ESC, and András Kállay-Saunders, the Hungarian representative in the 2014 ESC. The Greek-American Maria Menounos also co-hosted the 2006 ESC, while Sweeney was the most prominent example of an ESC host who went on to develop a career in the United States, where she began working for the Cable News Network after hosting the 1993 ESC.

25 Although the ESC seems an unsuitable stage for the Catholic Church's faith-based cultural diplomacy, there were examples of nuns competing in singing contests. In 2014, the nun Cristina Scuccia won *The Voice of Italy* television singing contest and later released a cover version of Madonna's 'Like a Virgin'. Her success was widely perceived as a reflection of Pope Francis' aim to make the Catholic Church more modern and open. A group of nuns also unsuccessfully competed in the Maltese national selection for the 2015 ESC. The hosts of the ESC in 2000 and 2015 also joked that Vatican City was not in the ESC and on the latter occasion invited it to join.

26 'Kosovo Seeks Full EBU Membership and Song Contest Slot', *EBU* (30 March 2012) [www.ebu.ch]. In its resolutions on the European integration of Kosovo, the EP also called for Kosovo to be admitted into the ESC. EP, 'European Integration Process of Kosovo', *Official Journal of the European Union: Information and Notices* (Brussels, 16 January 2014), 59, C 482 (23 December 2016), 133 [www.eur-lex.europa.eu]; EP, 'The European Integration Process of Kosovo', *Official Journal of the European Union: Information and Notices* (Brussels, 11 March 2015), 59, C 316 (30 August 2016), 73 [www.eur-lex.europa.eu].

28 'RTK Management Reacts Sternly over Eurovision Scandal', *RTK Live* (29 April 2016) [www.rtklive.com].

Sources

Archives

Council of Europe
Czech Television
German Broadcasting Archive
European Broadcasting Union
Historical Archives of the European Union
International Telecommunication Union
Polish Television

Books, Book Chapters and Journal Articles

Andjelić, Neven. 'National Promotion and Eurovision: From Besieged Sarajevo to the Floodlights of Europe'. *Contemporary Southeastern Europe* 2, no. 1 (2015): 94–109.

Ang, Ien, Gay Hawkins and Lamia Dabboussy. *The SBS Story: The Challenge of Cultural Diversity*. Sydney: University of New South Wales Press, 2008.

Aston, Elaine. 'Competing Femininities: A "Girl" for Eurovision'. In *Performing the 'New' Europe: Identities, Feelings, and Politics in the Eurovision Song Contest*, edited by Karen Fricker and Milija Gluhović, 163–77. Basingstoke and New York: Palgrave Macmillan, 2013.

Baker, Catherine. *Sounds of the Borderland: Popular Music, War and Nationalism in Croatia Since 1991*. Farnham and Burlington, VT: Ashgate Publishing, 2010.

Baumgartner, Michael. '*Chanson*, *canzone*, *Schlager*, and Song: Switzerland's Identity Struggle in the Eurovision Song Contest'. In *A Song for Europe: Popular Music and Politics in the Eurovision Song Contest*, edited by Ivan Raykoff and Robert Deam Tobin, 37–47. Aldershot and Burlington, VT: Ashgate Publishing, 2007.

Björnberg, Alf. 'Return to Ethnicity: The Cultural Significance of Musical Change in the Eurovision Song Contest'. In *A Song for Europe: Popular Music and Politics in the Eurovision Song Contest*, edited by Ivan Raykoff and Robert Deam Tobin, 13–23. Aldershot and Burlington, VT: Ashgate Publishing, 2007.

Björnberg, Alf. 'Invincible Heroes: The Musical Construction of National and European Identities in Swedish Eurovision Song Contest Entries'. In *Empire of Song: Europe and Nation in the Eurovision Song Contest*, edited by Dafni Tragaki, 203–19. Lanham, MD, and Plymouth: Scarecrow Press, 2013.

Bohlman, Andrea F., and Ioannis Polychronakis. 'Eurovision Everywhere: A Kaleidoscopic Vision of the Grand Prix'. In *Empire of Song: Europe and Nation in the Eurovision Song Contest*, edited by Dafni Tragaki, 57–77. Lanham, MD, and Plymouth: Scarecrow Press, 2013.

Bohlman, Andrea F., and Alexander Rehding. 'Doing the European Two-Step'. In *Empire of Song: Europe and Nation in the Eurovision Song Contest*, edited by Dafni Tragaki, 281–97. Lanham, MD, and Plymouth: Scarecrow Press, 2013.

Bohlman, Philip V. *World Music: A Very Short Introduction*. Oxford and New York: Oxford University Press, 2002.

Bohlman, Philip V. *Focus: Music, Nationalism, and the Making of the New Europe*. 2nd edition. New York and Abingdon: Routledge, 2011.

Bolton, Jonathan. *Worlds of Dissent: Charter 77, The Plastic People of the Universe, and Czech Culture Under Communism*. Cambridge, MA, and London: Harvard University Press, 2012.

Bourdon, Jérôme. 'Unhappy Engineers of the European Soul: The EBU and the Woes of Pan-European Television', *The International Communication Gazette* 69, no. 3 (2007): 263–80.

Buchanan, Jane. *'They Took Everything from Me': Forced Evictions, Unlawful Expropriations, and House Demolitions in Azerbaijan's Capital*. New York: Human Rights Watch, 2012.

Caroli, Menico. *Proibitissimo!: Censori e censurati della radiotelevisione italiana*. Milan: Garzanti, 2003.

Christensen, Miyase, and Christian Christensen. 'The After-Life of Eurovision 2003: Turkish and European Social Imaginaries and Ephemeral Communicative Space'. *Popular Communication* 6, no. 3 (2008): 155–72.

Cummings, Richard H. *Cold War Radio: The Dangerous History of American Broadcasting in Europe, 1950-1989*. Jefferson, NC, and London: McFarland & Company, 2009.

Dauvergne, Catherine. *The New Politics of Immigration and the End of Settler Societies*. New York: Cambridge University Press, 2016.

Eugster, Ernest. *Television Programming Across National Boundaries: The EBU and OIRT Experience*. Dedham, MA: Artech House, 1983.

Evans, Christine E. *Between Truth and Time: A History of Soviet Central Television*. New Haven, CT, and London: Yale University Press, 2016.

Fant, Kenne. *Alfred Nobel: A Biography*. Translated By Marianne Ruuth. New York: Arcade, 1993.

Feddersen, Jan. *Ein Lied kann eine Brücke sein: Die deutsche und internationale Geschichte des Grand Prix Eurovision*. Hamburg: Hoffmann und Campe, 2002.

Figueiredo, Cecília Amaral. *Ary dos Santos: A voz da resistência à ditadura salazarista*. Lisbon: Chiado Editora, 2014.

Fornäs, Johan. *Signifying Europe*. Bristol and Chicago: Intellect, 2012.

Fricker, Karen. '"It's Just Not Funny Any More": Terry Wogan, Melancholy Britain, and the Eurovision Song Contest'. In *Performing the 'New' Europe: Identities, Feelings, and Politics in the Eurovision Song Contest*, edited by Karen Fricker and Milija Gluhovic, 53–76. Basingstoke and New York: Palgrave Macmillan, 2013.

Frith, Simon. 'Euro Pop'. *Cultural Studies* 3, no. 2 (1989): 166–72.

Fulbrook, Mary. *The People's State: East German Society from Hitler to Honecker*. New Haven, CT, and London: Yale University Press, 2005.

Gatherer, Derek. 'Voting in Eurovision: Shared Tastes or Cultural Epidemic?', *Empirical Text and Culture Research* 3, no. 1 (2007): 72–84.

Ginsburgh, Victor, and Abdul G. Noury. 'The Eurovision Song Contest: Is Voting Political or Cultural?'. *European Journal of Political Economy* 24, no. 1 (2008): 41–52.

Gluhovic, Milija. 'Sing for Democracy: Human Rights and Sexuality Discourse in the Eurovision Song Contest'. In *Performing the 'New' Europe: Identities, Feelings, and Politics in the Eurovision Song Contest*, edited by Karen Fricker and Milija Gluhovic, 194–217. Basingstoke and New York: Palgrave Macmillan, 2013.

Gott, Karel. *Zwischen zwei Welten: Mein Leben*. Munich: Riva, 2014.

Grünlich, Peter. *12 Punkte beim Eurovision Song Contest gehen an Deutschland: Was ein Österreicher nie sagen würde*. Munich: Riva, 2014.

Gura, Caitlin. 'Österreichs Abschneiden beim Eurovision Song Contest zwischen 2000 und 2013: Und dessen Auswirkung auf die österreichische Identität'. In *Eurovision Song Contest: Eine kleine Geschichte zwischen Körper, Geschlecht und Nation*, edited by Christine Ehardt, Georg Vogt and Florian Wagner, 65–90. Vienna: Zaglossus, 2015.

Gutiérrez Lozano, Juan Francisco. 'Spain Was Not Living a Celebration: TVE and the Eurovision Song Contest During the Years of Franco's Dictatorship'. *View* 1, no. 2 (2012): 11–17.

Heller, Dana. '"Russian Body and Soul": t.A.T.u. Performs at Eurovision 2003'. In *A Song for Europe: Popular Music and Politics in the Eurovision Song Contest*, edited by Ivan Raykoff and Robert Deam Tobin, 111–21. Aldershot and Burlington, VT: Ashgate Publishing, 2007.

Herzog, Dagmar. *Sexuality in Europe: A Twentieth-Century History*. Cambridge and New York: Cambridge University Press, 2011.

Hilder, Thomas. *Sámi Musical Performance and the Politics of Indigeneity in Northern Europe*. Lanham, MD, and London: Rowman & Littlefield, 2015.

Hindrichs, Thorsten. 'Chasing the "Magic Formula" for Success: Ralph Siegel and the Grand Prix Eurovision de la Chanson'. In *A Song for Europe: Popular Music and Politics in the Eurovision Song Contest*, edited by Ivan Raykoff and Robert Deam Tobin, 49–59. Aldershot and Burlington, VT: Ashgate Publishing, 2007.

Hixson, Walter L. *Parting the Curtain: Propaganda, Culture, and the Cold War, 1945-1961*. New York: St. Martin's Press, 1997.

Iglesias, Julien Danero. 'Eurovision Song Contest and Identity Crisis in Moldova'. *Nationalities Papers* 43, no. 2 (2015): 233–47.

Ingvoldstad, Bjorn. 'Lithuanian Contests and European Dreams'. In *A Song for Europe: Popular Music and Politics in the Eurovision Song Contest*, edited by Ivan Raykoff and Robert Deam Tobin, 99-110. Aldershot and Burlington, VT: Ashgate Publishing, 2007.

Johansson, Ola. 'Beyond ABBA: The Globalization of Swedish Popular Music'. *Focus on Geography*, 53, no. 4 (2010): 134–41.

Jordan, Paul. *The Modern Fairy Tale: Nation Branding, National Identity and the Eurovision Song Contest in Estonia*. Tartu: University of Tartu Press, 2014.

Kater, Michael H. *Different Drummers: Jazz in the Culture of Nazi Germany*. New York: Oxford University Press, 1992.

Kirkegaard, Annemette. 'The Nordic Brotherhoods: Eurovision as a Platform for Partnership and Competition'. In *Empire of Song: Europe and Nation in the Eurovision Song Contest*, edited by Dafni Tragaki, 79–107. Lanham, MD, and Plymouth: Scarecrow Press, 2013.

Kraushaar, Elmar. *Freddy Quinn: Ein unwahrscheinliches Leben – Biografie*. Zurich: Atrium, 2011.

Kundera, Milan. 'The Tragedy of Central Europe'. Translated by Edmund White. *The New York Review of Books* 31, no. 7 (1984): 33-8.

Kundera, Milan. *The Unbearable Lightness of Being*. Translated by Michael Henry Heim. New York: Harper & Row, 1984.

Lampropoulos, Apostolos. 'Delimiting the Eurobody: Historicity, Politicization, Queerness'. In *Empire of Song: Europe and Nation in the Eurovision Song Contest*, edited by Dafni Tragaki, 151–72. Lanham, MD, and Plymouth: Scarecrow Press, 2013.

Langlois, Tony, 'The Rise and Fall of the Singing Tiger: Ireland and Eurovision'. In *Empire of Song: Europe and Nation in the Eurovision Song Contest*, edited by Dafni Tragaki, 261-279. Lanham, MD, and Plymouth: Scarecrow Press, 2013.

Lemish, Dafna. 'Gay Brotherhood: Israeli Gay Men and the Eurovision Song Contest'. In *A Song for Europe: Popular Music and Politics in the Eurovision Song*

Contest, edited by Ivan Raykoff and Robert Deam Tobin, 123-134. Aldershot and Burlington, VT: Ashgate Publishing, 2007.

Letschnig, Melanie. 'Hofburg, kurze Kleider und Knabenchor: Der Grand Prix de la Chanson 1967'. In *Eurovision Song Contest: Eine kleine Geschichte zwischen Körper, Geschlecht und Nation*, edited by Christine Ehardt, Georg Vogt and Florian Wagner, 214–26. Vienna: Zaglossus, 2015.

Lomartire, Carlo Maria. *Festival: L'Italia di Sanremo*. Milan: Mondadori, 2012.

Lommers, Suzanne. *Europe – On Air: Interwar Projects for Radio Broadcasting*. Amsterdam: Amsterdam University Press, 2012.

Lyall, Francis. *International Communications: The International Telecommunication Union and the Universal Postal Union*. Burlington, VT, and Farnham: Ashgate Publishing, 2011.

MacFadyen, David. *Red Stars: Personality and the Soviet Popular Song, 1955-1991*. Montreal: McGill-Queen's University Press, 2001.

Martínez, Sílvia, and Amparo Sales Casanova. 'Afterword: Mediterranean Love Songs – A Conversation with Joan Manuel Serrat'. In *Made in Spain: Studies in Popular Music*, edited by Sílvia Martínez and Héctor Fouce, 196–203. New York and Abingdon: Routledge, 2013.

Matei, Alexandru. 'The Golden Stag Festival in Ceausescu's Romania (1968-1971)'. *View* 1, no. 2 (2012): 18-24.

Mayer, Christoph Oliver. 'Die deutsch-französische Freundschaft und der Grand Prix de la Chanson de l'Eurovision'. In *Populärkultur und deutsch-französische Mittler: Akteure, Medien, Ausdrucksformen/Culture de masse et médiateurs franco-allemands: Acteurs, médias, articulations*, edited by Dietmar Hüser and Ulrich Pfeil, 153–66. Bielefeld: Transcript, 2015.

McIntyre, Stuart Hull. *Legal Effect of World War II on Treaties of the United States*. The Hague: Martinus Nijhoff, 1958.

Meerzon, Yana, and Dmitri Priven. 'Back to the Future: Imagining a New Russia at the Eurovision Song Contest'. In *Performing the 'New' Europe: Identities, Feelings, and Politics in the Eurovision Song Contest*, edited by Karen Fricker and Milija Gluhovic, 111–24. Basingstoke and New York: Palgrave Macmillan, 2013.

Miklóssy, Katalin. 'Competing for Popularity: Song Contests and Interactive Television in Communist Hungary'. In *Competition in Socialist Society*, edited by Katalin Miklóssy and Melanie Ilic, 107–24. Abingdon and New York: Routledge, 2014.

Milward, Alan S. *The European Rescue of the Nation-State*. 2nd edition. London and New York: Routledge, 2000.

Mitrović, Marijana. '"New Face of Serbia" at the Eurovision Song Contest: International Media Spectacle and National Identity'. *European Review of History – Revue européenne d'histoire* 17, no. 2 (2010): 171–85.

Mollin, Sandra. *Euro-English: Assessing Variety Status*. Tübingen: Gunter Narr, 2006.

Morrison, Donald, and Antoine Compagnon. *The Death of French Culture*. Cambridge and Malden, MA: Polity Press, 2010.

Morrison, Kenneth. *Montenegro: A Modern History*. London and New York: I. B. Tauris, 2009.

Musaraj, Smoki. 'Alternative Publics: Reflections on Marginal Collective Practices in Communist Albania'. In *Albania: Family, Society and Culture in the 20th Century*, edited by Andreas Hemming, Gentiana Kera and Enriketa Pandelejmoni, 175–86. Zurich and Berlin: Lit, 2012.

Mutsaers, Lutgard. 'Fernando, Filippo, and Milly: Bringing Blackness to the Eurovision Stage'. In *A Song for Europe: Popular Music and Politics in the Eurovision Song Contest*, edited by Ivan Raykoff and Robert Deam Tobin, 61-70. Aldershot and Burlington, VT: Ashgate Publishing, 2007.

O'Connor, John Kennedy. *The Eurovision Song Contest: The Official History*. Revised edition. London: Carlton Books, 2010.

Pajala, Mari. 'Finland, Zero Points: Nationality, Failure, and Shame in the Finnish Media'. In *A Song for Europe: Popular Music and Politics in the Eurovision Song Contest*, edited by Ivan Raykoff and Robert Deam Tobin, 71–82. Aldershot and Burlington, VT: Ashgate Publishing, 2007.

Pajala, Mari. 'Intervision Song Contests and Finnish Television Between East and West'. In *Airy Curtains in the European Ether: Broadcasting and the Cold War*, edited by Alexander Badenoch, Andreas Fickers and Christian Henrich-Franke, 215–39. Baden-Baden: Nomos, 2013.

Pavković, Aleksandar, and Christopher Kelen, *Anthems and the Making of Nation-States: Identity and Nationalism in the Balkans*. London and New York: I.B. Tauris, 2016.

Pavlyshyn, Marko. 'Envisioning Europe: Ruslana's Rhetoric of Identity'. *The Slavic and East European Journal* 50, no. 3 (2006): 469–85.

Pinto Teixeira, Luisa, and Martin Stokes. '"And After Love ...": Eurovision, Portuguese Popular Culture, and the Carnation Revolution'. In *Empire of Song: Europe and Nation in the Eurovision Song Contest*, edited by Dafni Tragaki, 221–39. Lanham, MD, and Plymouth: Scarecrow Press, 2013.

Poiger, Uta G. *Jazz, Rock, and Rebels: Cold War Politics and American Culture in a Divided Germany* (Berkeley, Los Angeles and London: University of California Press, 2000).

Potocki, Rodger. 'Belarus: A Tale of Two Elections'. *Journal of Democracy* 22, no. 3 (2011): 49-63.

Raber, Ralf Jörg. *Wir sind wie wir sind: Ein Jahrhundert homosexuelle Liebe auf Schallplatte und CD – Eine Dokumentation*. Hamburg: Männerschwarm Verlag, 2010.

Raykoff, Ivan. 'Camping on the Borders of Europe'. In *A Song for Europe: Popular Music and Politics in the Eurovision Song Contest*, edited by Ivan Raykoff and Robert Deam Tobin, 1–12. Aldershot and Burlington, VT: Ashgate Publishing, 2007.

Regev, Motti, and Edwin Seroussi. *Popular Music and National Culture in Israel.* (Berkeley, Los Angeles and London: University of California Press, 2004).

Roger, Philippe. *The American Enemy: The History of French Anti-Americanism.* Translated by Sharon Bowman. Chicago and London: The University of Chicago Press, 2005.

Roxburgh, Gordon. *Songs for Europe: The United Kingdom at the Eurovision Song Contest – Volume One: The 1950s and 1960s.* Prestatyn: Telos Publishing, 2012.

Ryback, Timothy W. *Rock Around the Bloc: A History of Rock Music in Eastern Europe and the Soviet Union.* New York and Oxford: Oxford University Press, 1990.

Scottish Government. *Scotland's Future: Your Guide to an Independent Scotland.* Edinburgh: Scottish Government, 2013.

Sieg, Katrin. 'Conundrums of Post-Socialist Belonging at the Eurovision Song Contest'. In *Performing the 'New' Europe: Identities, Feelings, and Politics in the Eurovision Song Contest*, edited by Karen Fricker and Milija Gluhovic, 218–37. Basingstoke and New York: Palgrave Macmillan, 2013.

Singleton, Brian. 'From Dana to Dustin: The Reputation of Old/New Ireland and the Eurovision Song Contest'. In *Performing the 'New' Europe: Identities, Feelings, and Politics in the Eurovision Song Contest*, edited by Karen Fricker and Milija Gluhovic, 142–59. Basingstoke and New York: Palgrave Macmillan, 2013.

Soffer, Oren. *Mass Communication in Israel: Nationalism, Globalization, and Segmentation.* Translated by Judith Yalon. New York and Oxford: Berghahn Books, 2015.

Solomon, Maynard. *Beethoven Essays.* Cambridge, MA, and London: Harvard University Press, 1988.

Solomon, Thomas. 'Articulating the Historical Moment: Turkey, Europe, and Eurovision 2003'. In *A Song for Europe: Popular Music and Politics in the Eurovision Song Contest*, edited by Ivan Raykoff and Robert Deam Tobin, 135–45. Aldershot and Burlington, VT: Ashgate Publishing, 2007.

Solomon, Thomas. 'The Oriental Body on the European Stage: Producing Turkish Cultural Identity on the Margins of Europe'. In *Empire of Song: Europe and Nation in the Eurovision Song Contest*, edited by Dafni Tragaki, 173–201. Lanham, MD, and Plymouth: Scarecrow Press, 2013.

Sontag, Susan. *Against Interpretation and Other Essays.* New York: Picador, 2001.

Starr, S. Frederick. *Red and Hot: The Fate of Jazz in the* Soviet Union *1917-1991.* 2nd edition. New York: Limelight Editions, 1994.

Sternberg, Claudia Schrag. *The Struggle for EU Legitimacy: Public Contestation, 1950-2005*. Basingstoke and New York: Palgrave Macmillan, 2013.

Štětka, Václav. 'Media Events and European Visions: Czech Republic in the 2007 Eurovision Song Contest', *Communications* 34, no. 1 (2009): 21–38.

Szabó, Ivan. *Bratislavská lýra*. Bratislava: Marenčin PT, 2010.

Szczygieł, Mariusz. *Gottland: Mostly True Stories from Half of Czechoslovakia*. Translated by Antonia Lloyd-Jones. New York and London: Melville House, 2014.

Taylor, Karin. *Let's Twist Again: Youth and Leisure in Socialist Bulgaria*. Vienna and Berlin: Lit, 2006.

Ternavasio, Maurizio. *La leggenda di mister Volare: Vita di Domenico Modugno* (Florence and Milan: Giunti, 2004).

Ther, Philipp. *Center Stage: Operatic Culture and Nation Building* in *Nineteenth-Century Central Europe*. Translated by Charlotte Hughes-Kreutzmuller. West Lafayette, IN: Purdue University Press, 2014.

Tobin, Robert Deam. 'Eurovision at 50: Post-Wall and Post-Stonewall'. In *A Song for Europe: Popular Music and Politics in the Eurovision Song Contest*, edited by Ivan Raykoff and Robert Deam Tobin, 25–35. Aldershot and Burlington, VT: Ashgate Publishing, 2007.

Tochka, Nicholas. *Audible States: Socialist Politics and Popular Music in Albania*. New York: Oxford University Press, 2016.

Van Rompuy, Ben, and Karen Donders. 'The EBU's Eurovision System Governing the Joint Buying of Sports Broadcasting Rights: Unfinished Competition Business'. *The Competition Law Review* 9, no. 1 (2013): 7–28.

Vick, Brian E. *The Congress of Vienna: Power and Politics After Napoleon*. Cambridge, MA, and London: Harvard University Press, 2014.

Vondráčková, Helena. *'Unter der Asche meiner Liebe ist noch Glut': Erinnerungen*. Berlin: Ullstein, 1997.

Vuletic, Dean. 'The Socialist Star: Yugoslavia, Cold War Politics and the Eurovision Song Contest'. In *A Song for Europe: Popular Music and Politics in the Eurovision Song Contest*, edited by Ivan Raykoff and Robert Deam Tobin, 83–97. Aldershot and Burlington, VT: Ashgate Publishing, 2007.

Vuletic, Dean. 'European Sounds, Yugoslav Visions: Performing Yugoslavia at the Eurovision Song Contest'. In *Remembering Utopia: The Culture of Everyday Life in Socialist Yugoslavia*, edited by Breda Luthar and Maruša Pušnik, 121–44. Washington, DC: New Academia, 2010.

Vuletic, Dean 'Sounds like America: Yugoslavia's Soft Power in Eastern Europe'. In *Divided Dreamworlds?: The Cultural Cold War in East and West*, edited by Peter Romijn, Giles Scott-Smith and Joes Segal, 115–31. Amsterdam: Amsterdam University Press, 2012.

Walzer, Lee. *Between Sodom and Eden: A Gay Journey Through Today's Changing Israel*. New York: Columbia University Press, 2000.

Weber, Cynthia. *Queer International Relations: Sovereignty, Sexuality and the Will to Knowledge*. New York: Oxford University Press, 2016.

Winter, Renée. '"Vielleicht geschieht ein Wunder": Österreichische Beiträge beim Eurovision Song Conest 1957-1963 im Zeichen geschichtspolitischer Rehabilitierung'. In *Eurovision Song Contest: Eine kleine Geschichte zwischen Körper, Geschlecht und Nation*, edited by Christine Ehardt, Georg Vogt and Florian Wagner, 15–29. Vienna: Zaglossus, 2015.

Wogan, Terry. 'Foreword'. *The Complete Eurovision Song Contest Companion*, by Paul Gambaccini, Tim Rice, Jonathan Rice and Tony Brown, 7–8. London: Pavilion Books, 1998.

Wolff, Larry. *Inventing Eastern Europe: The Map of Civilization on the Mind of the Enlightenment*. Stanford, CA: Stanford University Press, 1994.

Wolther, Irving. *'Kampf der Kulturen': Der Eurovision Song Contest als Mittel national-kultureller Repräsentation*. Würzburg: Königshausen & Neumann, 2006.

Woodhead, Leslie. *How the Beatles Rocked the Kremlin: The Untold Story of a Noisy Revolution*. London: Bloomsbury, 2013.

Yair, Gad, and Daniel Maman. 'The Persistent Structure of Hegemony in the Eurovision Song Contest'. *Acta Sociologica* 39, no. 3 (1996): 309–25.

Yair, Gad. 'Unite Unite Europe: The Political and Cultural Structures of Europe as Reflected in the Eurovision Song Contest'. *Social Networks* 17, no. 2 (1995): 147–61.

Yurchak, Alexei. *Everything Was Forever, Until It Was No More: The Last Soviet Generation*. Princeton and Oxford: Princeton University Press, 2005.

Yurtaeva, Yulia. 'Ein schwarzer Rabe gegen Conchita Wurst oder: Wovor hat Russland Angst?'. In *Eurovision Song Contest: Eine kleine Geschichte zwischen Körper, Geschlecht und Nation*, edited by Christine Ehardt, Georg Vogt and Florian Wagner, 111–35. Vienna: Zaglossus, 2015.

Zeller, Rüdiger. *Die EBU – Union Européene de Radio-Télévision (UER) – European Broadcasting Union (EBU): Internationale Rundfunkkooperation im Wandel*. Baden-Baden: Nomos, 1999.

Films and Television Shows

Cupcakes. Directed by Eytan Fox. Pro-Fun Media, 2013.

Eurotrash. Various directors. Channel 4, 1993-2016.

Eurovision Song Contest. Various directors. Various national broadcasting organizations, 1956-2016.

JRT izbor za pjesmu Evrovizije – Sarajevo '91. Directed by Slaviša Matić. Yugoslav Radio and Television, 1991.

The Pianist. Directed by Roman Polanski. Universal, 2002.

The Secret History of Eurovision. Directed by Stephen Oliver. Electric Pictures, 2011.

The Tony Ferrino Phenomenon. Directed by Geoff Posner. British Broadcasting Corporation, 1996.

Periodicals and Websites

Aftonbladet	www.aftonbladet.se
And the Conductor Is…	www.andtheconductoris.eu
AzerNews	www.azernews.az
Belarusian Telegraphic Agency	www.belta.by
Billboard	www.billboard.com
British Broadcasting Corporation	www.bbc.com
Business Insider	www.businessinsider.com
Corriere della Sera	www.corriere.it
Council of Europe	www.coe.int
Danmarks Radio	www.dr.dk
Delo	www.delo.si
Der Spiegel	www.spiegel.de
Der Standard	www.derstandard.at
Deutsche Welle	www.dw.com/en
Die Tageszeitung	www.taz.de
Diggiloo Thrush	www.diggiloo.net
Dnevnik	www.dnevnik.com.mk
E.B.U. Bulletin	
E.B.U. Review	
El Mundo	www.elmundo.es
EUR-Lex	www.eur-lex.europa.eu
European Broadcasting Union	www.ebu.ch
European Commission Press Release Database	www.europa.eu/rapid
European Commission	www.ec.europa.eu
European Parliament	www.europarl.europa.eu
Eurovision Song Contest Database	www.eschome.net
Eurovision.tv	www.eurovision.tv

Financial Times	www.ft.com
Forbes	www.forbes.com
Foreign Policy	www.foreignpolicy.com
Frankfurter Allgemeine Zeitung	www.faz.net
Freedom House	www.freedomhouse.org
Globus	www.jutarnji.hr/globus
Government Offices of Sweden	www.government.se
Haaretz	www.haaretz.com
ILGA-Europe	www.ilga-europe.org
Institute for War and Peace Reporting	www.iwpr.net
International Telecommunication Union	www.itu.int
Iris	www.obs.coe.int
Liechtensteiner Vaterland	www.vaterland.li
Literární noviny	www.literarky.cz
Ma'an News Agency	www.maannews.com
Ministry for Foreign Affairs of the Republic of Iceland	www.mfa.is
Ministry of Foreign Affairs of the Turkish Republic of North Cyprus	www.mfa.gov.ct.tr
Mitteldeutsche Zeitung	www.mz-web.de
NATO Review	www.nato.int/review
Neues Deutschland	www.neues-deutschland.de
New Europe	www.neweurope.eu
News.com.au	www.news.com.au
Newsweek	www.newsweek.com
Radio Free Europe/Radio Liberty	www.rferl.org
Radio Prague	www.radio.cz/en
Radio Televizioni i Kosovës Live	www.rtklive.com
Reputation Institute	www.reputationinstitute.com
Reuters	www.reuters.com
Royal Bank of Scotland	www.rbs.com
Russia Today	www.rt.com
Slate	www.slate.com
Sputnik International	www.sputniknews.com
Sveriges Television	www.svt.se
The Australian	www.theaustralian.com.au
The Economist	www.economist.com
The Guardian	www.theguardian.com
The Independent	www.independent.co.uk

The Jerusalem Post	www.jpost.com
The National	www.thenational.ae
The New York Times	www.nytimes.com
The Telegraph	www.telegraph.co.uk
The White House	www.whitehouse.gov
Time	www.time.com
Transitions Online	www.tol.org
United Nations	www.un.org
Wiener Zeitung	www.wienerzeitung.at
Wikipedia	www.wikipedia.org
Wiwibloggs	www.wiwibloggs.com
YouGov	www.yougov.co.uk
YouTube	www.youtube.com

Index

CPSIA information can be obtained
at www.ICGtesting.com
Printed in the USA
LVHW081511091221
705748LV00004B/151

9 781350 107397